The
Birth of Literary Fiction
in Ancient Greece

The
Birth of Literary Fiction
in Ancient Greece

MARGALIT FINKELBERG

CLARENDON PRESS · OXFORD
1998

Oxford University Press, Great Clarendon Street, Oxford OX2 6DP

Oxford New York

Athens Auckland Bangkok Bogota Bombay Buenos Aires
Calcutta Cape Town Dar es Salaam Delhi Florence Hong Kong Istanbul
Karachi Kuala Lumpur Madras Madrid Melbourne Mexico City
Nairobi Paris Singapore Taipei Tokyo Toronto Warsaw

and associated companies in
Berlin Ibadan

Oxford is a trade mark of Oxford University Press

Published in the United States
by Oxford University Press Inc., New York

British Library Cataloguing in Publication Data
Data available

Library of Congress Cataloging in Publication Data
The birth of literary fiction in ancient Greece
Margalit Finkelberg.
Includes bibliographical references and indexes.
1. Greek literature—History and criticism—Theory, etc.
2. Narrative poetry, Greek—History and criticism—Theory, etc.
3. Greek fiction—History and criticism—Theory, etc.   4. Homer—
Criticism and interpretation.   5. Civilization, Homeric.
6. Narration (Rhetoric).   7. Greece—Civilization.   8. Rhetoric,
Ancient.   9. Literary form.   I. Title.
PA3074.F56   1998   883'.0109—dc21   97-44154
ISBN 0-19-815095-4

1 3 5 7 9 10 8 6 4 2

Typeset by Regent Typesetting, London
Printed in Great Britain on acid-free paper by
Bookcraft (Bath) Ltd., Midsomer Norton

To the Memory of
Fanny and Shlomo Pines

Preface

THIS book is genetically related to my doctoral thesis submitted to the Hebrew University of Jerusalem in December 1985, but it cannot be called a revised version of it. Rather, the thesis itself was an intermediate stage in the realization of a project of long standing whose origins can be traced back to a paper written for a seminar on the history of aesthetics that I attended at Moscow University more than twenty years ago. It was published in 1973 by one of the university periodicals. Other articles, which appeared in various classical journals between 1986 and 1995, reflect my attempts to come to grips with the subject. Most of the work, however, was done in Jerusalem in the summer of 1995, when suddenly I felt myself able to cast my views on Greek poetics in the form of a book.

Marcel Dubois, John Glucker, and Ra'anana Meridor helped, in their different ways, to improve the presentation of my argument ten years ago, and I am still indebted to them for this. A debt of another nature, but belonging to the same period, is acknowledged in the dedication of this book. In a private conversation at Stanford in 1990, Scott Richardson made a remark to the effect that the Homeric poems apparently do not follow the poetics they overtly profess; this comment eventually gave an entirely new turn to my idea of Homeric composition. David Shulman's expert advice on Sanskrit poetics allowed me to identify the universal elements in the traditional poetics of the Greeks and therefore to delimit its specificity with a greater precision. Abraham Finkelberg taught me what living in a fictitious world is like and thus helped me to understand what Don Quixote's experience really was.

I wish to express my gratitude to my fellow participants at the round table on Poetry and Thought held at Mishkenot Sha'ananim in Jerusalem in 1994-5: the stimulating discussions that took place there gave me a fuller understanding of the idea of their art entertained by poets both ancient and modern, and enlarged my horizons. I am also grateful to the anonymous readers of the original typescript of this book for their useful and often challenging comments, and to Julian Ward, the OUP copy-editor, for a number of improvements he suggested in the course of his work. My special thanks go to Mira Reich for her collaboration, which surpassed by far the original target of English editing, and to Aryeh Finkelberg, without whose assistance this book would never have taken its final form.

The book incorporates slightly modified versions of my articles 'Enchantment and Other Effects of Poetry in the Homeric *Odyssey*' (1988), 'How Could Achilles' Fame Have Been Lost?' (1991–2), and 'The Shield of Achilles, or Homer's View of Representation in Art' (1994), all three of which appeared in *Scripta Classica Israelica*. I am grateful to the Editor, Professor Hannah M. Cotton, for her kind permission to publish them.

The translators of the various ancient works quoted in the text are named in the notes at their first appearance only; unless otherwise stated, each translation from a particular work is by the same hand.

M.F.

Tel Aviv
July 1997

Contents

Abbreviations   x

1. Introduction   1

2. Poetry Among Other Activities of Homeric Man   34

3. The Song of the Muse   68

4. Song and Artefact   100

5. 'Lies Resembling Truth'   131

6. Towards Fiction   161

Afterword   192

References   203

Index of Passages Cited   213

General Index   217

Abbreviations

AA	*Antike und Abendland*
AJP	*American Journal of Philology*
Allen	*Homeri Opera*, ed. T. W. Allen, 5 vols. (vols. i–ii with D. B. Monro) (Oxford, 1902–12)
AS	*Ancient Society*
CA	*Classical Antiquity*
CP	*Classical Philology*
CQ	*Classical Quarterly*
CR	*Classical Review*
DK	H. Diels and W. Kranz, (eds.), *Die Fragmente der Vorsokratiker*, 5th edn. (Berlin, 1934)
Ebeling	H. Ebeling, *Lexicon Homericum* (Leipzig, 1885)
FGrH	F. Jacoby (ed.), *Die Fragmente der griechischen Historiker*, 15 vols. (Berlin and Leiden, 1923–58)
GR	*Greece and Rome*
GRBS	*Greek, Roman and Byzantine Studies*
HSCP	*Harvard Studies in Classical Philology*
HThR	*Harvard Theological Review*
JHI	*Journal of the History of Ideas*
JHS	*Journal of Hellenic Studies*
JRSA	*Journal of the Royal Society of Arts*
Kinkel	G. Kinkel (ed.), *Epicorum Graecorum Fragmenta* (Leipzig, 1877)
Kock	T. Kock (ed.), *Comicorum Atticorum Fragmenta*, 3 vols. (Leipzig, 1880–8)
LfgrE	B. Snell, and H. Erbse (eds.), *Lexikon des frühgriechischen Epos* (Göttingen, 1955–)
LSJ	H. Liddell, R. Scott, and H. S. Jones, *A Greek-English Lexicon*, 9th edn. (Oxford, 1940)
MH	*Museum Helveticum*
MW	R. Merkelbach and M. L. West (eds.), *Fragmenta Hesiodea* (Oxford, 1967)

PLF	E. Lobel and D. L. Page (eds.), *Poetarum Lesbiorum Fragmenta* (Oxford, 1955)
PMG	D. L. Page (ed.), *Poetae Melici Graeci* (Oxford, 1962)
RE	G. Wissowa *et al.* (eds.), *Paulys Real-Encyclopädie der classischen Altertumswissenschaft* (Stuttgart, 1894–)
REG	*Revue des Études grecques*
RhM	*Rheinisches Museum*
SCI	*Scripta Classica Israelica*
Snell–Maehler	B. Snell and H. Maehler (eds.), *Pindarus: Fragmenta* (Leipzig, 1975)
TAPA	*Transactions and Proceedings of the American Philological Association*
West	M. L. West (ed.), *Iambi et Elegi Graeci ante Alexandrum Cantati*, 2 vols. (Oxford, 1971–2)
WS	*Wiener Studien*
YCS	*Yale Classical Studies*

1
Introduction

Inspiration versus Art

This study of the origins of the concept of literary fiction grew out of my attempts to settle a difficulty in a passage of the *Phaedrus*. The passage, describing a scale of human souls, runs as follows:

the soul that hath seen the most of being shall enter into the human babe that shall grow into a seeker after wisdom (*philosophos*) or beauty (*philokalos*), a follower of the Muses (*mousikos*) and a lover (*erōtikos*); the next, having seen less, shall dwell in a king that abides by law, or a warrior and ruler; the third in a statesman, a man of business, or a trader; the fourth in an athlete, or physical trainer, or physician; the fifth shall have the life of a prophet or a Mystery priest; to the sixth that of a poet (*poiētikos*) or other mimetic artist shall be fittingly given; the seventh shall live in an artisan or farmer; the eighth in a Sophist or demagogue; the ninth in a tyrant.[1]

Anyone who reads this passage with a view to fixing the place of the poet within this hierarchy (my original intention) will be struck by the fact that though it seems reasonable to expect the souls of the 'follower of the Muses' (*mousikos*) and the poet (*poiētikos*) to be referred to the same category, not only does Plato distinguish between them, he even places them at opposite ends of the scale.[2] That this dissociation between the poet and the Muses involves a puzzling contradiction is incontestable; far more important is the fact that attempts to resolve it against the background

---

[1] *Phdr*, 248de trans. R. Hackforth.
[2] Although it is generally true that 'Plato extends the meaning of μουσικός . . . far beyond art itself, to apply to the lover of all beauty, who . . . is again none other than the philosophos, the thinker' (Grube (1935), 187; cf. Hackforth (1952), 83; Tigerstedt (1969), 55; Ferrari (1989), 142–3; Asmis (1992), 358–9; Janaway (1995), 162–5), the very fact that in the passage in question Plato speaks of both *philosophos* and *mousikos* shows that in this context at least he does not regard the two as identical in every respect. Note also that above in the same dialogue (*Phdr*. 243a6) the term *mousikos* is applied to the poet Stesichorus.

of Plato's thought in general show that the contradiction is deeply rooted in his mind.

It is not difficult to discover exactly what is meant by *mousikos* and *poiētikos*. The passage in question is part of Plato's apology for 'divine madness' (*mania*). When Socrates proceeds to detail what is meant by divine madness, he specifies four types: prophetic, religious, poetic, and erotic (that is, for Plato, philosophic) madness. In three of these cases he carefully distinguishes between the two quite different forms an activity would take depending on whether it is 'blessed' by *mania* or lacks it entirely. Thus, there is prophecy as god-sent inspiration and prophecy practised by those who 'attained understanding and information by a purely human activity of thought belonging to their own intelligence'.[3] In love, too, a passionate lover is much superior to a sober-minded one, and though he is no longer master of himself and cannot account for his passion, his madness is 'the best of all forms of divine possession', because it brings him to the threshold of contemplation of true being.[4] Poetry is analysed similarly:

There is a third form of possession or madness, of which the Muses are the source. This seizes a tender, virgin soul and stimulates it to rapt passionate expression, especially in lyric poetry, glorifying the countless deeds of ancient times for the instruction of posterity. But if any man comes to the gates of poetry without the madness of the Muses, persuaded that skill alone (*technē*) will make him a good poet, then shall he and his works of sanity with him be brought to nought by the poetry of madness, and behold, their place is nowhere to be found.[5]

This seems to indicate that the distinction between the *mousikos* and the *poiētikos* is in fact the distinction between the poet possessed by the Muses and the poet creating by means of art (*technē*).[6] On the scale, the former is classed with the philosopher, while the latter is classed together with those whose main concern is imitation (*mimēsis*). Should we infer from this that Plato distinguishes

---

[3] *Phdr.* 244c; cf. also *Tim.* 72a.

[4] *Phdr.* 249d–256e.

[5] Ibid. 245a.

[6] Cf. Verdenius (1949), 43–4; Hackforth (1952), 84; Vicaire (1960), 53–4, 229–30, 266–7; Nussbaum (1982), 89; Murray (1996), 10–11. Tigerstedt (1969: 55–6), though arguing that the identification of the *mousikos* with the inspired poet 'has no support in the text', at the same time recognizes that 'we must accept the fact that after having exalted poetry as a kind of divine madness, Socrates-Plato ends by putting the poet low in the scale of human beings'.

between two types of poetry, non-mimetic poetry originating in inspiration and mimetic poetry originating in art? Plato's other dialogues, notably the *Ion* and the *Republic*, corroborate this suggestion.

According to the *Ion*, wholly based on the presumption that poetry is a product of divine inspiration, poetry cannot be considered an art because it does not meet the elementary demands that an art must, by definition, fulfil; unlike both the fine arts (painting, sculpture, playing musical instruments) and the useful arts (chariot-driving, medicine, fishing, divination), poetry cannot be defined as a special sphere of competence: the poet, being inspired, lacks the professional knowledge which is indispensable to the craftsman.[7] The *Ion* thus suggests a concept of poetry which conforms to the *mousikos* of the *Phaedrus*, and the same concept can also be discerned in the *Apology* and *Meno*.[8] Yet in the *Republic*, Plato explicitly refers to mimesis as the poet's sphere of competence. Notwithstanding the reservation that competence in mimesis does not lead to true knowledge, the identification of poetry as one of the two subdivisions of mimesis (painting being the other) permits him to associate poetry with the arts, specifically, with the lowest kinds of arts.[9] This concept of poetry unequivocally conforms to the *poiētikos* of the *Phaedrus*.

In so far as it is hardly possible for one and the same activity to be both excluded from and associated with the arts, it follows that by poetry in the *Ion* and poetry in the *Republic* Plato meant, in a sense, two distinct activities. Considering that the theory of mimesis was an innovatory theory developed by Plato himself, it can be suggested that the contradiction between the *Ion* on the one hand and the *Republic* and *Phaedrus* on the other can be resolved if approached in the perspective of the historical development of Plato's thought. Note in particular that the *Apology*, the *Ion*, and the *Meno*, all of which treat poetry as a product of divine

---

[7] *Ion* 532c–533d, 537a–542b. Cf. Murray (1996), 8–9.

[8] *Apol.* 22c: 'I realized that it was not owing to wisdom that they [the poets] compose their poems, but in virtue of some natural ability and inspiration (φύσει τινὶ καὶ ἐνθουσιάζοντες), just as seers and prophets who also deliver many fine messages without knowing in the least what they mean' trans. H. Tredennick cf. *Meno* 99cd. As Janaway (1995: 34) has reminded us only recently, it would be wrong to take the *Ion* as purporting to devalue inspired poetry: rather, Plato's criticism is directed against the inspired poets' claim to the knowledge which they by definition cannot possess.

[9] *Rep.* 600e–602a, 603bc, 605ab.

inspiration, are Plato's earlier dialogues, whereas both the *Phaedrus*
and the *Republic*, in which the theory of mimesis is already present
in a developed form, belong to his middle period. If this suggestion
is correct, then the discovery of the sphere of pseudo-crafts in the
Gorgias must have been the crucial point in the development of
Plato's poetics. Though mimesis is not yet mentioned in the *Gorgias*,
poetry is already characterized in this dialogue as a pseudo-craft, a
step which could well point the way to the reduction of all poetry
to the common denominator of mimesis.[10]

Plato's criteria for mimetic and non-mimetic poetry are made
explicit in book 3 of the *Republic*. Here, in what seems to be the first
extant classification of literary genres, Plato distinguishes the kinds
of poetry on the basis of their relation to mimesis. Using this
criterion, he introduces the following types: (i) mimetic poetry
proper, which works only through impersonation and is exemplified
by dramatic poetry; (ii) non-mimetic poetry, or 'plain discourse'
(*haplē diēgēsis*), which employs 'the report of the poet himself' and
is exemplified by lyric poetry (in fact, in the dithyramb); and
(iii) 'mixed' poetry (*di' amphoterōn* or *kekramenon*), which employs
both mimesis and 'plain discourse' and is best exemplified by epic
poetry.[11] Note that this classification proceeds from the presumption that there is both mimetic and non-mimetic poetry, that is, the
same presumption on which the *Phaedrus*-distinction between the
mousikos and the *poiētikos* is based. In the *Republic*, however, the
distinction is introduced not for its own sake, but in order to provide a criterion of the 'true' and 'beneficial' poetry which alone
would be permitted in the ideal state. In his search for such poetry
Plato proceeds from the premiss that 'poetry is not admitted to the
degree that it is mimetic'.[12] However, Plato's criterion of mimesis
proves to be twofold. Namely, in his search for true and beneficial
poetry he is applying not only the ontological but also the psychological criterion, that is, taking into account both the relation of
poetry to reality and its effect on the human soul; as a result,
mimetic poetry is found to be not only of an inferior status in
respect of reality, in that it produces only 'phantoms', but it is also
associated with the irrational and hence the inferior part of the

---

[10] *Gorg.* 501e–502d. Cf. Friedländer's general thesis that 'the *Republic* grew out
of the *Gorgias*' (Friedländer (1969), 122; see also ibid. 78–9, 92–3, 120–1, 124–5).
[11] *Rep.* 394bc; cf. also 392d–394a.
[12] Ibid. 595a.

soul, in that it causes pleasure.[13] Application of this criterion produces rather remarkable results.

That dramatic poetry, tragic as well as comic, is the first to be
rejected, comes as no surprise. But Plato intends to accomplish
'even more' than simply 'considering whether we shall admit
tragedy and comedy into our city or not.'[14] The dramatic genres are
followed by epic poetry, that is, by Homer, for though the mixed
kind he represents is supposed to be more acceptable from the ontological standpoint, Homer is deemed too 'pleasurable' to comply
with Plato's demands.[15] Nor is lyric poetry, though formally non-
mimetic, completely immune from the penetration of pleasure.[16]
Consequently, even this type of poetry must be 'purified', and only
'hymns to the gods' and 'the praises of good men', performed in
uniform rhythms and modes, are eventually allowed in Plato's ideal
state.[17] Thus, though Plato begins with the presumption that
poetry is not necessarily mimetic, his supplementing of the ontological criterion of mimesis with the psychological one makes
non-mimetic poetry into an ideal which is practically devoid of real
substance. Actually, most extant poetry is understood by Plato as a
product of the art of mimesis.

This, I believe, is the key to reconciling the view of poetry found
in book 3 of the *Republic* with that in book 10. While in book 3
Plato proceeds from the assumption that poetry can be either
mimetic or non-mimetic, in book 10 he seems to abandon this distinction and to characterize all poetry as mimetic.[18] Once we
realize that for Plato, non-mimetic poetry is 'ideal' poetry, however, we are able to explain the apparent inconsistency by referring
to the context of his discussion. In any case, it is irrelevant to our
discussion whether it is simply impersonation or representation in
a more general sense of making images that is meant by mimesis
in any given context. It has often been argued that since the

[13] *Rep.* 602c–606d. Cf. Koller (1954), 15–19; Belfiore (1983), 39–62; Ferrari
(1989), 118, 131ff.; Janaway (1995), 133–57. See also Ch. 6 below.
[14] *Rep.* 394d.
[15] Ibid. 606e–607e.
[16] Ibid. 607a. Cf. *Gorg.* 502a.
[17] *Rep.* 607a, 398d–400d. Cf. Murray (1996), 15: 'Hymns to the gods and
encomia to good men will be permitted in the ideal state, but there will be no place
for poetry as we know it.'
[18] See Tate (1928), 16–23 and (1932), 161–9; Verdenius (1949), 42; Havelock
(1963), 24–6; Lucas (1968), 260–1 n. 1; Russell (1981), 102–3; Janaway (1995),
131.

former comes to the fore in *Republic* 3, whereas *Republic* 10 stresses the latter, Plato entertains two mutually irreconcilable views of mimesis. For Plato, however, mimesis was a general philosophical concept purporting to account for the ontological status of representational arts, and impersonation was obviously taken by him as no more than one of the particular manifestations of the concept in question (see further below, Chapter 6).

It is characteristic that in the dialogues in which the theory of mimesis is being effectively developed Plato persistently avoids uniting mimesis and inspiration.[19] The attempts of some scholars to reconcile the two do not overcome the difficulty pointed out by W. J. Verdenius, namely, that

if it is the Muse herself who speaks through his mouth, it seems strange that the poet should involve himself in contradictions. There is no room for assuming a malignant intent on the part of the Muse, for Plato expressly assures that 'from every point of view the divine and the divinity are free from falsehood', and that 'God is altogether simple and true in deed and word, and neither changes himself nor deceives others by visions of words or the sending of signs in waking or in dreams' (*Rep.* 382e).[20]

It seems, however, that the contradiction between inspiration and mimesis runs even deeper than that, and this is why Verdenius's own attempt to solve this contradiction by assuming a sort of collaboration between the poet and the Muse and arguing that it is the artist himself who 'is to blame for confusing the inspiration of the Muse' is also unsatisfactory.[21] No collaboration can arise

[19] Cf. Stählin (1901), 29; Grube (1935), 182; Flashar (1958), 107 ff., 134 ff.; Hackforth (1952), 61; Vicaire (1960), 221, 225; Tigerstedt (1969), 60, 66, 71 n. 242; Murray (1996), 6–7. The only Platonic passage where inspiration and mimesis are brought together is *Laws* 719c: 'when a poet takes his seat on the Muse's tripod, his judgement takes leave of him. He is like a fountain which gives free course to the rush of its waters, and since his art is the art of mimesis must often contradict his own utterances in his presentation of contrasted characters, without knowing whether the truth is on the side of this speaker or of that', trans. A. E. Taylor. Note, however, that inspiration is interpreted here as the poet's identification with his characters rather than as his delivering of divine messages (for a different opinion see Murray (1996: 237–8), who takes the passage as referring to both). This is the interpretation ascribed to Agathon (and, by implication, to the Sophists) in Aristophanes' *Thesmophoriazusae* and which was to be expounded later in Aristotle's *Poetics*, see n. 37 below.

[20] Verdenius (1949), 4.

[21] Ibid. 5; cf. Verdenius (1983), 44. See the criticism of Verdenius's position by Tigerstedt (1969), 65, and Janaway (1995), 33–4.

where divine authority is involved: whether the poets' accounts are truthful or false, as far as the poet is divinely inspired, it is nevertheless the Muse who in any case would be held responsible for these accounts. Hesiod's introduction of lying Muses rather than lying poets immediately comes to mind in this connection (see further Chapter 5). Mimesis, however, is consistently treated by Plato as some kind of *technē* and therefore as the artist's own enterprise. That is to say, whether the poets' accounts are truthful or false, in the case of the mimetic poet it is the poet himself who in any case would be held responsible for them. Just as the poet cannot claim credit for what he does *qua* inspired by the Muse, there is no place for the Muse to the extent that the poet is considered the only cause of what he does. This is why inspiration and mimesis act as mutually exclusive.

Thus Plato's understanding of poetry acknowledges two mutually incompatible conceptions of this activity: on the one hand, poetry is a lofty enterprise not falling short of philosophy, which, in virtue of its origin in divine inspiration, delivers higher truth and thus benefits society; on the other, poetry is a trivial art of mimesis on a par with painting, which, in that it produces phantoms of things which exert a corrupting influence on the human soul, is socially dangerous.[22] While the former is set by Plato as an ideal which is only partly answered by the lyric genres, the latter corresponds to most poetry of the past, including Homer, but especially to poetry produced in Plato's own time. That such a discrimination between two kinds of poetry was not idiosyncratic to Plato is made clear by Aristophanes' *Frogs*, a comedy in the focus of which a fierce confrontation between the tragic poets Aeschylus and Euripides is placed:

> O surely with terrible wrath will the thunder-voiced monarch be
>   filled
> When he sees his opponent beside him, the tonguester, the
>   artifice-skilled,

---

[22] Cf. Tigerstedt (1969), 66: 'That Plato thus takes two different, mutually incompatible attitudes to poetry is a fact which the interpreter should loyally accept, however unpalatable to him it may be.' Cf. also Stählin (1901), 1; Vicaire (1960), 261ff; Annas (1982), 1–28; Halliwell (1986), 84. The latest attempt to gloss over the contradictions in Plato's theory of art is Janaway (1995). However, I agree with the opinion expressed by Julia Annas in the 12 July 1996 issue of the *Times Literary Supplement* (p. 31), that in spite of the other merits of Janaway's book, his 'unifying project' is on the whole unconvincing.

Stand, whetting his tusks for the fight! O surely, his eyes rolling-
fell
Will with terrible madness be fraught!
O then will be charging of plume-waving words with their wild-
floating mane,
And then will be whirling of splinters, and phrases smoothed
down with the plane,
When the man would the grand-stepping maxims, the language
gigantic, repel
Of the hero-creator of thought.
There will his shaggy-born crest upbristle for anger and woe,
Horribly frowning and growling, his fury will launch at the foe
Huge-clamped masses of words, with exertion Titanic up-tearing
Great ship-timber planks for the fray.
But here will the tongue be at work, uncoiling, word-testing,
refining,
Sophist-creator of phrases, dissecting, detracting, maligning,
Shaking the envious bits, and with subtle analysis paring
The lung's large labour away.[23]

Although Aristophanes formally sets up his contest as between rival claims to superior *technē*, both the characters of Aeschylus and Euripides and the nature of their poetry as portrayed in the *Frogs* fit in well with Plato's distinction between the *mousikos* and the *poiētikos*. Like the possessed poet of the *Phaedrus*, Aeschylus of the *Frogs* is characterized by 'madness' (*mania*)[24] and is incapable of controlling his speech, which pours out 'like a stream'.[25] In contrast to this, Euripides is a master of his art who approaches poetry, both Aeschylus' and his own, rationally and analytically.[26] As Plato's *mousikos* was classified with the philosopher, so

[23] *Frogs* 814–29, trans. B. B. Rogers.

[24] *Frogs* 816; cf. *Phdr.* 245a, 256b; *Symp.* 218b. Cf. also τὸν βακχεῖον ἄνακτα at *Frogs* 1259 and *Symp.* 218b. Pohlenz (1965: 440 n. 3) comments on Aeschylus' madness: 'Es ist die μανία des platonischen Phaidros (245a), das ἱερὸν πνεῦμα Demokrits (B 18 und 21), das schon Klemens mit Platos Ion 534b zusammenstellt und Cicero Div. I 80 platonisierend mit *furor* wiedergibt.' Cf. also Lucas (1968), 178.

[25] *Frogs* 1005; cf. also 838, 1198–9, 1407. Harriott (1969: 88–90) showed that the image of a stream was a literary cliché of the time, intended to express the 'unconscious stage in the genesis of a poem'. The closest parallel seems to be *Phdr.* 235c: 'There is something welling up within my breast. . . . I am of course well aware it can't be anything originating in my own mind, for I know my own ignorance; so I suppose it can only be that it has been poured into me, through my ears, as into a vessel, from some external stream. . . .' Cf. also *Laws* 719c and Emped. DK 31 B 4.

[26] *Frogs* 973–4, 945, 1178–9. Cf. Radermacher (1967), 284–5.

Aeschylus is ranked among the great educators of the Greeks together with Orpheus, Museus, Homer, and Hesiod;[27] conversely, Euripides is described, like Plato's *poiētikos*, first and foremost as an artisan—he 'weighs', 'measures', 'plans', and 'models' his verses by means of scales, rulers, yardsticks, and so on.[28] Finally, like the inspired poet of the *Phaedrus*, Aeschylus instructs the citizens by providing them with examples of military prowess and thus greatly benefits society,[29] whereas Euripides, like Plato's mimetic poet, is competent in a wrongful art—his plays, though they please the audience, are morally corrupting:

> Of what ills is he not the creator and cause?
> Consider the scandalous scenes that he draws,
> His bawds, and his panders, his women who give
>   Give birth in the sacredest shrine,
> Whilst others with brothers are wedded and bedded,
>   And others opine
> That 'not to be living' is truly 'to live'
> And therefore our city is swarming today
> With clerks and with demagogue-monkeys, who play
> Deluding the people of Athens. . . .[30]

At the same time, it can be observed that the conflict between Aeschylus and Euripides as represented in the *Frogs* is far from being a conflict between two individual poets. For Aristophanes, Aeschylus and Euripides are two authentic representatives of 'old' and 'new' poetry, respectively.[31] The poetry of Aeschylus is 'old' not only because Aristophanes associates it with the poetic tradition and social standards of the past, but also because he is aware that it is Euripides rather than Aeschylus who is favoured by the contemporary Athenian public.[32] In Aristophanes' eyes, Euripides is a representative of a whole generation of 'new' Athenian poets creating in the Sophistic tenor. Perhaps even closer to Plato's *poiētikos* is the Agathon of the *Thesmophoriazusae* who is not only described in the same vein as the Euripides of the *Frogs* but even characterized by the term *mimēsis*.[33]

---

[27] *Frogs* 1030-44.
[28] Ibid. 797-801, 819, 881, 956. Cf. also *Thesm.* 52-7 and Radermacher (1967), 257-8.   [29] *Frogs* 1019-29, cf. 1052-6.
[30] Ibid. 1078-86; cf. 1010-11, 1069-71, 1413.
[31] Cf. Pohlenz (1965), 459; Snell (1953), 114.
[32] *Frogs* 66-103, 771-8, cf. also 1069-88. Cf. Radermacher (1967), 335-6.
[33] *Thesm.* 156.

Thus a generation before Plato, Aristophanes had drawn a similar distinction between two types of poetry, the beneficial, originating in divine inspiration, and the corrupting, originating in art, and had similarly associated the latter with contemporary poetic practice. Yet in the case of Aristophanes this distinction seems to be far better balanced: while Plato's ideal poetry is reduced to the lyric genre alone, the ideal poetry of Aristophanes embraces all the epic and dramatic poetry of the past, and Aeschylus and Sophocles are its representatives among more recent poets.[34] In view of this, the respective positions of Aristophanes and Plato can tentatively be accounted for in terms of historical development: the concept of poetry as based on either inspiration or art had evolved into a concept of poetry as based on art alone. That this understanding of the relation between Aristophanes and Plato would make sense is corroborated by Aristotle's *Poetics*.

It was Aristotle, indeed, who revised Plato's doctrine of poetry and came to conclusions that had only been implied by his predecessor. Plato, we saw, reduced almost all actual poetry to mimesis, and the only thing that prevented him from overtly admitting this was his ideal of a non-mimetic, that is, inspired, poetry. Aristotle too assumes mimesis as a basis for his poetics, but whereas Plato regarded it as the art of producing phantoms of reality, for Aristotle, not committed to Plato's ontology,[35] mimesis is an art that enables the representation of the universal, purified of the accidental aspects of empirical reality. Aristotle uses Plato's view of poetry as a mimetic art to build a hierarchy of preferences directly opposed to Plato's. Thus, while Plato considered tragedy the least acceptable of all literary genres, for Aristotle it was the most acceptable; while Plato faulted Homer for his deviations from 'plain discourse', that is, for the considerable part played by impersonation in his poems, Aristotle saw this as one of Homer's greatest virtues; while Plato thought poetry has a harmful effect on the soul in that it feeds the emotions that destroy its rational part, in Aristotle's eyes the emotions aroused by poetry have a purifying effect on the soul, and so on. To borrow G. F. Else's formulation, 'Aristotle puts highest what Plato puts lowest'.[36]

[34] On Aristophanes' attitude to Sophocles see *Frogs* 786-94.

[35] That Aristotle's rejection of Plato's theory of Forms was the main reason for their different attitudes to the issue of mimesis is often overlooked: Janko (1987, p. xiii) is a notable exception.

[36] *Poet.* 1461^{b}26-1462^{b}15, 1460^{a}5-8, 1449^{b}24-8. Else (1957), 98.

Aristotle's view of mimesis as essential to poetry leaves no room for Plato's ideal of non-mimetic poetry, and the fact is that in the *Poetics*, the very concept of which presupposes that poetry is a product of deliberate activity, inspiration no longer plays any significant part. It is treated there as an auxiliary tool which provides the poet with a 'natural sympathy', enabling him to make his characters more convincing: it is the empathy of Aristophanes' Agathon, rather than the divine enthusiasm of the Platonic poet.[37] It is not surprising, therefore, that lyric poetry, the only genre which, in virtue of being non-mimetic, was partly admitted by Plato into his ideal state, finds no classificatory niche of its own in Aristotle's *Poetics*.[38]

Now, if Aristophanes proceeds from a distinction between the poetry deriving from inspiration and the poetry deriving from art, and Plato in the *Republic*, although nominally keeping this distinction, treats all existing poetry as deriving from art alone, whereas Aristotle makes no provision at all for the poetry deriving from inspiration, then it can be suggested that the conflict between the two concepts of poetry as found in Aristophanes and Plato is indicative of transition from one concept to another. That is, the concept of poetry as deriving from inspiration was superseded by the concept of poetry as deriving from art. With this in view, let us turn again to Plato, the Sophists, and Aristotle.

As we have seen, the only thing that prevented Plato from reducing all poetry to mimesis was that he felt it necessary to retain, even if only as an ideal, the possibility of 'true' and 'beneficial', that is, inspired, poetry. For Plato, therefore, the character of a work of poetry was strictly conditioned by its source—a work of poetry was 'true' and 'beneficial' if derived from divine inspiration, but 'false' and 'harmful' if derived from art. Since the Sophists and Aristotle derived poetry from art, it is hardly surprising that they exhibit a very different attitude to the work of poetry.

---

[37] See *Poet.* 1455ᵃ32-4; *Thesm.* 149-52. Cf. Lucas's commentary on *Poet.* 1455ᵃ32-4 in Lucas (1968), 178: 'Aristotle has nothing to say on this aspect of the poet's activities. There was no room in his philosophy for powers which expressed themselves through the mouths of poets. He recognized ἐνθουσιασμός, a word which can cover the condition of the inspired poetry, but only as a nervous condition.' Cf. Halliwell (1986), 82-92.

[38] On Aristotle's neglect of the chorus in tragedy and the first-person poetic genres in general see esp. Halliwell (1986), 238-52, 276-84. On the lyric see also below, Ch. 6 and the Afterword.

To be sure, the Sophists did not proclaim poetry to be false and harmful, but, in fact, whether it was true and beneficial was of no relevance to them. In the Sophists' eyes, poetry was one subdivision of *logos* ('speech', 'discourse'), the other being rhetoric. 'I regard and designate poetry as a whole', Gorgias wrote in his *Encomium of Helen*, 'as speech (*logos*) accompanied with metre.'[39] Since *logos* was held by the Sophists to be neutral with respect to values, such criteria as 'true' and 'beneficial' were not applicable to it. The only criterion for evaluating speech thus understood could be a criterion immanent to speech itself. Note that the criterion of truth was considered irrelevant from the very first days of rhetoric in the Sicilian school of Corax and Tisias, who replaced it by the criterion of plausibility (*eikos*).[40] Among the Sophists, it was Protagoras who asserted that there are two contradictory propositions on every matter, while Gorgias never professed to teach virtue, claiming only to make his pupils skilled speakers.[41] And just as plausibility (*eikos*) was the essence of rhetoric, and persuasion (*peithō*) its object, so the essence of poetry was illusion (*apatē*), and its end pleasure (*hēdonē*).[42]

Although Aristotle did not share the Sophists' view of poetry as drawing no distinction between just and unjust,[43] neither did he regard it as subject to ordinary standards of 'true' and 'false'. Unlike history, which relates 'what has happened' (*ta genomena*) and deals with 'the particular' (*kath' hekaston*), or 'what Alcibiades did or suffered', poetry relates 'what may happen' (*hoia an genoito*) and deals with 'the universal' (*ta katholou*), or 'how a person of a certain type will on occasion speak or act, according to the law of probability and necessity'. 'What has happened' is thus just raw material to be rearranged anew into an organic unity in accordance with the principle of 'probability (or: plausibility) and

[39] DK 82 B 11, 9 λόγον ἔχοντα μέτρον. Cf. Pl. *Gorg.* 502c.

[40] See e.g. Pl. *Phdr.* 257a; *Gorg.* 453a; cf. Diels's note on DK 82 A 28.

[41] DK 80 A 20, B 6a; 82 A 21. The metaphysical foundation of the Sophists' doctrine of *logos* was most likely Gorgias' dissociation of *logos* from 'being' (*ta onta*) in the treatise *On Being*, see DK 82 B 3, 84. Cf. Untersteiner (1954), 140–75; Rosenmeyer (1955), 230–2; Kerferd (1981), 80–2.

[42] See Gorgias, *Hel.* 8–10 (DK 82 B 11) and, especially, his definition of tragedy as *apatē* (B 23), which is justly thought to point the way to Plato's theory of mimetic poetry, see Pohlenz (1965), 463, and below, Ch. 6. On *apatē* and pleasure in Gorgias see Untersteiner (1954), 108, 185 ff., 189–90.

[43] As expressed e.g. in *Dialexeis* 90. 3. 17 DK. On Aristotle's attitude to the ethical impact of poetry see the discussion of pleasure below in this section and the Afterword.

necessity' (*kata to eikos kai anagkaion*).[44] In other words, like the
other arts, Aristotle provides poetry with laws of its own, laws
according to which 'not to know that a hind has no horns is a less
serious matter than to paint it inartistically'.[45] In Aristotle's eyes,
therefore, the existence of a work of art was justified by no other
factor than the work of art itself or, to use his own words, 'the
products of arts have their goodness in themselves, so that it is
enough that they should have a certain character'.[46] In the case
of poetry, this 'goodness' was certainly equivalent to the inner
coherence of the poem's plot (*muthos*).

Aristotle thus dismisses Plato's demand for factual truth in
poetry, subordinating it to the specific requirements of poetry and
viewing it as only 'accidental':

the standard of correctness (*orthotēs*) is not the same in poetry and
politics, any more than in poetry and any other art. Within poetry itself
there are two kinds of faults,—those which concern the poetry proper
(*kath' hautēn*), and those which are accidental (*sumbebēkos*). If a poet has
chosen to imitate something, ⟨but has imitated it incorrectly⟩ through
want of capacity, the error is inherent in the poetry. But if the failure is
due to a wrong choice—if he has represented a horse as throwing out both
his off legs at once, or introduced technical inaccuracies in medicine, for
example, or in any other art—the error is not essential to the poetry.
These are the points of view from which we should consider and answer
the objections raised by the critics.[47]

To illustrate Aristotle's attitude to questions of factual truth in
poetry, it suffices to recall that he praises Homer for having taught
other poets how 'to tell lies skilfully'.[48] In Aristotle's eyes, poetry is
of greater value than simply an account of 'what has happened':
in virtue of its dealing with the universal rather than with the
particular it is 'a more philosophical and a more serious thing than
history'.[49]

And just as the truth of poetry is a special kind of truth, not
commensurable with factual correctness, so too its end, as stressed

[44] *Poet.* 1451ᵃ37-ᵇ11. On *eikos* as 'plausibility' see esp. Halliwell (1986), 101-4.
[45] *Poet.* 1460ᵇ32-3. Cf. Butcher (1951), 163-97; Else (1957), 262; Lucas
(1968), 111; Halliwell (1986), 132-7.
[46] *Eth. Nic.* 1105ᵃ27-32, trans. D. Ross.
[47] *Poet.* 1460ᵇ13-23, trans. S. H. Butcher. See Lucas (1968), 236, 235; cf.
Butcher (1951), 163-97; Else (1957), 284, 630.
[48] *Poet.* 1460ᵃ18-19.
[49] Ibid. 1451ᵇ5-7.

in the *Poetics* on more than one occasion, is a specific pleasure which is proper to poetry alone (*oikeia hēdonē*): 'For we must not demand of tragedy any and every kind of pleasure, but only that which is proper to it.'[50] That for Aristotle the sole object of poetry is pleasure is a conclusion with which the majority of twentieth-century commentators on the *Poetics* would agree.[51] At the same time, since in many recent studies of the *Poetics* there can be discerned a tendency to put more emphasis on the moral and educational effects of poetry rather than simply on the pleasure caused by it, the statement that for Aristotle the end of poetry is pleasure can no longer pass without further qualification. The thorough treatment of pleasure in book 10 of the *Nicomachean Ethics* seems to be of especial importance in this respect. Since the bearing of the *Nicomachean Ethics* on the issue of pleasure in the *Poetics* is usually not taken into account in discussions of the latter, I shall dwell on this subject at some length.

According to Aristotle, pleasure is inseparable from the activity which causes it. Every activity is bound to be completed by the kind of pleasure proper to it. 'Pleasure completes the activity not as the correspondent permanent state does, by its immanence, but as an end (*telos*) which supervenes as the bloom of youth does on those in the flower of their age.' Or: 'For they [the activity and pleasure] seem to be bound up together and not to admit of separation, since without activity pleasure does not arise, and every activity is completed by the attendant pleasure.'[52] But this is true only of the pleasure which is specific to the activity in question (*oikeia hēdonē*).[53] Pleasures arising from other sources hinder the corresponding activities and eventually destroy them:

This will be even more apparent from the fact that activities are hindered by pleasures arising from other sources. For people who are fond of playing the flute are incapable of attending to arguments if they overhear

---

[50] *Poet.* 1453^{b}10-11. See also 1451^{b}23, 1452^{b}33, 1453^{a}36, 1459^{a}21, 1462^{a}16, 1462^{b}13.

[51] As Allan (1970: 155) put it, 'the poet, according to him [Aristotle], should have but one aim, that of giving pleasure by representation'; cf. Hulton (1982), 11: 'pleasure is the only external purpose which the *Poetics* recognizes'. See also Collingwood (1938), 51-2, 81, 98; Butcher (1951), 198-314; Lucas (1968), 105, 239; Russell (1981), 91, 159-62. *Poet.* 1462^{b}13 clearly implies that Aristotle meant the epic to produce the same kind of pleasure as tragedy, cf. Lucas (1968), 139, 257; Else (1957), 651-3; Halliwell (1986), 65.

[52] *Eth. Nic.* 1174^{b}31-4, 1175^{a}19-21.

[53] Ibid. 1175^{a}30-1 ff.

someone playing the flute, since they enjoy flute-playing more than the activity in hand; so the pleasure connected with flute-playing destroys the activity connected with argument. This happens, similarly, in all other cases, when one is active about two things at once; the more pleasant activity drives out the other, and if it is much more pleasant does so all the more, so that one even ceases from the other. This is why when we enjoy anything very much we do not throw ourselves into anything else, and do one thing only when we are not much pleased by another; e.g. in the theatre the people who eat sweets do so most when the actors are poor. Now since activities are made precise and more enduring and better by their proper pleasure, and injured by alien pleasures, evidently the two kinds of pleasure are far apart.[54]

On this argument, to endow poetry with a didactic by-purpose in the vein of Plato's exegesis would be equivalent to eating sweets during a theatrical performance, that is, it would be equal to annihilation of the activity itself. Pleasure aroused by poetry must therefore not be seen as instrumental of something other than poetry itself.

This is not to say that Aristotle thought poetry served no good purpose. But, since pleasure only accompanies a given activity and has no separate status of its own, this goodness should be sought for not in the effect of poetry but in the nature of this activity itself:

Now since activities differ in respect of goodness and badness, and some are worthy to be chosen, others to be avoided, and others neutral, so, too, are the pleasures; for to each activity there is a proper pleasure. The pleasure proper to a worthy activity is good and that proper to an unworthy activity bad; just as the appetites for noble objects are laudable, those for base objects culpable.[55]

Aristotle's criteria for a worthy activity are found further in book 10. Those things are both valuable and pleasant which are such to the good man, and the activities which are valuable and pleasant to the good man are those which are in accordance with virtue.[56] If, then, a work of poetry is ethically unworthy (and in chapter 13 of the *Poetics* Aristotle supplies well-defined criteria for distinguishing between ethically worthy and unworthy plots), then the pleasure by which it is accompanied would be unworthy as well.

[54] Ibid. 1175^{b}1-16.
[55] Ibid. 1175^{b}24-9.
[56] Ibid. 1176^{b}24-7; cf. 1099^{a}13, 1113^{a}22-33, 1166^{a}12, 1170^{a}14-16, 1176^{a}15-22.

'Those which are admittedly disgraceful plainly should not be said to be pleasures, except to a perverted taste.'[57] But if poetry is in accordance with virtue, then the pleasure accompanying it would lead, as with other virtuous activities, to the attainment of happiness (*eudaimonia*).[58] 'Whether, then, the perfect and supremely happy man has one or more activities, the pleasures that complete these will be said in the strict sense to be pleasures proper to man.'[59]

This seems to place pleasure caused by poetry among the pleasures which complete the activities of the 'perfect and supremely happy man'. These are activities that are desirable in themselves, that is, those 'from which nothing is sought beyond the activity'.[60] Such is first and foremost the activity of reason, 'which is contemplative, seems both to be superior in serious worth and to aim at no end beyond itself, and to have its pleasure proper to itself'.[61] 'It is clear', Aristotle wrote in the *Politics*,

that there are some branches of learning and education which ought to be studied with a view to the proper use of leisure in the cultivation of the mind. It is clear, too, that these studies should be regarded as ends in themselves, while studies pursued with a view to an occupation should be regarded merely as means and matters of necessity. This will explain why our forefathers made music a part of education. They did not do so because it was necessary: it is nothing of the sort. Nor did they do so because it is useful, as some other subjects are. . . . We are thus left with its value for the cultivation of mind in leisure. This is evidently the reason of its being introduced into education: it ranks as a part of the cultivation which men think proper to freemen.[62]

If we take into account that the Greek word 'music' (*mousikē*) habitually designated not only music proper but also poetry, we shall be able to conclude that the pleasure deriving from poetry was seen by Aristotle as akin to the highest intellectual pleasure that only 'the cultivation of mind in leisure' can produce. One can see that on this interpretation, there would be no discrepancy

[57] *Eth. Nic.* 1176ᵃ22–3. On *Poetics* 13 see also the Afterword.
[58] Cf. *Eth. Nic.* 1177ᵃ2–11.
[59] Ibid. 1176ᵃ26–8. Cf. *Pol.* 1338ᵃ8–9: 'the pleasure of the best men is the best, and springs from the noblest sources.'
[60] *Eth. Nic.* 1176ᵇ5–6.
[61] Ibid. 1177ᵇ19–21.
[62] *Pol.* 1338ᵃ9–23, trans. E. Barker; 'the cultivation of mind in leisure' ἡ ἐν τῇ σχολῇ διαγωγή. On Aristotle's conception of leisure see Barker (1946), 323–4.

between those who see the end of poetry in Aristotle as identical to self-contained aesthetic pleasure and those who prefer to stress its philosophical and moral (but by no means plainly didactic!) character.

Nothing could contrast more sharply with Plato's idea of art. It is hard to improve on Verdenius's formulation of this idea:

Plato never tires of emphasizing the limitations of art. In his opinion art does not possess any independent value in the sense of having its aim in itself. It is important only in so far as it points to something more important. It derives its right of existence from a higher standard founded in a more essential realm of being of which it is an indirect reflection. . . . In short, art cannot be autonomous creation . . .[63]

Though he rightly points out that the tendency to regard a work of art as an autonomous phenomenon conforming to laws of its own is essentially anti-Platonic, at the same time, Verdenius avoids naming Aristotle as the main proponent of this view. Yet, in view of the fact that Aristotle expresses opinions opposite to those of Plato on practically every issue concerning poetry, it would be hard not to agree with those who see in Aristotle's *Poetics* a direct answer to the theory of poetry developed by Plato.[64]

It should not be forgotten, however, that, as is the case with other ideas found in the *Poetics*, the idea of the work of art as an autonomous phenomenon is also present in Plato, although he gives it an unambiguously negative estimation. We saw indeed that, like the Sophists and Aristotle, Plato saw mimetic poetry as not being commensurable with factual truth and having its effect in pleasure. Yet, as distinct from the Sophists and Aristotle, in Plato's system everything 'plausible' and 'pleasurable' inevitably transforms itself into 'false' and 'harmful'. It goes without saying that these qualifications of the product of art are polarly opposed to the characteristics 'truthful' and 'beneficial' by means of which Plato qualifies the work of inspired poetry. This seems to indicate that the character of a poem was conceived as strictly conditioned by its cause—depending on whether the cause of poetry was traced to inspiration or to art, the poem acquired such mutually exclusive

---

[63] Verdenius (1949), 27–8; cf. Annas (1982), 13–19; Janaway (1995), 80.

[64] On the opposition between the aesthetics of Plato and Aristotle see e.g. Collingwood (1938), 51–2, 81, 98, 114; Butcher (1951), 158–62, 203–6, 220–3; Else (1957), 97ff., 306, and *passim*; Lucas (1968), 228, 235–6, 299; Halliwell (1986), *passim*; Janko (1987), pp. x–xiv.

characteristics as 'truth' versus 'plausibility', or 'usefulness' versus 'pleasure'. In view of this, there is good reason to suppose that the conflicting fifth-century attitudes to poetry reflect not only the conflict between two opposite ideas regarding the source of the poet's creative ability ('inspiration' vs. 'art'), but also the conflict between two opposite evaluatory frameworks for the ontological and teleological status of the work of art.

If we take into account that traditional Greek poetry, that of Homer and Hesiod, invariably proceeds from the idea of the poet's inspiration by the Muses, whereas Aristophanes, in both the *Thesmophoriazusae* (411) and the *Frogs* (405), treats the poetry deriving from art as 'new' and unambiguously associates it with the influence of the Sophists, it can further be suggested that the traditional concept of poetry as deriving from divine inspiration historically preceded the concept of poetry as deriving from art, and that the latter should be traced back no further than the emergence of the Sophistic movement in the fifth century BC.[65] If this is correct, the same conclusion should also apply to the criteria by which the products of inspired poetry and those of poetry deriving from art were judged respectively. As we have seen, these criteria were 'truth' and 'usefulness' in the case of inspired poetry and 'plausibility' and 'pleasure' in the case of poetry deriving from art.

The 'Poetics of Truth' and the 'Poetics of Fiction'

At this point of our discussion, it may be useful to draw a distinction between 'inspiration' as a general idea accounting for artistic creativity, and 'divine inspiration' as a concept ascribing the work of art to factors other than the artist himself. Consider, for

---

[65] According to the influential hypothesis put forward by A. Delatte, the concept of poetic enthusiasm as found in Plato's *Ion* must have originated with Democritus: see Delatte (1934); cf. Koller (1954), 148–51; Flashar (1958), 53, 56ff.; Halliwell (1986), 83. Yet to claim this is to ignore the evidence of traditional Greek poetry which invariably sees its source in the poet's inspiration by the Muses. In view of this, Friedländer's position, according to which Democritus and Plato 'drew from the same source', namely, from the common Greek belief in divine inspiration, seems to be methodologically preferable, see Friedländer (1964), 324 n. 8; cf. Finsler (1900), 172–4; Vicaire (1960), 215–16. Consequently, the doctrine of poetic enthusiasm as a state of possession, which did become extremely popular in the fifth century BC, can be explained as a sort of polemical reinforcement of the traditional idea of divine inspiration against the new concept of poetry as an art.

example, the distinction between 'modern' and 'primitive' ideas of inspiration as formulated by C. M. Bowra: 'The primitive poet asserts that everything comes to him from some external, super-natural power and that he himself is little more than its mouth-piece, while the modern takes more credit to himself for what he does, and indeed usually does a good deal to polish and complete what has come to him in inspired moments.'[66] While in the case of Bowra's 'modern' poet it is the poet who holds himself, and is held by others, responsible for his work, in the case of the 'primi-tive', or 'divinely inspired', poet, the factor responsible for the poet's work is the deity behind him. This is also true of the dis-tinction, drawn by D. A. Russell, between attitudes to inspiration in ages 'when religious belief is strong' and in ages 'when belief is questioned by rational speculation'.[67] In the latter, since belief in 'prophecy or direct divine intervention' is replaced by 'more plausible explanations' founded on psychology or physiology, the product of inspiration ceases to be ascribed to divine forces, and forces within man himself begin to be considered responsible for the poem's coming into being. Since this shift inevitably entails a corresponding change in the status of the work of poetry, these are in fact two different ideas, though both are designated by the term 'inspiration'.[68]

Helpful in distinguishing the early Greek idea of inspiration from its later Greek, Roman, and modern counterparts, the issue of the poet's responsibility for his work also highlights some irrelevant distinctions within the concept of divine inspiration itself—primarily, the distinction between inspiration and posses-sion. The importance of distinguishing between inspiration and possession was argued by E. N. Tigerstedt, in whose opinion the concept of poetic inspiration as a state of possession was Plato's invention, whereas the earlier poets 'called themselves inspired but not possessed'.[69] Though certainly implying different degrees of intensity in the poet's emotion, the distinction between inspiration

---

[66] Bowra (1955), 3.

[67] Russell (1981), 70.

[68] Cf. Russell's contention (1981: 79-80), that though Hellenistic and Roman poets proclaimed belief in divine inspiration, this belief was essentially a convention. Cf. also the discussion of Horace in Bowra (1955), 26-44.

[69] Tigerstedt (1969), 26, 64; see also Tigerstedt (1970), 163-78. Cf. Dodds (1951), 67ff. According to Taylor (1960: 38ff., 162 n. 1, 234, 256, 306 n. 1), the idea originated with Socrates.

and possession does not imply any essential difference in the poet's relation to the poem, for whether divinely inspired or divinely possessed, the poet is not responsible for his creation, and this is the only thing that matters for the status of his work.[70] Indeed, whether or not the poet is held responsible for his work inevitably affects the status of the work of poetry, for where the poet *is* held responsible, the work will be considered his personal creation, whereas in the case of the 'divinely inspired' or 'divinely possessed' poet, his work will be considered a divine message.

In dealing with the distinction between early and late, or ancient and modern concepts of inspiration, or the distinction between inspiration and possession, the fundamental issue seems to be that of the poet's individual responsibility for the product of his work. What is the relevance of the issue of individual responsibility to the status of the work of art?

A priori, there seem to be two ways in which the author's relation to his work can be envisaged: either (*a*) the author is considered the only cause of his work, in which case the latter can only be seen as the author's own creation, or (*b*) factors other than the author are considered to have caused his work, in which case it cannot be seen as his creation. Now, if the author is considered the only cause of his work, it is reasonable to suppose that this would affect its ontological status, in that its existence would be justified by nothing other than itself; consequently, the product created in this way would be evaluated for its own sake. Conversely, in a case where factors other than the author are seen as having caused his work, it is reasonable to suppose that this would affect its ontological status, in that its existence would be justified by things other than itself; consequently, the product created in this way would be evaluated for the sake of those entities which justify its existence rather than for its own sake.

In other words, the whole of one's assessment of the ontological and teleological status of the work of art depends upon how the artist is related to his activity from his own or from the interpreter's

[70] While Tigerstedt recognizes that both inspiration and possession involve creative passivity on the part of the poet, Murray (1981: 88–9) maintains that 'it is a mistake therefore to assume that inspiration either in theory or in practice necessarily involves total abandonment of responsibility for his creation on the part of the poet'; for a similar position see also Pratt (1993), 50–2. However, the question as to whom, poet or god, the poem is ascribed, remains the principal one determining the poem's status.

point of view. When the artist is envisaged as individually responsible for his activity, the work of art would be considered a reality *sui generis* and an end in itself; conversely, when the artist is not held individually responsible for his activity, the work of art would be conceived as a message and a means to an end. Since the dichotomous author–creation relationships are thus found to necessitate dichotomous evaluatory frameworks for the work of poetry, we can conclude that the distinctions dealt with are of a typological nature. This seems to indicate that the opposition between inspiration and art as discussed above is in fact an opposition between two different poetics, that is, two different assessments of the mode of existence of the work of art.

It can of course be argued that the distinction between the two poetics does not stipulate the cases where the typologically opposed criteria of approaching the work of art are employed as mutually complementary. The most typical case is a synthetic use of the teleological criterion, that is, a sort of Horatian harmonizing between *prodesse* and *delectare*, exemplified everywhere in neo-classicist poetics (see e.g. the *Don Quixote* quotation adduced in the Afterword, Dryden's definition of drama in his *Essay of Dramatic Poesy*, or *L'Art poétique* of Boileau). The only relevant question in such cases, however, is that of the interpreter's priorities.[71] Thus neither Aristotle nor even Gorgias was against factual truth in literature, but the former saw it as an accidental factor (*sumbebēkos*), and the latter considered it a mere embellishment (*kosmos*). Similarly, it would be wrong to say that Plato demanded that poetry be 'unpleasant'; the point, however, is that when he had to choose between 'usefulness' and 'pleasure', provided that it was 'beneficial', he preferred 'more austere' and 'more unpleasant' poetry.[72]

Let us try now to look at the historically conditioned opposition between inspiration and art from a more general point of view. As has been emphasized already, the 'inspiration:art' opposition is a special case of a more general dichotomy between the author's being or not being individually responsible for his work. But the author may not be held individually responsible for his work, and that work may be conceived as a message and a means to an end not only in cases where he is believed to be the mouthpiece of a divine force. One whose main objective is to give a report of events

---

[71] Cf. Russell (1981), 86.
[72] Arist. *Poet.* 1460[b]17; Gorg. *Hel.* 1; Pl. *Rep.* 398a.

which he has witnessed can well be seen as not 'responsible' for his account either, in that he did not create the events reported. In both cases, the justification for the existence of a given work would be the 'reality' of which it is an account, while deviations from this reality, whatever their artistic merits may be, would be seen as blurring the message and damaging the value of the work. Thus, from a more general point of view, a poetics placing its source in divine inspiration falls into the broader category of a poetics which approaches its object by transcendent criteria.

Note that in the last analysis this poetics does not construe its object as the work of art at all. And obviously, this is the reason why, as Bowra pointed out, 'primitive poetry, however inspired, [is not] always at a high level': as far as the proclaimed goal of such poetry is to deliver divine messages, its artistic merits, if there are any, would always be regarded as secondary to this goal.[73] This was already known to Plutarch. In his discussion of why most of the oracles delivered at Delphi are of a poor artistic quality, he introduces the following comparison between Sappho and the Sybil:

'Do you not see', he [Sarapion] continued, 'what grace the songs of Sappho have, charming and bewitching all who listen to them? But the Sibyl "with frenzied lips", as Heraclitus has it, "uttering words mirthless, unembellished, unperfumed, reaches to a thousand years with her voice through the god." '[74]

If indeed the only demand addressed to the author is to deliver truth, and the only object envisaged is to be useful, any documentary report, provided that it fulfils these requirements, will do.[75]

Not so in the case of poetry deriving from art. 'And even if he [the poet] chances to be putting things that have happened into his poetry,' Aristotle writes in the *Poetics*, 'he is none the less the

---

[73] Bowra (1955), 3. Cf. Russell's view that 'there are obvious links between the notion of a poet's inspiration and that of his didactic or social function', in Russell (1981), 84, see also 76.

[74] Plut. *Mor.* 397A, trans. F. C. Babbitt; see also ibid. 396 C-F.

[75] That messages delivered by the inspired poet (or the inspired prophet, for that matter) are sometimes denounced as false (e.g. the claims of Hesiod discussed in Ch. 5 below) cannot deny the poets in general their professional status of deliverers of divine truth. The activity of the inspired poet owes its very existence to the fact that both the poet himself and his community take it for granted that he is engaged in an activity which as a rule proves efficient. It goes without saying that this can only be possible if the messages delivered by the poet are generally believed to be true.

poet; for there is no reason why some events that have actually happened should not conform to the law of plausible and possible, and in virtue of that quality in them he is their poet or maker.' G. F. Else comments on this: 'These events are already there, they have happened, and yet the poet "makes" them just as much as if he had invented them himself. . . . Their having happened is accidental to their being composed, and vice versa. It is not their own status that matters, but the poet's creative intervention.'[76] This is obviously why Aristotle did not entertain the possibility that those tragedies, few as they were, that used newly invented rather than traditional subjects should be regarded as constituting a separate category:

Still there are some tragedies in which there are only one or two well-known names, the rest being fictitious. In others, none are well known— as in Agathon's *Antheus*, where incidents and names alike are fictitious— and yet they give none the less pleasure. We must not, therefore, at all costs keep to the received legends, which are the usual subjects of tragedy.[77]

Aristotle's words supply an important caveat against attempts at drawing a distinction between the works of literature whose subject-matter is (or is believed to be) historical and those whose subject-matter is purely fictitious, and accordingly at seeing in the Hellenistic novel—the first narrative genre in Greek literature that used invented rather than traditional subjects—the only true ancestor of the modern fiction.[78] Yet, setting the rules of art above what is considered as reality and thus inventing reality of a different order is inevitable, not only for historical fiction but even for those forms of art that sometimes naïvely claim to approximate reality to the degree of becoming indistinguishable from it; for, as was known already to Plato, even the art that aims at producing exact replicas of existing things eventually falsifies reality.[79] As was

[76] *Poet.* 1451ᵇ29–32; Else (1957), 321.

[77] *Poet.* 1451ᵇ19–25.

[78] Thus, Pratt (1993: 37–42) proposes distinguishing between the kind of fiction represented by the modern novel, 'in which most of the characters and events are presumed to be the author's invention', and 'commemorative', or 'historical', fiction, which is based on real events; the latter is accordingly taken to be less of a 'fiction' than the former. Likewise, Gill (1993: 41, 79) maintains that of the genres of Greek literature only the Hellenistic novel can be considered true fiction and therefore it cannot be accounted along the lines of Aristotelian interpretation.

[79] As Halliwell (1987: 108) reminds us, 'even a movement such as nineteenth-century naturalism, which brought with it an often meticulous concern with the

powerfully argued by Goethe, the double light on a picture by Rubens, exactly because it is 'against' nature, testifies to the fact that the artist is placed above nature and his art 'is not subordinated completely to the necessity of nature but has its own laws'.[80] This is why transcendent criteria such as 'true:false' are of little relevance in this kind of poetics. Thus a poetics placing its source in art is a poetics which approaches its object by immanent criteria.

Consequently, the distinction between the two poetics should not be confused with ostensibly similar distinctions which are often drawn within the poetics of art itself. These distinctions have been generalized by W. C. Booth as follows: 'A dialectical history of modern criticism could be written in terms of the warfare between those who think of fiction as something that must above all be real and those who ask that it be pure.'[81] This would be true, for example, of the distinction, made by Goethe in *Über Wahrheit und Wahrscheinlichkeit*, between 'reproduction of reality' and 'reality *sui generis*' as two alternative ways of approaching the ontological status of the work of art; it would also be true of the distinction made in *The Principles of Art* by R. G. Collingwood, who proposes a typology of art by its teleological status, i.e. 'magic' versus 'amusement'; of that made in *The Dehumanization of Art* by Ortega y Gasset, who opposes a 'popular', or 'realistic', art to an 'artistic' art, which is a 'thing of no consequence'; and, in the context of classical antiquity, it would be true of the distinction made in *Idea* by Erwin Panofsky, who wrote,

Insofar as art was an object of thought in classical antiquity, two opposing motives were from the very beginning set naively side by side. . . . There was the notion that the work of art is inferior to nature, insofar as it merely imitates nature, at best to the point of deception; and then there was the notion that the work of art is superior to nature because, improving upon the deficiencies of nature's individual products, art independently confronts nature with a newly created image of beauty.[82]

presentation of life-like particulars, rested in origin on certain convictions about the universal conditions and determinants of human existence: the extreme particularity of artistic fabric was believed to mediate an insight into larger, non-particular truths.' Cf. also Booth (1983), 23–64.

[80] Eckerman (1955), conversation of 18 April 1827.
[81] Booth (1983), 38.
[82] Goethe (1974), 67–74; Collingwood (1938), esp. book 1; Gasset (1956), 8–13, 45; Panofsky (1968), 14.

However, in all these cases the distinctions drawn are those between different principles of representation within the poetics deriving from art, whereas the distinction between this poetics and the poetics deriving from inspiration is that between a poetics whose subject is and a poetics whose subject is not construed as a work of art.

Proceeding from the assumption that inspiration and art are conceptions of creativity which suggest typologically different poetics, that is, different relations between the artist and his activity and different assessments of the ontological and teleological status of the product of this activity, we can conjecture that the conflict discussed in the preceding section between the criteria of 'truth' and 'usefulness' as applied to the inspired poetry, and the criteria of 'plausibility' and 'pleasure' as applied to poetry deriving from art was not only a conflict between two opposite ideas regarding the source of the poet's creativity, i.e. 'inspiration' versus 'art', but also the conflict between two poetics, a 'poetics of truth' and 'a poetics of fiction', of which the former approached poetry by transcendent and the latter by immanent criteria.

It follows from this that, in the search for relevant distinctions between the two poetics, it would not be enough to see such a distinction in the fact that in Archaic Greece it was often recognized that poetry contains lies. When Hesiod and Solon admit that poets' accounts can be false, when Xenophanes accuses Homer and Hesiod of having attributed to the gods 'everything that is a shame and reproach among men', when Hecataeus doubts the reliability of the mythological tradition, when Heraclitus blames Homer for having made Achilles pray that strife would depart from gods and men and Hesiod for his extensive learning that 'teaches no sense', in all these cases poetry is taken as information which may be true or false, or opinion which may be right or wrong. Neither the immanent virtues of a given piece of poetry nor the goal set by the poet are relevant.[83] It is not here, then, that the beginnings of the 'poetics of fiction' should be sought. Only when a piece of poetry is

---

[83] Hes. *Th.* 27–8; Solon 29 West; Xenoph. DK 21 B 11 (cf. also 21 B 1. 19–23); Hecat. *FGrH* 264 F 1, cf. F 19; Heraclit. DK 22 A 22 (cf. B 42, B 56) and B 40 (cf. B 57, B 106). Cf. Rösler (1980), 286–9. In her discussion of the same sources, Pratt (1993: 136–46) confuses fiction with lie, which brings her to the erroneous conclusion that the criticism of the epic tradition by early philosophers and historians amounted to a theory of fiction. 'Lie', however, is just as transcendent a criterion as 'truth', and in virtue of it is equally inapplicable to fiction.

approached from the inner standpoint of the poem itself, will we be in a position to state conclusively that the traditional understanding of poetry has undergone a radical change.

Consider now the following report on Protagoras: 'Protagoras says that the purpose of the episode immediately following the fight between the river Xanthus and mortal men is to divide the battle and make a transition to the theomachy, perhaps also to glorify Achilles.'[84] For Protagoras, the question of whether or not Homer's account is true is of no relevance, the only considerations being those of the text itself. On the assumption that the relevance or irrelevance of immanent criteria in approaching poetry is what basically distinguishes the 'poetics of truth' and the 'poetics of fiction', it follows that the distinction between the modes of criticism found in Hesiod, Solon, Xenophanes, Hecataeus, and Heraclitus, on the one hand, and in Protagoras, on the other, is in fact the distinction between the two poetics. If we locate Protagoras' floruit about 450 BC, we can tentatively assume that the first half of the fifth century BC was the period during which the new approach to poetry was articulated on a conscious level.

Aristotle's *Poetics* was thus the culmination of one of the trends in pre-Aristotelian thought, arising with the Sophists and continued, though evaluated negatively, in Plato's theory of mimetic poetry. But the development of the concept of poetry as deriving from art was paralleled by the gradual decline of another concept, that which saw the source of poetry in divine inspiration. This concept was still alive with Aristophanes in the second half of the fifth century BC, and held as an ideal by Plato in the first half of the fourth, but it had completely disappeared by the time of Aristotle in the middle of the same century.

Above we concluded that the approach to poetry as divinely inspired was superseded by the approach to it as a product of art; now, we may restate this conclusion in terms of the typological opposition between two kinds of poetics: an earlier 'poetics of truth', which in the last analysis did not construe its object as the work of art, clashed with the new 'poetics of fiction' at some point in the fifth century BC, and was eventually superseded by it. It is evident that this event must have amounted to an aesthetic revolution, because as a result of it literary fiction, which since

[84] DK 80 A 30, cf. A 29; trans. W. K. C. Guthrie. Cf. Guthrie (1969), 269; Heath (1989), 157.

then has become a necessary framework for both the theory and the practice of literature in Western tradition, was for the first time separated from non-fiction and given a status of its own. To find out how and why the 'poetics of fiction' arose, what were its sources and the materials from which it was created is the purpose of the present book. The starting-point of our inquiry will naturally be in the traditional 'poetics of truth'.

Approaches to Traditional Poetics

As a matter of fact, it has never been seriously challenged that, to the extent that the traditional poet saw himself as a mouthpiece of the Muse, Greek epic tradition derived poetry from divine inspiration. In Homer, the poet is 'divine' and his song 'inspired';[85] invocations of the Muses found in Homer and Hesiod, as well as such Homeric lines as 'the Muse stirred the bard to sing' or Hesiod's description of how the Muses 'breathed' the divine song into him, show that it was the Muse rather than the poet himself who was believed to be responsible for the poet's song;[86] moreover, like Plato's Ion, both Homer and Hesiod admit their own ignorance of the subject-matter of their poetry.[87] But to admit that the idea of divine inspiration is relevant to Homer and Hesiod is not the same as to argue that traditional Greek poetics was a 'poetics of truth'. We have seen, indeed, that the 'poetics of truth' and the 'poetics of fiction' each imply different assessments of the ontological and the teleological status of poetry. That is to say, to argue that traditional Greek poetics was the 'poetics of truth' would amount to acknowledging that Homer, Hesiod, and other traditional poets saw their poetry as a message of something beyond poetry proper and as a means to an end, which of course is a much stronger claim than merely referring the source of the poet's activity to divine inspiration. The trouble, however, is that the nature of the evidence involved prevents the relevance or irrelevance of this or any other

[85] θεῖος ἀοιδός *Il.* 18. 604; *Od.* 1. 336, 4. 17, 8. 43, 47, 87, and 539, 13. 27, 16. 252, 17. 359, 23, 133 and 143, 24. 439; θέσπις (the song) *Od.* 1. 328, 8. 498, see also ἀοιδὴν θεσπεσίην at *Il.* 2. 599–600; (the singer) *Od.* 17. 385.
[86] *Il.* 1. 1, 2. 484, 761, 11. 218, 14. 508, 16. 112; *Od.* 1. 1, 10, 8. 73, 499; Hes. *Erga* 1–2; *Th.* 1–115, esp. 31–4.
[87] *Il.* 2. 484–7; *Erga* 648–9 and 662.

claim as to the character of traditional poetics from becoming immediately obvious.

Taken together, remarks about poetry scattered throughout the poems of Homer and Hesiod do throw light on various aspects of what could be called 'traditional poetics'. But, in classifying and interpreting the evidence at our disposal, we begin to realize that Hesiod's evidence is not sufficiently detailed, whereas the evidence of Homer, ample though it is, is for the most part of a casual nature, and what we possess are actually inconclusive and sometimes even apparently mutually contradictory *testimonia*. This is probably why it has become habitual to treat Homer's materials on poetry as no more than 'stray hints' whose only value is that they contain grains of ideas which were developed by later writers.[88] Perhaps the most important caveat is that these materials do not supply criteria allowing us to determine Homer's priorities with regard to poetry. This point is best made by way of illustration.

Though the effect of poetry most frequently mentioned in the Homeric poems is pleasure, it is far from clear that pleasure was the only effect that Homer intended poetry to produce. In the *Iliad*, the poet's request for knowledge in the invocation of the Muses preceding the Catalogue of Ships cannot be accounted for in terms of pleasure; an example from the *Odyssey* is the song of the Sirens, described as bringing both pleasure and knowledge to those who hear it.[89] Consequently, scholars are divided as to whether the end of poetry in Homer is pleasure, or knowledge, or both together. The situation with regard to inspiration and art is not very different. Though Homer's invocations of the Muses and the prologue of Hesiod's *Theogony* have led many scholars to take it for granted that the traditional poet considered inspiration the sole source of poetry, there are also indications in the Homeric poems (which will be discussed in detail later in this book) which imply that Homer's understanding of the sources of his poetic ability was quite the opposite. As a result, there are scholars who hold that the source of poetry in Homer is art alone and consider the idea of inspiration to be essentially post-Homeric. Those who decline to single out specific remarks and prefer to keep in mind all the relevant Homeric material generally adopt a compromise position, which

---

[88] Atkins (1934), 11; cf. Sikes (1931), 1–2; Verdenius (1983), 15.
[89] *Il.* 2. 484–93; *Od.* 12. 188. The issue is treated in detail in Ch. 3 below.

sees in inspiration and art two mutually complementary principles equally active in Homer's poetics.

In view of the fact that Homeric texts on poetry seem to support any position whatsoever as to the nature of traditional poetics, we are compelled to conclude that inductive inferences from Homer's materials on poetry to Homer's view of poetry as a whole do not constitute a satisfactory means for analysing his poetics. Accordingly, I have chosen *deduction*, which seems a more profitable procedure for analysing Homer's poetics or, indeed, any subject whose place in a given system is only peripheral. It can be safely presumed that Homer's view of poetry is an inseparable part of the epic system of views, and that the regularities underlying his treatment of poetry and those that underlie his treatment of any other activity are the same. Consequently, inference, whether direct or indirect, from Homer's system of views to his view of poetry as an integral part of this system, seems to be an especially promising procedure for establishing a consistent and reliable picture of the traditional poetics of the Greeks.

Yet, in the case of Homer, application of such a deductive procedure involves a number of difficulties which do not arise when the system being analysed is more self-conscious than that of the epics. Inference from the general to the particular is, in fact, a simple procedure only in cases where class membership is explicit. Thus, for example, from Aristotle's definition of art (*technē*) as a 'state concerned with making, involving a true course of reasoning' in the *Nicomachean Ethics*[90] and his reference to poetry as an 'art' (*technē*) everywhere in the *Poetics*, we are able to infer the place of poetry in Aristotle's system with a considerable degree of certainty. This was, basically, the approach adopted by S. H. Butcher in his classic commentary on the *Poetics*: 'If it is necessary, then, to interpret Aristotle by himself, it will not be unfair in dealing with so coherent a thinker to credit him with seeing the obvious conclusions which flow from his principles, even when he has not formally stated them.'[91] In contrast, in cases like that of Homer, one has to discover not only the way in which a peripheral subject (like poetry) is classified under general

---

[90] *Eth. Nic.* 1140ᵃ21-2 ἡ τέχνη . . . ἕξις τις μετὰ λόγου ἀληθοῦς ποιητική.

[91] Butcher (1951), 114-15. See also Else's discussion (1957: 2-7) on the meaning of *poiētikē* in Aristotle, and Halliwell's discussion (1986: 43) of Butcher's approach.

categories (like 'art'), but also the nature of these general categories themselves.

As we saw above, whether the poet creates by inspiration or by art is a particular instance of a more general question: whether or not the poet is seen as individually responsible for his activity. It follows that if we aim to establish whether the Homeric poet was creating by inspiration or by art, we must enquire whether or not the poet's activity belongs to the class of activities for which Homeric man was held responsible. This amounts to a subsumption of poetry under more general categories which, if performed correctly, would eventually lead to establishing the place of poetry within the system underlying Homeric usage, whether or not this system was consciously articulated by Homer himself. At the same time, it would be wrong to assume that the analytical procedure can proceed mechanically or that its application can by itself guarantee the correctness or relevance of the results. To prove that an established system is relevant to the text under analysis, the results obtained must be tested against something, and this 'something' is the evidence about meanings that the system under analysis would admit or reject. To quote Jonathan Culler, 'whatever one's procedure, results must still be checked by their ability to account for facts about the system in question, and thus the analyst's task is not simply to describe a corpus but to account for the structure and meaning that items of the corpus have for those who have assimilated the rules and norms of the system.'[92] Thus, the analyst must simultaneously work from two perspectives, that of structure and that of meaning, the latter providing a means of assessing the former.

Naturally, the most effective way to check one's results is to bring them into correspondence with the competence of native speakers, which alone can assure the analyst of their correctness.[93] But if the perspective of meaning is essential to any analysis, how much more so in the case of remote civilizations with regard to which one has very little of what might correspond to the competence of native speakers. Consequently, the discovery of meaning constitutes the essential part of any analysis of this kind. To render meaningful the results of an analytical procedure dealing with data of whose meaning one can never be absolutely

---

[92] Culler (1975), 31.
[93] On the theory of literary competence see Culler (1975), 20-4, 113-30.

certain, one has to reconstruct the cultural context that may provide clues as to the nature of the relations established. This, in fact, is one of the major problems I have had to confront in *Chapter 2*. The classification of Homeric man's activities and the establishment of the place of poetry within this classification, which resulted from this approach, have set much of the framework for the treatment of Greek poetics in the subsequent chapters of this book.

Since the introduction of the 'poetics of truth' and the 'poetics of fiction' issued from considerations of a general nature, I could hardly expect that my inferences concerning the nature of traditional poetics should be accepted without my having demonstrated the relevance of these inferences to the cultural context in question. In other words, the contention that the source of a given activity, inspiration or art, determines different understandings of the ontological and teleological status of the product of this activity ought also to be verified. *Chapter 3*, discussing how Homer saw the ontological and the teleological status of the traditional poem, is intended to supply such verification.

Although the 'poetics of fiction' proves not applicable to the traditional Greek view of the epic song, this does not mean that this poetics was altogether alien to the traditional Greek outlook as a whole. *Chapter 4* is an attempt at demonstrating that in Greek tradition the sphere to which the 'poetics of fiction' was considered relevant was represented not by poetry but by handicrafts. Handicrafts thus acted in Homer as a typological counterpart to poetry. It can be expected, therefore, that, as soon as poetry begins to be treated as deriving from art, the productive ability of the poet would be conceived along the lines of handicrafts.

No study of Homer's poetics can be complete unless it is brought into correspondence with the actual practice of Homer as reflected in his poems. As we shall see, there is an intriguing incompatibility between Homer's views on poetry and the Homeric poems themselves. The meaning and the historical significance of this phenomenon will be discussed in *Chapter 5*.

Relinquishment of the idea of inspiration and the ensuing recognition that the poem is the poet's own creation were a result of cultural developments of which the *Poetics* of Aristotle was only the last stage. These developments are examined in *Chapter 6*. The new approach to poetry as a product of art brought forth the acknowledgement that the 'true:false' criterion is not applicable to the work of poetry, and that poetry is at its best when creating an illusionary world of its own that is to be judged for its own sake.

The 'Aristotelian galaxy' of fiction remained unchallenged in Western tradition until the emergence of the Romantic movement at the end of the eighteenth and beginning of the nineteenth century. Some aspects of the rebirth of the 'poetics of truth' which followed this development and its relation to mimesis-based mass culture are discussed in the *Afterword*.

'Rather than seeking the permanence of themes, images, and opinions through time,' Michel Foucault wrote, 'rather than retracing groups of statements, could one not rather mark out the dispersion of the points of choice, and define prior to any option, to any thematic preference, a field of strategic possibilities?'[94] The concept of literary fiction as it is known to Western tradition was formed as a result of a series of cultural choices made in Archaic and Classical Greece, choices which made possible a radical revision of the inherited idiom of the divinely inspired poet. As we shall see, the crucial points of this development were the Archaic Greek preference for some forms of representation in the arts to the exclusion of others; the characteristic interpretation given to the poet's inspiration by the Muse in the Homeric tradition to the exclusion of other epic traditions of Archaic Greece; the codification and the subsequent canonization of the Homeric poems in sixth-century Athens; the intellectual revolution of the fifth century, which allowed for explicit formulation of the new status of poetry; the preference shown by the fifth-century Athenian public for some particular forms of theatrical performance to the exclusion of others; Plato's rejection of the popular taste and Aristotle's rejection of this rejection. At every single stage, any particular development could have taken another course, and the final outcome would accordingly have been different.

This is not to say that all the factors involved were changeable and all the choices arbitrary. Strategic possibilities at issue are always culturally bounded and therefore not unlimited, and there were certainly things of which the Greeks could not conceive differently than they in fact did. The constants of the process dealt with in this book consisted in the inherited view, attested as early as Homer, that the human self encompasses both a rational and an

[94] Foucault (1976), 37.

irrational part and that interaction between the two is possible; in the inherited view of creation or, to be more precise, the absence of such a view, which a priori excluded the idea of artistic creativity which became prominent in the modern period; in the inherited idea of art as a competitor of nature; in the limits within which production by art was deemed possible. All the choices, both those that were made and those that eventually were not, could be placed only within these boundaries, and it is mainly the interplay between the changeable and the unchangeable factors, between the freedom of every given choice and the necessity of the framework within which these choices were being made that imparted to the Greek concept of literary fiction the singular form in which it was taken over by Western tradition.

2

Poetry Among Other Activities of Homeric Man

Homer's Classification of Human Activities

If we assemble all the manifestations of Homeric man—from physiological instincts to the higher forms of intellectual activity—and take them, provisionally at least, as a corpus representative of the entire spectrum of Homeric man's functioning, we shall see that the way in which poetry is treated in Homer is far from being peculiar to this activity alone. Thus, Homer's poets sing either when 'incited' by the Muse, 'moved' by a god, or 'stirred' by their *thumos* ('spirit') or *noos* ('mind'), and Hesiod says about himself that the Muses 'ordered' him to sing[1]—but 'to incite', 'to move', 'to stir', 'to order' can motivate many other actions of Homeric man. Helen's elopement with Paris, Patroclus' fatal onslaught on Troy, Telemachus' decision to call the assembly and to go to Pylos are explained exactly like Demodocus' starting of his performances,[2] not to mention the stereotyped acts of fighting, speaking, or even eating and drinking that are regularly the result of being 'stirred', 'incited', 'moved', or 'ordered'. Again, Hesiod says about himself that the Muses 'breathed' into him 'divine song'[3]—but communication of martial valour and strength (*menos*, *tharsos*, *alkē*, *sthenos*) by one of the gods, sudden surges of anger (*kotos*) and infatuation (*atē*) are also quite often explained by Homer as either 'put' or 'thrown' into someone's heart, either 'sent' or 'breathed' into man by the gods; and the same is true of fortunate or ill-fated ideas, of desires, oracles, and so on.

[1] *Od.* 8. 73, 499, 45; 1. 347, 8. 539; *Th.* 33–4. See also n. 54 below.

[2] Helen, *Il.* 5. 422, *Od.* 23. 222; Patroclus, *Il.* 16. 691; Telemachus, *Od.* 1. 89, 4. 712–13; Demodocus, *Od.* 8. 73, 499.

[3] *Th.* 31–2 ἐνέπνευσαν δέ μ' ἀοιδὴν | θέσπιν (μ' ἀοιδήν Rzach; v. l. μοι αὐδήν). I am not persuaded by West (1966: 165) that the latter reading is superior in sense: note that θέσπιν is a fixed epithet of ἀοιδήν in Homer, see *Od.* 1. 328, 8. 498 and that ἀοιδὴν | θεσπεσίην at *Il.* 2. 599–600 gives a close parallel to Hesiod's usage.

This encourages us to investigate further into the nature of the activities in question. Since poetry is the activity whose status we intend to establish, it will not be considered together with the others, but examined in a separate section.

Now, regardless of whether a given action or state of mind is 'thrown' or 'sent', 'put' or 'breathed' into one's heart by a god, 'stirred', 'moved', 'ordered', or 'impelled' by either a god or man's *thumos*, it is not regarded as effected by a compulsion of the will, as premeditated or deliberate. When his actions and states of mind arise in this way, man neither intentionally produces nor controls them, just as he does not produce or control his natural instincts, and the fact is that man's physiological instincts, such as hunger and thirst, and the instinctive behaviour of animals are described in exactly the same way.[4] To use M. P. Nilsson's expression, in situations like these man becomes a 'stranger' to his own behaviour and, consequently, cannot see himself as its real cause.[5] Clearly, this is where the 'argument from non-responsibility'[6] as represented in Agamemnon's famous apology originates:

The Achaeans have often said these words to me, and upbraided me; but I am not to blame (*aitios*), but rather Zeus and Fate and Erinys that walks in darkness: they threw a cruel blindness (*atē*) in my mind at the assembly on that day when nobody else than I took away his prize of Achilles.[7]

Elsewhere, Agamemnon's *thumos* ('spirit') and *phrenes* ('mind') are held to be the cause of the same act. Consider also the motivation

[4] See *Il.* 4. 263, 12. 300, 17. 456, 20. 171, 22. 142, 23. 390 and 399-400, 24. 442; *Od.* 6. 133, 7. 217 and 220, 8. 70.

[5] Nilsson was the first to interpret Homeric man's behaviour in terms of alienation in his 'Götter und Psychologie bei Homer' (1924; rep. in Nilsson (1951), 355-91; summarized in Nilsson (1949), 163-7); however, Nilsson's purely psychological approach caused him to reduce the phenomenon to the states of passion and infatuation only.

[6] The range of application of the terms 'responsibility' and 'non-responsibility' here and elsewhere in this book follows that of the Homeric terms *aitios* and *ouk aitios*. These can apply to any situation in which the agent is or is not recognized as an autonomous causer of what he has done, from the most trivial situations to more complex cases of moral responsibility such as those of Helen and Agamemnon (*Il.* 3. 164, 19. 86). Characteristically, the poets' lack of responsibility for the content of their songs is expressed by the same term (*Od.* 1. 348). On distribution of responsibility in Homer cf. Finkelberg (1995), 15-28.

[7] *Il.* 19. 86-9. The English quotations from the *Iliad* are given here in the translation by Martin Hammond, and those from the *Odyssey* in the translation by Walter Shewring; minor changes have been introduced whenever necessary.

of Sarpedon's attack on the Greeks through his being stirred by
Zeus and his own *thumos* alternately. It seems that in cases such as
these, that is, when the same act is given both divine and human
motivation, Homer, rather than providing two different explanations of it, is suggesting that the act can be accounted for on two
levels, the psychological and the divine.[8] This seems to indicate that
regardless of whether a god or man's own *thumos* is the agent, in
neither case will man be held responsible for what he is doing.

Let us, then, provisionally designate the kind of motivation in
which man is treated as suddenly 'filled' with something or 'stirred'
towards doing something as *motivation by non-responsibility*.[9]
Human activities which are regularly associated with this kind of
motivation are physical abilities, heroic valour, emotions, instincts,
and insight. The most characteristic example (and the one that
has attracted most scholarly attention) is when a sudden surge of
physical energy or bodily strength (*menos*, *sthenos*) is described as
being communicated or stirred by the gods or by man himself.[10]
Likewise, Homeric man's valour (*tharsos*, *alkē*), the characteristic

---

[8] *Il.* 9. 109–10 and 119 (Agamemnon); 12. 292–3 and 307 (Sarpedon). That
Homer gives two different motivations for Agamemnon's act, through the gods in
Iliad 19 and through Agamemnon's mental organs in *Iliad* 9, is sometimes seen as
inconsistency. Thus Wilamowitz (1931–2: ii. 117) saw in the diverse motivations
of *Iliad* 9 and 19 the work of different poets, whereas Lesky (1961: 41–2) argued
that Agamemnon's psychological states in *Iliad* 9 and 19 were different. Yet, the
psychological state of Agamemnon, who ascribes his insulting of Achilles to his
phrenes at *Il.* 9. 119, cannot be projected onto Nestor, who, a few lines above
(ll. 109–10), gives a similar explanation of Agamemnon's act, while later in
the same book (l. 377) Achilles attributes a divine motivation to this same act. This
seems to indicate that divine and human motivation were not seen as mutually
contradictory. On the so-called 'double motivation' in Homer see Dodds (1951),
1–27; Lesky (1961), 22–32. That the gods and *thumos* (as well as the other
mental organs) invariably conform in their interventions in Homeric man's
behaviour has recently been argued in Pelliccia (1995), 250–68.

[9] The most detailed treatment of this kind of motivation is Kullmann (1956),
72–80, but see also Lesky (1961), 11–12; Dodds (1995), 8–13; Pelliccia (1995),
37–57, 256–8.

[10] 'To put', 'to throw', 'to breath into', 'to fill', and the like: μένος δέ οἱ ἐν φρεσὶ
θῆκε *Il.* 21. 145; μένος δέ οἱ ἔμβαλε θυμῷ *Il.* 16. 529, cf. 5. 513, 10. 366, 17. 451;
ἐνῆκε δέ οἱ μένος ἠΰ *Il.* 20. 80, cf. 5. 125, 17. 156, 19. 37, 23. 90, *Od.* 13. 387;
ἔμπνευσε μένος *Il.* 10. 482, cf. 15. 262, 17. 456, 19. 159, 20. 110, 24. 442, *Od.*
24. 520; μένεος δ' ἐμπλήσατο θυμόν *Il.* 22. 312, cf. 1. 103–4, 9. 679, 13. 60, *Od.*
4. 661–2; σθένος ἔμβαλε *Il.* 11. 11 = 14. 151, cf. 21. 304; πλῆσθεν δ' ἄρα οἱ μέλε'
ἐντὸς | ἀλκῆς καὶ σθένεος *Il.* 17. 211, cf. ibid. 499; ἐν δὲ βίην ὤμοισι καὶ ἐν γούνεσσιν
ἔθηκε *Il.* 17. 569. 'To stir', 'to incite', 'to order', and the like: τοῦ δ' ὄτρυνεν μένος
Ἄρης *Il.* 5. 563; Ἕκτορος ὄρσωμεν κρατερὸν μένος *Il.* 7. 38, cf. 13. 78, 20. 93, 22.
204; σθένος ὦρσεν *Il.* 2. 451, cf. 11. 827.

feature of which is its close connection with physical strength, is instantly 'put' or 'thrown' into one's heart, 'sent' or 'breathed' into one, and man can be 'filled' with it exactly as he can be filled with physical strength.[11] Sudden surges of moral courage, expressed by adapting the martial terms *menos* and *tharsos*, are communicated in the same way.[12] Anger, joy, fright, sorrow, etc. are also regularly referred to by Homer as either 'put' or 'thrown' into one's heart, either 'sent' or 'breathed' into one by the gods, or 'stirred' by one's own *thumos*,[13] and the same is true of Homeric man's physiological impulses, primarily those of hunger and thirst.[14] Finally, sudden understanding or, conversely, inexplicable lapses of understanding are regularly accounted for by Homer's people in such phrases as 'the gods threw this into my mind' or 'the gods took away my understanding'.[15]

This does not necessarily indicate that, as is sometimes claimed, motivations like those described above are representative of the entire spectrum of Homeric man's behaviour.[16] As a matter of fact, by no means all the activities of Homer's people are motivated in

[11] θάρσος ἐνὶ φρεσὶ θῆκε *Od.* 6. 140, cf. 1. 320-1, 3. 76-7; ἐν μέν οἱ κραδίῃ θάρσος βάλε *Il.* 21. 547; θάρσος ἐνὶ στήθεσσιν ἐνῆκεν *Il.* 17. 570; θάρσος ἐνέπνευσεν μέγα δαίμων *Od.* 9. 381; θάρσευς πλῆσε φρένας *Il.* 17. 573; ἀλκῆς καὶ σθένεος πλῆτο φρένας *Il.* 17. 499, cf. ibid. 211-12. Cf. Jaeger (1947), 6: 'such valour is not considered as a moral quality distinct from strength, in the modern sense; it is always closely bound up with physical power'. Cf. the doublet ἀλκῆς καὶ σθένεος *Il.* 17. 212, 499.

[12] *Od.* 1. 89, 320-1, 3. 76-7, 6. 140. See Dodds (1951), 10.

[13] 'To put', 'to throw', and the like: χόλον τόνδ' ἔνθεο θυμῷ *Il.* 6. 326, cf. 9. 629; κότον ἔνθετο θυμῷ *Od.* 11. 102 = 13. 342; κότον αἰνὸν ἐνήσεις *Il.* 16. 449, cf. 1. 103-4, 9. 679, *Od.* 4. 661-2; σὺ δ' ἵλαον θυμὸν θυμόν *Il.* 9. 639; φόβον ἔμβαλε *Il.* 17. 118; ἧκε φόβον *Il.* 15. 327, cf. 16. 656; ἐκ δέος εἵλετο γυίων *Od.* 6. 140; γλυκὺν ἵμερον ἔμβαλε θυμῷ *Il.* 3. 139. 'To stir', 'to incite', 'to order', and the like: χόλος δέ τε καὶ τὰ κελεύει *Il.* 20. 255; ὅτε τε Ζεὺς ἐν φόβον ὄρσῃ *Il.* 14. 522; μνηστῆρσι δὲ Παλλὰς Ἀθήνη | ἄσβεστον γέλω ὦρσε *Od.* 20. 345-6, cf. 8. 343; γόου ἵμερον ὦρσε *Il.* 23. 14, cf. *Od.* 16. 215; μοι ὀρώρεται ἔνδοθι θυμός | κήδεσιν *Od.* 19. 377.

[14] πιέειν ὅτε θυμὸς ἀνώγοι *Il.* 4. 263, cf. 8. 189, *Od.* 8. 70; κέλεται δέ ἑ γαστήρ *Od.* 6. 133, cf. *Il.* 12. 300, *Od.* 7. 217, 221.

[15] μαντεύσομαι, ὡς ἐνὶ θυμῷ | ἀθάνατοι βάλλουσι *Od.* 1. 200-1 = 15. 172-3; ἀλλ' ἐπεὶ ἐφράσθης καί τοι θεὸς ἔμβαλε θυμῷ *Od.* 19. 485 = 23. 260; φάρος . . . ἐνέπνευσε φρεσὶ δαίμων *Od.* 19. 138; καὶ τόδε μεῖζον ἐνὶ φρεσὶν ἔμβαλε δαίμων *Od.* 19. 10; middle μὴ . . . φύξιν . . . ἐμβάλλεο θυμῷ *Il.* 10. 447; μῆτιν ἐμβάλλεο θυμῷ *Il.* 23. 313, cf. *Il.* 9. 434-5, *Od.* 11. 428; φρεσὶν ἔμβαλον ἄγριον ἄτην *Il.* 19. 88; τὴν δ' ἄτην . . . ἑῷ ἐγκάτθετο θυμῷ *Od.* 23. 223; ἐκ γὰρ εὖ φρένας εἵλετο μητίετα Ζεύς *Il.* 9. 377, or: Παλλὰς Ἀθήνη 18. 311; φρένας ἐξέλετο Ζεύς *Il.* 6. 234, 19. 137, cf. 17. 470.

[16] Cf. e.g. Russo and Simon (1968), esp. 497. This view owes its existence to E. R. Dodds's famous study of Homeric motivations in the first chapter of *The Greeks and the Irrational* (Dodds (1951)). Of course, Dodds, who introduced the 'irrational' into Homeric man's behaviour only to supplement the 'rational', not to supersede it, cannot be held responsible for all the conclusions drawn on the basis of his book.

this way. Activities which are never combined with motivation that presumes non-responsibility are sports, crafts, skills, and practical wisdom. This distinction in the mode of motivation is important enough to allow us provisionally to distribute the activities of Homeric man into two classes, one compatible with motivation presuming man's lack of responsibility for his behaviour, and the other not compatible with such motivation. Instincts, emotions, insight, and heroic valour would belong to the first, and sports, crafts, skills, and practical wisdom to the second class.

I fully realize that putting physiological manifestations such as hunger or thirst in the same list as insight or heroic valour, or uniting sports with practical wisdom may look incongruous. However, to follow Homeric usage as faithfully as possible seems to be the only way to put things exactly as Homer himself put them, without foisting on him our own modes of classification. That is to say, if Homer gives strength or natural instincts the same kind of motivation as, say, understanding or courage, we have no right to ignore this simply because our way of classifying things is different. In this connection, Foucault's remark on a Chinese classification of animals, surpassing in its oddity anything found in Homer, is pertinent: 'In the wonderment of this taxonomy, the thing we apprehend in one great leap, the thing that, by means of the fable, is demonstrated as the exotic charm of another system of thought, is the limitation of our own, the stark impossibility of thinking *that*.'[17]

At the same time, it is doubtful whether a distributional analysis, that is, a registration of compatibilities and incompatibilities within a given text, can of itself produce a set of classes which need not be justified by any explanatory function.[18] Indeed, it is obvious that our distribution only reflects the way in which the activities of Homeric man are combined with kinds of motivation in the Homeric poems. The problem, however, is that, if we do no more than follow the epic usage, our description, though faithfully reproducing the state of things fixed in the epics, does not provide information about what has made this state of things possible. But as long as the rules underlying the compatibilities and incompatibilities revealed in the distributional analysis are unknown to us,

---

[17] Foucault (1970), p. xv.
[18] Culler's illuminating criticism of Barthes and Lévi-Strauss saves me any lengthy discussion here, see Culler (1975), 32–54.

we cannot be certain as to whether the regularities observed are of a systematic nature. We must, therefore, not only describe the way in which a given activity is combined with a given kind of motivation, but also explain why Homer chose a given kind of motivation for a given activity. Only when we are able to state conclusively that a given activity is not combined with the motivation presuming lack of responsibility because this would be at variance with the epic system of views, and not merely because this happens to be the case in Homer, shall we be in a position to say what the Homeric view of this activity really is. This is why semantic interpretation of the results of the distributional analysis is essential for our purpose.

Clearly, what prevents us from immediately understanding why members of one class of human activities are compatible with the motivation presuming non-responsibility whereas members of the other class are not compatible with it is our lack of competence in the semantic system underlying the epic mind. To be sure, there is no need to penetrate deeply into the epic mind to understand why the physical, physiological, and emotional manifestations of Homeric man are motivated by non-responsibility: the explanation is supplied by the very spontaneous and impulsive character of the manifestations in question. The same, however, cannot be said of the other class of activities. It is indeed difficult to explain why handicrafts, for example, cannot be combined with the motivation presuming non-responsibility as well. Biblical passages such as the following naturally come to mind in this connection:

And the Lord spake unto Moses, saying,
    See, I have called by name Bezaleel the son of Uri, the son of Hur, of the tribe of Judah:
    And I have filled him with the spirit of God, in wisdom, and in understanding, and in knowledge, and in all manner of workmanship,
    To devise cunning works, to work in gold, and in silver, and in brass,
    And in cutting of stones, to set *them*, and in carving of timber, to work in all manner of workmanship.[19]

Nothing of the kind can be found in the Greek sources. Consistent as they may appear to us, expressions like 'the gods threw his work into a craftsman's heart' or 'his *thumos* stirred the craftsman to perform the work' never occur in the Homeric poems, and the

[19] Exodus 31: 1–5; see also Exod. 36–9.

same is true of other skills, of sports, and of various manifestations of Homeric man's practical wisdom. This can only mean that there must have been something in the activities themselves that led Homer to choose consistently one type of motivation over another, but what this factor consists in is far from obvious. To discover it, we must uncover the broader cultural context that renders meaningful the regularities observed. This can only be achieved by examining the semantic characteristics of the activities in question.

The constant semantic characteristic of the activities of Homeric man which are not compatible with the motivation presuming lack of responsibility is *knowledge*.[20] Thus, the carpenter is 'competent', 'well-knowing', 'expert with his hands', and performs his work 'expertly', while the goldsmith is twice characterized as a 'knowing man'.[21] A good sportsman, too, is 'competent' in sports, and 'not ignorant' of them, as well as 'well-knowing' either in all kinds of competitions or in only one of them.[22] Likewise, navigators are 'knowing', dancers are 'competent' and possessed of 'expert legs', physicians are 'knowing' and 'expert', cooking is performed 'expertly', and women are either 'expert in all kind of work' or 'knowing splendid works'.[23]

The same would be true of Homeric man's practical wisdom. Consider in particular the outstanding role that life-experience plays in this aspect of Homeric man's functioning. That people become wise owing to their life-experience follows from the very fact that wisdom in Homer is generally associated with old age. The words of the relatively young Odysseus to the yet younger Achilles 'I might claim to surpass you in judgement by far, since I was born older than you and have greater knowledge' shows Homeric

---

[20] Actually, characteristics with a connotation of 'knowledge' are rendered in Homer by derivatives of three verbs: οἶδα (ἴδρις, ἰδρείη, εὖ εἰδώς, νῆϊς), ἐπίσταμαι (ἐπιστάμενος, ἐπισταμένως), and *δάω (δαήμων, ἀδαήμων). To preserve this distinction, I use 'to know' to translate οἶδα and its derivatives, 'to be expert' for ἐπίσταμαι and its derivatives, and 'to be competent' for *δάω and its derivatives.

[21] ἴδρις ἀνήρ Od. 6. 233, 23. 159; εὖ εἰδῇ Il. 15. 412, Od. 5. 250; δαήμων Il. 15. 411; ἐπίσταμαι Il. 5. 60; ἐπισταμένως Od. 5. 245, 17. 341, 21. 44, 23. 197.

[22] οἶδα, εὖ οἶδα Il. 15. 679, 23. 309, Od. 8. 134, 146, 215; εἰδώς Il. 23. 665; νῆϊς Od. 8. 179; δαήμων Il. 23. 671, Od. 8. 159.

[23] οἶδα Il. 11. 741 (of physicians), 9. 128, 278, 18. 420 (of women); ἴδρις Od. 7. 108 (of navigators); εἰδώς Il. 4. 218 (of physicians); εἰδυῖα Il. 18. 420, 23. 263, Od. 13. 289, 15. 418, 16. 158 (of women); δαήμων Od. 8. 263 (of dancers); ἐπίσταμαι Il. 23. 705, Od. 2. 117, 7. 111 (of women); ἐπιστάμενος Od. 4. 231 (of physicians); Il. 18. 599 (of dancers' legs); ἐπισταμένως Il. 7. 317, 24. 623, Od. 12. 307, 19. 422, 20. 161 (of cooks); 19. 457 (of medical treatment).

man's wisdom in the dynamics of its growth.²⁴ But even one who has not lived a long life like Nestor or Phoenix may compensate for his lack of experience by learning. 'We both know each other's birth, and we know each other's parents', Aeneas says to Achilles, 'from hearing the tales that mortal men have long made famous—though I have never seen your parents, nor you mine.'²⁵ Like his acquisition of knowledge about the past, Homeric man acquires social norms by learning them, generally from a tutor, as Achilles does from Phoenix.²⁶ It is not surprising, then, that Homeric man's practical wisdom is often conveyed in terms of knowledge.²⁷

Even the most superficial examination confirms that no qualification which involves the meaning 'knowledge' is ever applied to activities motivated by non-responsibility, that is, to instincts, emotions, insight, and heroic valour. Moreover, there is at least one instance in which one of the activities of this class, namely, insight, is explicitly associated with the opposite characteristic of ignorance: 'But now I will give you a prophecy—truth to tell, I am not a prophet, and I have no clear knowledge of the signs of the birds, but the immortals have thrown this into my mind, and I am sure it will happen as I say.'²⁸ Clearly, whether the idea conveyed concerns his private affairs or contains a divine message of a more universal significance, the recipient, being only a mouthpiece of the gods, possesses no real knowledge of it. It goes without saying that insight thus understood is nothing other than 'wisdom through ignorance', a phenomenon which we will discuss in more detail with reference to the activity of the Homeric poet.

Furthermore, the activities of Homeric man which are described in terms of knowledge are regularly represented as derived from *teaching*.²⁹ Handicrafts are taught by Athene and Hephaestus, chariot-driving by Zeus and Poseidon, hunting by Artemis,

---

²⁴ *Il.* 19. 218–19 ἐγώ δέ κε σεῖο νοήματί γε προβαλοίμην | πολλόν, ἐπεὶ πρότερος γενόμην καὶ πλείονα οἶδα, cf. 13. 355, 21. 440.

²⁵ *Il.* 20. 203–5, cf. n. 85 below.

²⁶ *Il.* 9. 438–43, cf. 11. 710, 719.

²⁷ *Od.* 2. 188, 7. 157, 24. 51 παλαιά τε πολλά τε εἰδώς.

²⁸ *Od.* 1. 200–2, cf. 15. 172–3.

²⁹ The meaning of 'teaching' is conveyed in Homer by the verbs 'to teach' (διδάσκω, cf. *Il.* 5. 51, 11. 831, 23. 307; *Od.* 8. 481, 488; *δάω *Od.* 6. 233, 17. 519, 20. 72, 23. 160) and 'to learn' (*δάω *Od.* 8. 134, 146; see also μανθάνω at *Il.* 6. 444 and διδάσκομαι at *Il.* 16. 811). In one place, a nominal equivalent of 'to teach' is employed (ὑποθημοσύνῃσιν Ἀθήνης at *Il.* 15. 412).

women's work by Athene, Patroclus was taught medicine by Achilles, and so on.[30] But when one turns to activities whose motivation presumes non-responsibility, it soon becomes evident that they are derived not from teaching, but from *giving*.[31] Thus far, no scholarly attention seems to have been paid to the fact that the spheres of application of 'to give' and 'to teach', the two ways in which man's excellences, advantages, and properties are communicated in Homer, do not coincide. 'To give' and 'to teach' are usually treated as synonyms, mainly because it is taken for granted that the 'divine gift' and 'divine instruction' are simply two different ways of designating one and the same thing. However, 'to give' and 'to teach' do not apply, as a rule, to the same realms of human experience. Whereas 'to teach' is used for communicating crafts and skills of any kind, 'to give' is used for communicating constitutional qualities such as strength, beauty, intellect, valour, and so on.[32] An illuminating example of Homer's differential use of 'to give' and 'to teach' is afforded by a passage in the *Odyssey* describing the upbringing of Pandareus' daughters by Olympian goddesses: 'Hera *gave* them beauty and wisdom beyond all other women; holy Artemis *furnished* them with stature, and Athene *taught* the making of famous works.'[33]

The reasons for the distinction between 'to teach' and 'to give' become clear as soon as one takes into account how they relate to the criterion of individual responsibility. There can be no doubt that as far as 'giving' is concerned, any responsibility on the part of a recipient of the 'gift' would be out of the question. The only role assigned to man in this type of communication is passive acceptance of the 'gift', whatever its nature. 'There is no discarding the glorious gifts that come of the gods' own giving, though a man would not take them of his choice.'[34] This, however, is

[30] *Il.* 5. 51-2, 11. 830-2, 15. 411-12, 23. 307-9; *Od.* 6. 232-4, 20. 72, 23. 159-60.

[31] 'Giving' is conveyed both by 'to give' proper (δίδωμι *Il.* 1. 178, 7. 288, 13. 730; *Od.* 8. 44, 64, 167, 14. 216, 19. 396, 20. 70) and by its synonyms, 'to grant' (ὀπάζω *Il.* 6. 157; *Od.* 8. 498, 13. 45) and 'to furnish' (*πόρω *Il.* 1. 72; *Od.* 20. 71).

[32] See e.g. *Il.* 1. 178, 6. 156-7, 7. 288-9; *Od.* 2. 116-18, 7. 110-11, 8. 166-7, 14. 216-17, 20. 70-1 in contrast with the examples cited in n. 30 above.

[33] *Od.* 20. 70-2 (my italics). Cf. however *Od.* 12. 116 and 7. 110, where a similar conjunction of gifts and skills typical of Homer's descriptions of standard female virtues is introduced by the verb 'to give' alone.

[34] *Il.* 3. 65-6. Generally speaking, there is no compelling reason why a gift bestowed by a god cannot be used subsequently by man as he likes. Nevertheless, correlation between the 'to give' type of communication and the kind of motivation

not true in the case of 'teaching'. In order to be taught, one has to learn, and this makes the pupil's active participation absolutely indispensable. This is why man can be taught not only by the gods, but also by another man or even by himself.[35] It follows, then, that not only are 'to give' and 'to teach' not synonymous with each other, they are even, in a sense, semantically opposite.[36]

The effect of this conclusion on the relations between the two different classes of Homeric man's activities will be made clearer if we consider that 'teaching' is regularly represented by Homer as a precondition of knowledge. The causal relationship between the two is revealed from passages describing a 'competent carpenter, a man who is well-knowing in every manner of craft, by the instructions of Athene', a 'knowing man . . . whom Hephaestus and Pallas Athene have taught every manner of craft', or from Nestor's address to Antilochus: 'Zeus and Poseidon . . . have taught you every manner of horsemanship: so . . . you know well how to wheel round the turning-posts.'[37] Naturally, one who learns something has gained knowledge of the things learned. As in the case of handicrafts and sports, knowledge is identified as a direct derivative of teaching in the words of Phoenix addressed to Achilles:

implying lack of responsibility on man's part is a Homeric norm. A good example of such a correlation is *Od.* 8. 44–5: 'on him more than on any other the god has bestowed the gift of song, to delight men in whatever way his spirit (*thumos*) moves him to sing.' That is to say, what has been 'given' by the god would further be regarded as belonging to the spontaneous rather than to the deliberate behaviour of Homeric man.

[35] See e.g. *Il.* 6. 444–5, 16. 811; *Od.* 8. 134, 146.

[36] In many respects, the relation between 'giving' and 'teaching' in Homer foreshadows the opposition between 'nature' and 'teaching', which was hotly debated in the 5th cent. BC. Indeed, if one takes into account that the bodily and mental properties which Homer believed to be the result of 'divine gift' were later treated as inherent 'by nature', and that the concept 'by nature' was so alien to him that he considered even the characteristic properties of the gods to be 'given' (as in *Il.* 5. 428), it will become clear that in Homer 'giving' covered the same range of content as that covered by 'nature' in later Greek thought. The first distinction between 'given' and 'innate' seems to have been made in the Homeric *H. Herm.* 440–2, where Apollo questions Hermes about how he came to play the lyre: 'has this marvellous thing been with you from your birth (ἐκ γενετῆς), or did some god or mortal give it you as a gift (δῶρον . . . ἔδωκε)?'

[37] *Il.* 15. 411–12; *Od.* 6. 232–4 and 23. 159–62; *Il.* 23. 307–9. Cf. the formula εἰ δ᾽ ἐθέλεις καὶ ταῦτα δαήμεναι, ὄφρ᾽ εὖ εἰδῇς *Il.* 6. 150, 20. 213. 'To be taught' and 'to know' appear as synonyms in the doublet οἶδε τε καὶ δεδάηκε at *Od.* 8. 134.

The old horseman Peleus sent me out with you . . . you were a child, with
no knowledge yet of levelling war or of debate, where men win distinction.
So he sent me to teach you all these things, to make you a speaker of
words and a doer of deeds.[38]

It is in this context, then, that Odysseus' famous saying, 'I know
that it is only unworthy ones (*kakoi*) who keep clear of fighting,'
must be understood—the hero remains alone against the enemy
not because of his martial valour (which, as we have seen, is
not exercised deliberately), but as a result of a moral judgement
deriving from his knowledge of the norms of the society to which
he belongs.[39]

Since 'teaching:giving' and 'knowledge:lack of knowledge', or
'knowledge:ignorance', characterize the two classes of Homeric
man's activities which we have found to be mutually opposed,
they can be identified as the distinctive features that condition
the distribution of the activities of Homeric man into these two
classes. This provides us with the cultural context allowing for
the communication of meaning to the regularities established in
the distributional analysis. If, in the epic mind, a given activity
is conceived as involving 'giving' and 'lack of knowledge', it is
only natural that its motivation will be carried out in terms of
non-responsibility. By the same token, in so far as the activity is
conceived as involving 'teaching' and 'knowledge', it is natural for
it not to be motivated in terms of non-responsibility. In other
words, compatibilities and incompatibilities observed in the distributional analysis are the outward expression of the opposed
semantic characteristics of the activities themselves. The two
classes of Homeric man's activities established on this basis are,
again, instincts, emotions, heroic valour, and insight, on the one
hand, and crafts, skills, sports, and practical wisdom, on the other.

At the same time, it is not difficult to see that there are
activities which do not fall unequivocally into either of these two
categories. Thus, martial activities can be characterized by either
knowledge or ignorance, either giving or teaching, and the

[38] *Il.* 9. 438–43.
[39] *Il.* 11. 408. That moral (as distinct from physical) courage is thus found
to belong to Homeric man's practical wisdom results directly from the fact that
in Homer moral acts are usually associated with practical advantage, see Snell
(1953), 157: 'the moral gains in plausibility if it can be shown in the guise of
an advantage; more than that, this is the specific form in which the act may be
recommended as practicable.' Cf. Dihle (1982), 26–7.

same holds good for prophecy. In other words, martial activities and prophecy participate in both mutually opposed classes of Homeric man's activities. This necessitates a closer examination of the activities in question.

On the one hand, *martial activities* can appear as an innate warlikeness, such as that of Achilles, who is said ever to love 'strife and wars and battle'.[40] When manifested in man's behaviour, warlikeness usually takes the form of warlike inspiration, which emerges whenever one is 'set in motion' or 'stirred' towards fighting, or whenever martial prowess is represented as 'thrown' or 'breathed' into one's heart; it seizes the warrior in spite of himself and leaves him as suddenly as it came.[41] It goes without saying that since man can neither invoke this martial fury deliberately nor control it (the gods and his *thumos* being the only forces acting in such cases), he can only be ignorant of it, just as he is ignorant of his urges and drives. Like Patroclus in his final battle, the Homeric warrior is unable to take control of his martial fury—he can only follow it blindly even if it leads him to his death.[42]

But this is not to say that Homeric man's martial activities include only warlike disposition and martial fury. Otherwise, it would be difficult to explain why even Achilles needed to be taught 'levelling war' by Phoenix, or to account for a passage mentioning a young warrior who came to the battlefield 'to teach himself war', or Hector's evidence about himself: 'I have learnt always to be brave and to fight in the forefront of the Trojans'.[43] Moreover, like a good craftsman or sportsman, so a good warrior is 'competent' in the skill of war, 'not ignorant' of it, 'well-knowing' and 'expert', either in the military sphere as a whole or in one particular kind of military practice; and he is guided by knowledge (*idreiē*) when taking part in battle.[44] In this regard, nothing can better

---

[40] *Il.* 1. 177, cf. *Od.* 14. 216-28.

[41] On martial inspiration as an inseparable part of battlefield behaviour see Dodds (1951), 9-10; Kirk (1976), 43.   [42] *Il.* 16. 684-91.

[43] *Il.* 9. 440-3, 16. 811, 6. 444-5. Plutarch's comment on *Il.* 6. 444 seems pertinent: 'For by declaring that bravery is a thing to be learned (τὴν ἀνδρείαν . . . μάθημα) . . . the poet urges us not to neglect ourselves, but to learn what is good, and to give heed to our teachers, intimating that both boorishness and cowardice are but ignorance and defects of learning (ἀμαθίαν καὶ ἄγνοιαν)' (*Mor.* 31 F).

[44] οἶδα, εὖ οἶδα *Il.* 7. 237-41, 9. 440; εὖ εἰδώς *Il.* 2. 718, 720, 923, 4. 196, 310, 5. 11, 245, 549, 12. 100, 350, 363, 15. 525; ἰδρείη *Il.* 7. 198, 16. 359; νῆϊς *Il.* 7. 198; δαήμων, ἀδαήμων *Il.* 5. 634, 13. 811, 23. 671; ἐπιστάμενος *Il.* 2. 611, 13. 223, 15. 282, 16. 243.

complement martial fury than Hector's lavish praise of his own
military competence:

I know well about fighting and the killing of men. I know how to swing
the tanned ox-hide of my shield to the right, I know how to swing it to
the left—that I call true shield-fighting. I know how to charge into the fury
of speeding chariots. I know the steps of Ares' deadly dance in the close
fighting.[45]

Since one and the same activity can hardly have such contradictory characteristics as 'ignorance' and 'knowledge', it follows
that the ambivalent treatment of martial activity in Homer gives
outward expression to the fact that what is being dealt with is
actually a complex activity which can be divided into simpler
ones belonging to the opposed classes of Homeric man's activities.
It is not difficult to see that the aspect of martial activitiy which
encompasses Homeric man's warlikeness and martial fury can be
reduced to *physical ability* and *heroic valour*, which already appear
on our list. On the other hand, the aspect encompassing military
experience and competence in the techniques of war coincides
with another item in our inventory, namely, *sports*, which are
basically equivalent to exercises in military skills aimed at acquiring the experience necessary for the battlefield. That this division
of Homeric man's martial activities would not be at variance
with Homer's usage is corroborated by the instances in which
the complex character of martial practice is made explicit by Homer
himself. Thus in Ajax' challenge to Hector, the elements constituting the hero's martial fitness are identified as physical ability
(*biē*), on the one hand, and military competence (*idreiē*), on
the other, while on another occasion martial activities are
dichotomized by Nestor into valour (*ēnoreē*) and skill with horses
(*hipposunē*).[46]

Prophecy, too, can be analysed similarly. The term 'prophecy'
designates a wide range of practices conventionally considered to
be the occupation of the 'seer' (*mantis*). Actually, however, the seer
is also referred to as a 'soothsayer', as an 'interpreter of dreams',
or as 'one who takes the omens from the flight and cries of birds'.[47]
Like martial activity, prophecy is described by Homer in ambivalent terms: although an oracle is only referred to as 'thrown' into

---

[45] *Il.* 7. 237–41.   [46] *Il.* 7. 197–8, 4. 303; cf. 18. 341.
[47] θεοπρόπος *Il.* 12. 228, *Od.* 1. 416; ὀνειροπόλος *Il.* 1. 63, 5. 149; οἰωνοπόλος *Il.*
1. 69, 6. 76; οἰωνιστής *Il.* 2. 858, 17. 218.

someone's heart, and prophecy in general as 'given' by Apollo,[48] in both poems the soothsayers are often defined as 'well-knowing' of their skill, just as ordinary artisans are.[49]

Since the relevant activities usually involve techniques for taking omens from the flight and cries of birds, interpretation of dreams and portents, and so on, it is no mere coincidence that, whenever the seer is characterized as 'knowing', it is to this skill of divination that the characteristic generally refers.[50] Yet I find it difficult to agree with Dodds that 'the *Iliad* admits only inductive divination from omens', for neither the insight of Helenus, who 'had understood their plan in his mind, the plan the gods had settled on as they conferred', nor the foretelling of the future by the dying Patroclus and Hector—both spontaneous utterances resulting from direct communication with the divine—can be subsumed under the category of inductive divination.[51] That the insight which comes directly from the god, on the one hand, and the professional techniques of divination, on the other, are not only two distinct practices but may also be thought to conflict with each other is best illustrated by Hector's outburst against Polydamas in *Iliad* 12:

You would have me put my trust in birds flapping their wings—I have no thought for them, I care nothing for them, whether they fly to the right towards the east and to the sunrise, or to the left towards the western darkness. No, let us put our trust in the counsel of great Zeus, who is king over all mortals and immortals.[52]

As distinct from one who is a professional in divination, the recipient of the divine message, being only a mouthpiece of the gods, possesses no real knowledge of it; this, however, does not make that message less effective:

But now I will give you a prophecy—truth to tell, I am not a prophet, and I have no clear knowledge of the signs of the birds, but the immortals have thrown this into my mind, and I am sure it will happen as I say.[53]

---

[48] *Od.* I. 200–1, 15. 172–3; *ll.* I. 72.

[49] οἶδα *ll.* 2. 832, 11. 330; εὖ εἰδώς *ll.* I. 384, 2. 170, 6. 438; σάφα εἰδώς *Od.* I. 202, cf. *ll.* 12. 228–9. Prophecy is never actually presented as resulting from teaching, but see *H. Herm.* 556 μαντείης διδάσκαλοι.

[50] See e.g. σάφα θυμῷ εἰδείη τεράων at *ll.* 12. 228–9 and οἰωνῶν σάφα εἰδώς at *Od.* I. 202, 2. 159, 15. 532. Cf. Pl. *Phdr.* 244bd.

[51] Dodds (1951), 70. Helenus, *ll.* 7. 44–5; Patroclus, 16. 851–4; Hector, 22. 355–60.

[52] *ll.* 12. 237–42.

[53] *Od.* I. 200–2.

Thus there is good reason to view prophecy, together with martial activity, as a complex kind of activity which actually consists of two simpler ones. In the case of prophecy these will be *insight*, on the one hand, and the *skill of divination*, on the other. With this in view, we can at last apply ourselves to our primary interest—the determination of the class membership of the activity of the Homeric poet.

The Place of Poetry

Both in Homer and in Hesiod poetry is only found combined with the kind of motivation defined above as a motivation presuming non-responsibility. Thus Homer's poets sing either when 'incited' by the Muse, 'moved' by a god, or 'stirred' by their own mental organs. Hesiod says about himself that he was 'ordered' by the goddesses to sing, and that the song was 'breathed' into him by the Muses.[54] In view of this, it is not surprising to find poetry being explicitly characterized by 'ignorance' in the invocation of the Muses introducing the Catalogue of Ships:

Tell me now, you Muses who have your homes on Olympus—you are gods, and attend all things and know all things, but we hear only the report and have no knowledge—tell me who were the leaders of the Danaans and their rulers.

This compares well with a passage in the *Works and Days* where Hesiod promises his brother to explain 'the measures of the resounding sea': 'quite without instruction as I am in seafaring or in ships . . . but even so I will tell the design of Zeus the aegis-bearer, since the Muses have taught me to make song without limit.'[55] On the basis of this evidence, there seems reason to regard poetry as belonging to the same class as instincts, emotions, heroic valour, and insight.

Since poetry is compatible with the motivation presuming non-responsibility, we would not expect this activity to be characterized by 'knowledge'. Surprisingly, our examination of Homeric evidence proves this assumption wrong. Three times poetry is referred to

---

[54] ἀνίημι *Od.* 8. 73, ὁρμάω 8. 499, ἐποτρύνω 8. 45, ὅρνυμι 1. 347, 8. 539; ἐμπνεύω *Th.* 31, κέλομαι 33.

[55] *Il.* 2. 484–7; *Erga* 648–9 . . . 661–2 (trans. M. L. West).

in terms of knowledge,[56] and on the basis of this evidence there seems reason to regard it as belonging to the same class as sports, crafts, skills, and practical wisdom. This seems to indicate that, like martial activity and prophecy, poetry cannot be unequivocally classed as an activity for which Homeric man either is or is not responsible. This conclusion is corroborated by the fact that both 'giving' and 'teaching' are far from incompatible with the activity of the Homeric poet: poetry is described as either 'given' by the Muse or a 'god' or 'taught' by the gods.[57] That is to say, if the activities of Homeric man are represented as divided into two mutually opposed classes, the one presuming non-responsibility, giving, and lack of knowledge, and the other presuming responsibility, teaching, and knowledge on the agent's part, poetry, together with martial activity and prophecy, would participate in both. It thus proves to belong with more complex forms of Homeric man's behaviour which cannot be reduced unambiguously to such simple ones as instincts and emotions, on the one hand, and crafts and skills, on the other. The precedent of martial activity and of prophecy, the ambivalent status of which has been resolved by distribution of their components among two opposed classes, allows us to expect that poetry, too, will fall into this classification.

I use the term *poetry* to designate all the activities of the 'singers' (*aoidoi*) described in Homer.[58] Whether the Homeric poems themselves were composed orally or in writing (see Ch. 5), there is no doubt that the performances of Phemius and Demodocus, the two epic poets described in the *Odyssey*, refer to the practice of oral poetry. In everything concerning the latter, the *Singer of Tales* by Albert Lord, a book which emerged from field research in the oral tradition which was still alive in the former Yugoslavia up to the middle of this century, is unrivalled.[59] As Lord has shown, the signal feature of oral composition is that the oral poem, or the 'song', is created by the poet at the time of performance. This is

---

[56] οἶδας *Od*. I. 337, ἐπισταμένως II. 368, ἐπιστάμενος 21. 406.

[57] Giving: δίδωμι *Il*. 13. 730, *Od*. 8. 44, 64; ὀπάζω *Od*. 8. 498. Teaching: διδάσκω *Od*. 8. 481, 488; *δάω *Od*. 17. 519.

[58] Essentially a professional occupation of a particular group of specialists, poetry, like other professional activities, is occasionally represented by Homer as practised by non-specialists as well. The episode of Achilles' occupying himself by playing the lyre and singing an epic song (*Il*. 9. 186–9) provides the best illustration of this.   [59] Lord (1960).

possible because, in the years of acquiring his profession, while still a child in fact, the oral poet not only learns the repertoire of the epic subjects current in his tradition but also takes in the stock of traditional expressions, the 'formulae', and the traditional narrative units, the 'themes', and masters the rules of their combination. The process involved is not unlike that of a child's learning the vocabulary and syntax of language. Versatility in oral composition acquired in this way allowed the poets to extemporize their songs at the time of performance. Since the essence of oral poetry thus proves to be the improvisation rather than the memorizing of songs, it comes as no surprise that the concept of song as a fixed text is altogether alien to the oral poets. As in jazz (Eric Havelock's parallel), no orally composed song is ever identical to another: if the poet is asked to repeat his song, he would not reproduce it verbatim but would give another version of it. Each oral poem is thus a unique creation, never identical to any other poem on the same subject.

In Homer, the function of the *aoidos* included, in addition to the recitation of heroic songs, a wide range of activities, from the singing of dirges and marriage songs to the musical accompaniment of festivities and even dance. Obviously, musical accompaniment on the lyre, inseparable as it is from the bards' performances in Homer, is a technical activity *par excellence*. It is not surprising, then, that when Homer refers to poetic activity in terms of knowledge, he is speaking of the playing of the lyre, as, for example, in the following simile: 'then, like a man expert in lyre and song who with utmost ease winds a new string round a peg, fitting the pliant sheep-gut at either end, so did Odysseus string the great bow tranquilly.'[60] Though the term *epistamenos* ('expert') is applied here to 'lyre and song', the way in which the simile is developed leaves no doubt that the poet actually had in mind the playing of the lyre. In the Homeric *Hymn to Hermes*, which deals at length with playing the lyre, this activity is treated only in terms of knowledge: it is described as a 'skill' (*technē, sophiē*), which must be learned, and in which one ought to be competent and not ignorant.[61] On one occasion, in the description of Thamyris' punishment by the Muses, 'song' (*aoidē*) is explicitly dichotomized

---

[60] *Od.* 21. 406-9.
[61] τέχνη *H. Herm.* 447, 465, 483, 511; σοφίη 483, 511; δαήμεναι 483, 489, 510; νῆϊς 487.

by Homer into 'song' proper (*aoidē* again) and 'playing the lyre' (*kitharistus*).[62]

But in *Odyssey* 1 Penelope says to Phemius, 'you know many other spells of mortals, deeds of men and deeds of gods that the bards celebrate'.[63] Obviously, this passage cannot refer to the playing of the lyre. What Penelope's words clearly imply is that the sphere of the poet's competence is connected with the epic subjects he sings about. Now, Homer's special term for an epic subject seems to be *oimē*.[64] This follows both from the proper meaning of the word, namely 'path', 'route', and, especially, from its occurrence at *Odyssey* 8. 74: 'an *oimē* whose fame then reached to broad heaven itself, the quarrel between Odysseus and Achilles, son of Peleus'. That *oimē* should not be taken as synonymous to *aoidē*, 'song' proper, follows from the expression 'the route of song' occurring in the Homeric *Hymn to Hermes*.[65] Characteristically, it is the term *oimē* rather than *aoidē* that emerges when poetic activity as such is referred to as the object of teaching. Thus, in *Odyssey* 8. 481 we find: 'the Muse has taught the singers *oimas*'. Since *oimē* is found to refer to epic stories and since *oimē* is taught, we can conclude that, in addition to playing the lyre, the sphere of the Homeric poet's technical competence is his knowledge of epic stories, gained as a result of learning.

The other case of treating poetry in terms of knowledge which cannot be referred to the playing of the lyre is Alcinous' praise of Odysseus for having told his story 'expertly', 'like a singer'.[66] Rather than the poet's familiarity with the range of epic subjects, the phrase emphasizes his mastery in the presentation of the given single subject. That the exact nature of this mastery primarily consists in the poet's carefully following the proper sequence of events within a given story is made explicit in *Odyssey* 8, where Demodocus is said to have been taught by the Muse or Apollo to sing 'the doom of the Achaeans' in 'perfectly good order', as if he were an eyewitness of those events.[67] We can thus conclude that,

---

[62] *Il.* 2. 595–600.

[63] *Od.* 1. 337–8 πολλὰ γὰρ ἄλλα βροτῶν θελκτήρια οἶδας, | ἔργ' ἀνδρῶν τε θεῶν τε, τά τε κλείουσιν ἀοιδοί.

[64] On οἴμη and the related οἶμος see Lanata (1963), 11–12 (with the bibliography); on οἴμη as Homer's technical term for 'an individual story within the heroic repertoire' see Ford (1992), 41–3.   [65] *H. Herm.* 451 οἶμος ἀοιδῆς.

[66] *Od.* 11. 368 μῦθον δ' ὡς ὅτ' ἀοιδὸς ἐπισταμένως κατέλεξας.

[67] *Od.* 8. 489. On the expressions ἐπισταμένως, ('expertly') and κατὰ κόσμον, ('in order') see also below, Ch. 4.

besides the playing of the lyre, Homer also considered acquaintance
with the epic subjects and their proper presentation to be another
technical component of the poet's activity.

But if the Muse teaches the poet the epic stories so that he will
be competent to recount them in the correct order, what does she
give him as a gift? Now, in all contexts, without exception, the
Muses' gift to the poet is designated by the term *aoidē*.[68] To understand the difference between the *oimē* learned by the poet and the
aoidē given to him by the Muses, we must see exactly what the poet
proclaims himself to be ignorant of. We saw above that Homer
explicitly acknowledges himself to be incompetent in the case of the
Catalogue of Ships, a detailed enumeration of the Achaean troops
that came to Troy. Now, if the poet asks for the Muses' help in
relating such specific information, we can only conclude that the
information at his disposal is envisaged as not sufficiently detailed.
This means that the *oimē* in which the poet is competent cannot be
more than basic knowledge of the principal events constituting the
story and of the order of their succession; Homer's own summary
of Odysseus' wanderings in *Odyssey* 23 comes to mind in this
connection.[69] This fits in well with the fact, as pointed out above,
that the professional competence of the poet is seen in his recounting given events in the correct order. Yet, the Catalogue of Ships
is more than just such an account; it is, rather, an expansion, or
elaboration of the subject beyond its basic plot.[70] It follows that
it is owing to the Muses' intervention that the poet is able to
elaborate an elementary sequence of events within a given story
into a developed and detailed narrative, that is, to transform a
given plot into an epic poem. The *aoidē* which the Muse 'gives' to
the poet is therefore the very act of singing in which the creation
of the epic song takes place. This seems to be why *aoidē*, as distinct
from *oimē*, is never employed in the plural.[71]

---

[68] *Od.* 8. 44, 64, 498.

[69] *Od.* 23. 310–41. Cf. Lord (1960), 99: 'When the singer of tales, equipped
with a store of formulas and a technique of composition, takes his place before an
audience and tells his story, he follows the plan which he has learned along with
the other elements of his profession.' Cf. Hainsworth (1991), 21.

[70] On the extended catalogue as a form of expansion typical of the epic style see
Lord (1960), 106. Cf. Arist. *Poet.* 1459ᵃ 35–7.

[71] It is significant that the distinction between the story (plot) and the song
developed on the basis of the story, which we were required to make in order to
account for our material, is essentially the same as that arrived at by Lord in his
investigation of the practice of oral poets in Yugoslavia, see e.g. Lord (1960), 100:

In the elaborated invocation of the Muse at the beginning of the *Odyssey*, after having proclaimed to the audience that the subject of his poem will be the wanderings of Odysseus, the poet asks the Muse to tell him of these 'from somewhere'.[72] He opens his narrative at the moment when, nearly ten years after the fall of Troy, Odysseus is about to leave the island of Calypso and embark on his last enterprise, which will eventually bring him home. The Muse is represented in these lines as responsible for the point from which the poet's narrative starts. The same conclusion follows from Homer's description in *Odyssey* 8 of how Demodocus, fulfilling the request of Odysseus, starts his song of the Wooden Horse:

The bard was stirred by the god and began his performance (*aoidē*), taking up where the Argives had set huts aflame, had boarded their ships and were under sail already, while the few left behind with great Odysseus were crouched inside the sheltering horse in the Trojans' own assembly-place etc.[73]

Again, the point at which the poet starts his song is presented here as associated with the divine stimulus which stirs him to sing. That is to say, not only the stimulus to the poet's beginning his performance but also the very point at which any given performance would open are seen as lying in the sphere of responsibility of the Muse rather than of the poet himself.

Thus, what the Homeric poet sees himself as competent in is the range of epic subjects at his disposal and their basic plots, and what he sees himself as ignorant of is the way in which he should expand these subjects by elaborating on them within these basic plots, and the point within the epic saga at which his narrative should start. Obviously, in terms of the practice of oral poetry, the area of competence would stand for the technical and the area of ignorance for the improvisatory side of the poet's activity. If my previous argument is correct, it is only the latter that was

'We must distinguish then two concepts of song in oral poetry. One is the general idea of the story, which we use when we speak in larger terms, for example, of the song of the wedding of Smailagić Meho, which actually includes all singing of it. The other concept of song is that of a particular performance or text, such as Avdo Međedović's song, "The Wedding of Smailagić Meho", dictated during the month of July, 1935.'

[72] *Od.* 1. 10 τῶν ἀμόθεν γε, θεά, θύγατερ Διός, εἰπὲ καὶ ἡμῖν.

[73] *Od.* 8. 499–503: 'was stirred by the god and began' ὁ δ' ὁρμηθεὶς θεοῦ ἄρχετο, 'taking up where' ἔνθεν ἑλών.

seen as issuing from inspiration sent by the Muses.[74] As far as I can see, this analysis may be further supported by one of the more problematic Homeric passages referring to poetry. The passage in question is the famous plea of Phemius in *Odyssey* 22.

During the episode of Odysseus' killing of the suitors, the Ithacan bard Phemius begs Odysseus to spare his life, addressing him, *inter alia*, in the following words:

> You yourself will repent it afterwards if you kill a man like me, a bard, singing for gods and men alike. I am self-taught; the god has implanted in my heart all manner of lays, and I am worthy to sing before you just as before a god. Do not behead me in thoughtless passion.[75]

The interpretation of Phemius' statement, 'I am self-taught; the god has implanted in my heart all manner of lays', raises a number of difficulties, the principal one being the apparent contradiction between the messages in the two clauses. For, if the singer has 'taught' himself (as seems to be implied by the first clause), how can this be reconciled with the god's having 'implanted' all manner of lays in his heart, as the second part of the passage clearly states?[76] This difficulty is increased in view of the fact that neither *autodidaktos* ('self-taught') nor *emphuein* ('to implant'), the keywords in Phemius' plea, are regular epic terms, so that their meaning cannot be ascertained by examining their usage in the broader context of the Homeric poems.[77] We have seen, however, that the activity of the Homeric poet is far from homogeneous. Hence, there is reason to suggest that the apparent inconsistency of Phemius' appeal reflects that activity's heterogeneity. To check this, let us consider the terms *emphuein* and *autodidaktos*.

Though it has no parallels in Homer, the verb *emphuein* clearly belongs to the series of terms, covered by the 'teaching:giving' opposition, which designate the sources of human activities in Homer. The fact that its connotations lie in the sphere of natural

---

[74] That the Muses should not be regarded as inspiring the poets' songs in their totality has recently been argued in Bowie (1993), 12–14.

[75] *Od.* 22. 345–9. 'I am self-taught; the god has implanted in my heart all manner of lays' αὐτοδίδακτος δ' εἰμί, θεός δέ μοι ἐν φρεσὶν οἴμας | παντοίας ἐνέφυσεν.

[76] Cf. Murray (1981), 96–7; Verdenius (1983), 21, 38–9.

[77] The passive voice of the verb ἐμφύω is employed in Homer once, in connection with horses' hairs (*Il.* 8. 84), but it is only in Hdt. 3. 80 that it is found applied to human qualities; *autodidaktos* is a *hapax legomenon* in Homer and in epic poetry in general, and it is not until Aesch. *Ag.* 991 that the word re-emerges in our sources.

growth seems to be compatible with Homer's understanding of learning as a gradual process of acquiring a given profession or property. The fact that in another Homeric context the object of the verb, namely *oimas*, is explicitly presented as a result of teaching, as well as the conclusion that the term *oimē* stands for that side of the Homeric poet's activity in which he sees himself competent, also seems to make the association of *emphuein* with the 'to teach' type of communication more plausible.

A similar attempt to reduce the term *autodidaktos* to conventional Homeric terms leads to two other passages in the *Odyssey* where the poet's creative ability is simultaneously traced to both divine and human sources. The first passage is Alcinous' characterization of another singer, Demodocus the Phaeacian, in *Odyssey* 8: 'on him more than on any other the god has bestowed the gift of song, to delight men in whatever way his spirit (*thumos*) moves him to sing.'[78] Telemachus' rebuke of Penelope in *Odyssey* 1 is yet another instance: 'Mother, why grudge the sweet bard to please us in whatever way his mind (*noos*) stirs itself? In all such things it is not the bards who are accountable (*aitioi*); Zeus, it may be, is accountable, when he allots to toiling men to each one as he will.'[79] In his plea, Phemius also derives his song from two sources: his being 'self-taught' and the god's having 'implanted' into him various *oimas*. Yet, while the language of Phemius' plea is unique, the two other passages use traditional epic language.[80] In both, the human elements in the poet's activity are rendered by the poet's being 'stirred' (*epotrunein, ornusthai*) by his mental organs (*thumos, noos*). The equivalent of these in Phemius' words is 'I am self-taught'. The structural similarity of the three passages seems to suggest that Phemius' *autodidaktos* is synonymous with the poet's being 'stirred' by his *thumos* or *noos*.

To be sure, such an interpretation of *autodidaktos* strikes one as incompatible with the word's literal meaning 'self-taught'. Yet,

---

[78] *Od.* 8. 44–5: τῷ γάρ ῥα θεὸς πέρι δῶκεν ἀοιδὴν | τέρπειν, ὅππῃ θυμὸς ἐποτρύνῃσιν ἀείδειν. The parallel between this passage and Phemius' plea is noted in Schmidt (1995) and Lesky (1961), 31.

[79] *Od.* 1. 346–9: μῆτερ ἐμή, τί τ' ἄρα φθονέεις ἐρίηρον ἀοιδὸν | τέρπειν ὅππῃ οἱ νόος ὄρνυται; οὔ νύ τ' ἀοιδοὶ | αἴτιοι, ἀλλά ποθι Ζεὺς αἴτιος, ὅς τε δίδωσιν | ἀνδράσιν ἀλφηστῇσιν ὅπως ἐθέλῃσιν ἑκάστῳ. Cf. Schmidt (1955).

[80] The formulaic character of these expressions follows from the fact that both have the words τέρπειν ὅππῃ at the beginning of the verse, followed by two slightly different expressions of the same idea, θυμὸς ἐποτρύνῃσιν and νόος ὄρνυται, 'thumos moves' and 'noos stirs itself'.

the way in which the term *autodidaktos* is employed in Greek makes it clear that its association with 'teaching' proper is far from certain. It seems to me that a clue to the correct understanding of the term can be found in a choral song of Aeschylus' *Agamemnon*: 'from within my heart sings, self-taught, a dirge of Erinys without the lyre.'[81] Everything in this passage, from its general context to the details of its terminology, reveals a striking resemblance to the three Homeric passages discussed above, blending their most salient features into one consistent picture. Indeed, the correspondence between the *thumos* that 'sings from within' in Aeschylus' verses and the *thumos* (or *noos*) that 'stirs to sing' in Homer is immediately obvious. Moreover, in Aeschylus this *thumos* is 'self-taught', exactly as Phemius says he is himself. Aeschylus' usage of the term is illuminating. As an epithet of the *thumos* that 'sings from within', *autodidaktos* implies neither a deliberate process of acquiring knowledge nor the subject's active participation in this process, as seems to be suggested by its literal meaning of 'self-taught'. What the *autodidaktos* of Aeschylus does imply is that the *thumos* sings of itself, that is, in an unprompted and spontaneous manner. In this, it resembles *automatos*, the Greek term for 'self-acting' and 'spontaneous'.[82] Consequently, semantic associations of *autodidaktos* should be sought not in the area of 'self-teaching' but in that of 'self-acting', and this is precisely how the term was employed in later Greek. The most salient example is Galen's 'self-taught element of the parts of the body', where *to autodidakton*, 'the self-taught', stands for 'instinct'.[83]

It can be concluded, therefore, that Phemius' 'I am self-taught' stands for the improvisatory aspect of the poet's activity,[84] that is, the one we have rendered by *aoidē*, or 'singing' proper. Considering that the other clause of Phemius' plea deals with 'implanting'

[81] *Ag.* 990–3 τὸν δ' ἄνευ λύρας ὅμως ὑμνῳδεῖ θρῆνον Ἐρινύος αὐτοδίδακτος ἔσωθεν θυμός.

[82] 'Spontaneous' is the translation proposed for Aeschylus' *autodidaktos* in Denniston and Page (1957), 156. Cf. Schrade (1952), 235: 'Es [Phemius' *auto-didaktos*] hat als Wortbildung seine unmittelbare Entsprechung *automatos*.' Note that in Greek tradition *automatos* is one of the attributes of nature, and is found in opposition to 'teaching' as early as Democritus (DK 68 D 182).

[83] Galen 8. 445 τὸ τῶν ὀργάνων αὐτοδίδακτον, cf. ibid. 19. 175. It is characteristic that the other Greek term for 'self-taught', αὐτομαθής, also has 'spontaneous' among its meanings. See Philod. *On Poems* 2. 47: συγγένειαν εἶναι μούσαις αὐτομαθῆ. See LSJ s.vv. αὐτοδίδακτος, αὐτομαθής.

[84] This interpretation coincides in its essentials with that proposed by M. Schmidt in his article on αὐτοδίδακτος in *LfgrE*.

(probably, teaching) 'various lays', and that *oimē* ('lay') seems to represent the technical side of the activity of the Homeric poet, Phemius' words as a whole can be taken as referring to the complex character of the poetic activity that has been detailed in this chapter.

To recapitulate: the part of the poetic activity for which the poet is held individually responsible consists in the technical skill of playing the lyre and competence in a range of epic subjects and their basic plots, whereas the part for which he is not held individually responsible consists in his ability, guaranteed by the 'gift' of the Muses, to transform a given subject into an epic song, an ability manifested in the poet's improvisation at the time of performance. Thus, like the other ambivalent activities of Homeric man, poetry can be divided into simple components belonging to the two mutually opposed classes.

Now, knowledge of stories from the past is certainly not the exclusive province of the poet. 'We both know each other's birth, and we know each other's parents', Aenaeas says to Achilles, 'from hearing the tales that mortal men have long made famous—although I have never seen your parents, nor you mine'; and Phoenix says of the story about Meleager's wrath, 'we heard the glories of men that were of old'.[85] Characteristically, 'glories of men' and related expressions used in such contexts in Homer can equally well designate the subject-matter of both poetry and story-telling.[86] Note that the kind of knowledge meant here—that is, knowledge of the past—does not differ essentially from Homeric man's practical wisdom. It is characteristic in this connection that Homer renders the knowledge of old men and the poet's knowledge in only slightly different terms: while the former know 'many things of old' the latter knows 'many deeds of men and gods'.[87] On the other hand, the 'spontaneous' element of the activity of the Homeric poet, namely, his ability to be 'stirred' so as to elaborate a given story into an epic song, should be classified with instincts,

[85] *Il.* 20. 204 πρόκλυτ' ἀκούοντες ἔπεα θνητῶν ἀνθρώπων, 9. 524 τῶν πρόσθεν ἐπευθόμεθα κλέα ἀνδρῶν.

[86] Thus, the expression κλέα ἀνδρῶν is applied to poetry at *Il.* 9. 189 and *Od.* 8. 73 and to story-telling at *Il.* 9. 524; see also Hes. *Th.* 100 κλεῖα προτέρων ἀνθρώπων (of poetry).

[87] Cf. παλαιά τε πολλά τε εἰδώς (*Od.* 2. 188, 7. 157, 24. 51) as against πολλὰ . . . οἶδας ἔργ' ἀνδρῶν τε θεῶν τε, Penelope to Phemius in *Od.* 1. 337–8. See also πλείονα εἰδώς, one of the two effects of the Sirens' song as described in *Od.* 12. 188. On the Sirens see below, Ch. 3.

emotions, and other activities for which Homeric man is not considered individually responsible: this element of the poet's activity will henceforth be designated 'singing'.

Applying the same criteria to what may be called the 'poetics' of Hesiod shows that his approach to poetry does not differ essentially from that of Homer. We have seen already that Hesiod describes poetry, or 'song', as being 'breathed' into the poet's heart by the Muses, and the poet himself as one who has been 'ordered' by the goddesses to sing and thus is not individually responsible for his activity.[88] Again, Hesiod's song, like Homer's, is a 'sacred gift' of the Muses,[89] while the poet himself, although 'not competent' in the things he sings about, delivers truthful messages owing to his contact with the goddesses.[90] It is true of course that the expressions 'they [the Muses] have taught me the beautiful song' and 'the Muses have taught me to sing the marvellous hymn'[91] differ from the Homeric usage in that they admit application of 'teaching' to 'song' (*aoidē*) and 'singing' (*aeidein*), but Hesiod has no designation for song which, like Homer's *oimē*, would stand for an aspect of the poet's activity other than that designated by the term *aoidē*; as a result, *aoidē* functions as an inclusive term which can be combined both with the characteristics presuming the lack of responsibility (such as 'to breathe into', 'to order', 'to give') and with those presuming responsibility (such as 'to teach'). At the same time, it is obvious that although Hesiod speaks of his song as being 'taught' by the Muses, teaching cannot cover the whole of his poetic experience. That is to say, although the vocabularies of the Homeric and the Hesiodic tradition may be different, the basic idea of the nature of the poet's activity is the same. To prove this, it suffices to turn to Hesiod's own description of how he became a poet:

and they [the Muses] gave me a branch of springing bay to pluck for a staff, a handsome one, and they breathed into me divine song, so that I should celebrate things of the future and things that were aforetime. And they told me to sing of the family of the blessed ones who are for ever, etc.[92]

---

[88] *Th.* 30–1 ἐνέπνευσαν δέ μ' ἀοιδήν; 33–4 μ' ἐκέλονθ' ὑμνεῖν . . . ἀείδειν. See n. 3 above.

[89] *Th.* 93 Μουσάων ἱερὴ δόσις; 103 δῶρα θεάων.

[90] *Erga* 649 οὔτε τι . . . σεσοφισμένος; *Th.* 28 ἀληθέα γηρύσασθαι. Cf. n. 55 above.

[91] *Th.* 22 καλὴν ἐδίδαξαν ἀοιδήν; *Erga* 662 Μοῦσαι γάρ μ' ἐδίδαξαν ἀθέσφατον ὕμνον ἀείδειν.

[92] *Th.* 30–3, trans. M. L. West. On the translation 'divine song' see n. 3 above.

This is how a shepherd becomes the 'divine singer'—neither teaching nor training of any kind whatsoever is supposed to be connected with this transformation.

We can see now that the category of 'poetry' or 'poetic activity' covers more than one simple constituent. What may be called 'poetry' in Homer consists in fact of *singing*, on the one hand, and *playing the lyre* and possessing *knowledge of the past*, on the other. In view of this, our answer to the question as to the nature of the poet's activity in the traditional poetics addressed in Chapter I cannot be a simple one. In so far as poetry is associated with playing the lyre and with knowledge of the past acquired by learning, and is practised by virtue of competence accumulated through experience and exercise, it belongs, together with the crafts and skills and other manifestations of Homeric man's practical wisdom, in the category of activities for which Homeric man is responsible. On the other hand, in so far as poetry is associated with the ability to 'sing' guaranteed by the divine gift and manifested spontaneously at the time of performance, it should be classed, together with instincts, emotions, heroic valour, and insight, with the activities for which Homeric man is not held individually responsible. Thus, like warrior or seer, the poet in Homer simultaneously manifests two different modes of functioning.

At the same time, it is clear that among the constituents of poetry, only *singing* should be regarded as unique to this activity alone. Playing the lyre is no more intrinsically related to poetry than, for example, dancing, which is also quite commonly associated with the poet's activity in Homer.[93] Likewise, knowledge of the past is indispensable for epic poetry, but not for poetry as such: the genre of lyric monody, concentrated as it was on the poet's individual experience, immediately comes to mind in this connection (see Chapter 6). Moreover, knowledge of the past is, as we have seen, far from being the exclusive province of the poet, but can belong to anyone who has assimilated this knowledge as a result of his own experience or the testimony of others; it is clear, however, that the difference between 'knowing' a story and transforming it into a song is as great as that between the general plot of the *Iliad* and the *Iliad* as an epic poem.[94]

[93] Cf. West (1981), 115: 'The implication is that the lyre was a valuable adjunct, but its use or non-use did not determine the nature of the vocal performance.'

[94] Cf. Hainsworth (1991), 17–18: 'To recount the tales of the Heroic Age

It is indeed a well-known phenomenon of traditional poetry that, though each of the limited range of subjects, or 'stories', dealt with by a given tradition is fixed in respect of its main outline, each version of a song treating the same story is individual, differing from one poet to another.[95] This difference is due to the fact that while the essence of a story remains the same in all its versions, its expansion by means of recurring typical motifs, or 'themes', varies according to the stock of such themes at a given poet's disposal, his taste for expansion, and his ability to expand. Thus there is a tension between the fixity of the story and the looseness of its expansion, which amounts in effect to the tension between the poet's commitment to preserve his tradition and his creative freedom.[96] Hence, only *singing*, that is, the poet's creating an original song of his own out of a given traditional story, can truly be regarded as the very essence of his activity. Accordingly, the subject of our inquiry is singing proper, and it is the place of this activity that should be established.

On the basis of its position among other activities of Homeric man, poetry ('singing') can be defined as an activity of Homeric man that belongs to the class of activities (constituted by instincts, emotions, heroic valour, and insight) which possesses the semantic characteristics 'giving' and 'lack of knowledge' and for which, therefore, man is not held individually responsible; and by the same token, poetry is opposed to the class of activities (constituted by sports, practical wisdom, crafts, and skills) which possesses the semantic characteristics 'teaching' and 'knowledge' and for which, therefore, man is held individually responsible. In so far as the opposition between 'art' and 'inspiration' is only a particular application of the opposition between the artist's being and not being responsible for his activity as an artist, the question of whether the poet *qua* poet was guided in Homer by inspiration or by art is answered unequivocally.

The *Preface to Plato* by E. A. Havelock is, to my knowledge, the only systematic attempt thus far to represent skill, or *technē*, as the

was not a task for amateurs. The events and personnel of that distant epoch constituted a corpus of "knowledge" that was not to be learned without much application. But that knowledge, though necessary, was not sufficient to tell the stories. The singer had to tell the tale in verse, and at short notice or none at all . . . what he actually did was to re-create the song in the act of performance.'

[95] See Lord (1960), 100; A. Parry (1966), 182; Hainsworth (1984), 115.

[96] See Lord (1960), 28–9; Bowra (1963), 39; Finkelberg (1990), 296–303.

sole basis of Homer's poetics. Havelock's general concept of the development of the Greek view of poetry aside, there are only two concrete arguments in his book against the relevance of divine inspiration to Homer's concept of poetry. The first runs as follows: 'A god to be sure could "breathe songs" into Phemius . . . but he could also put courage, fear, intention, and the like into any hero.'[97] Actually, the example adduced proves just the opposite of what Havelock intended. That the poet's behaviour is motivated in the same way as the behaviour of 'any hero' does not prove that the poet was not inspired, but rather, that 'any hero' could be 'inspired', that is, would not be able to control his behaviour if it was 'put' into him by a god.

Havelock's other argument (ibid.) proceeds from the assumption that the terminology of 'skill' used by post-Homeric poets would be relevant to Homer as well. The objection here is not only that any assumption of the kind is purely speculative: in fact, it disagrees with the actual situation observed in Homer. For Homer, both 'skilled singer' and 'inspired craftsman' would have been verbal nonentities with no cultural content to support them. To become treated as a product of art in the vein of Havelock's interpretation, poetry as conceived of by Homer had to undergo a process of cultural re-evaluation as a result of which it changed its class membership and began to be envisaged as one skill among many.

Some Strategic Possibilities

In Homer, poetry proper, or 'singing', derives from divine inspiration and thus is one of the activities for which man is not held individually responsible. Centuries later, we find poetry deriving from art and therefore belonging with the activities for which man *is* held responsible. What could have caused this change? We have seen that the class membership of a given activity is ultimately determined by the semantic qualification it possesses in the minds of the 'native speakers'. We have also seen that the activities for which man is held responsible are found to be regularly qualified through 'knowledge', while those for which he is not held

---

[97] Havelock (1963), 163–4 n. 29. Havelock misreads ἐνέφυσε at *Od.* 22. 348, which means not 'breathed into', but 'implanted', but this is of little relevance to my point.

responsible are qualified through 'lack of knowledge' or 'ignorance'. Knowledge, therefore, is the distinctive feature that divides the two classes of Homeric man's activities and thus determines the class membership of each individual activity. To understand what makes knowledge so important a category in Homer's treatment of man, we need to dwell at some length on the early Greek idea of knowledge.

We have already touched on the close causal relationship between experience and knowledge in Homer (pp. 40-1 above). It is thanks to this relationship that an eyewitness possesses greater knowledge than the recipient of hearsay, that the older man has the same advantage over the younger, and that, in general, mortal men can never approach in their knowledge the omnipresent and immortal gods. It can be seen from this that the knowledge meant by Homer is of an extensive rather than an intensive character: it is invariably 'knowledge of many things'.[98] Given the extensive character of knowledge, it is little wonder that the acquiring of knowledge, or learning, would invariably be perceived as a process of accumulation. That is to say, nobody is able to become 'knowing many things' (a formula designating the wisdom of old men) in a moment; man has to acquire his knowledge step by step in the course of his life or by incessant exercise of a craft or skill. This seems to be the reason why not only crafts and skills but also practical wisdom like that of Nestor are never presented in Homer as communicated by the gods. To make someone a Nestor the gods would have to give him the entire lifetime of experience, to reproduce all the circumstances of the real life, in short, to make him 'live' every moment of Nestor's life.

This fact throws light on another important characteristic of knowledge in Homer, namely, its inalienable character. In so far as knowledge is understood as a derivative of experience, it should be as inalienable from a person as the years of his or her life and training. A peculiar expression of this 'possessive' connotation of Homeric knowledge is found in the tendency to describe character in terms of knowledge: thus, Achilles 'knows wild things, like a

---

[98] See further Snell (1953), 18; Fränkel (1962), 519-20. It is noteworthy that the 'knowledge of many things' that served as a guarantee of wisdom in the Archaic age would later become, under the name of *polumathiē*, the target of Heraclitus' intellectual invective, see DK 22 B 40.

lion', Polyphemus 'knows lawless things', and so on.[99] This seems to indicate that everything entering man's knowledge was envisaged as forming an integral part of man's self. One of the possible implications of this situation is that everything not entering one's knowledge should not be recognized as part of the self. This was indeed the conclusion arrived at by M. P. Nilsson, E. R. Dodds, and others as a result of their study of Homeric man's 'psychische Labilität'. Dodds was especially explicit on this point:

> If the character is knowledge, what is not knowledge is not part of the character, but comes to a man from outside. When he acts in a manner contrary to the system of conscious dispositions which he is said to 'know', his action is not properly his own, but has been dictated to him. In other words, unsystematised, nonrational impulses, and the acts resulting from them, tend to be excluded from the self and ascribed to an alien origin.[100]

If we take into account that Homer had no special term for 'self', 'soul', or 'character', it should not be difficult to understand why scholars have so often arrived at the conclusion that Homeric man possessed no integrated personality whatsoever.

Note that one of the observations on which this conclusion is founded is that Homeric man's *thumos*, or 'spirit', which almost invariably stands for irrational factors in Homeric psychology, 'tends not to be felt part of the self'.[101] The difficulty, however, is that this observation is based in turn on the tacit presumption— which has never undergone a proper examination—that the interaction between man and his *thumos* is always one-sided: that is, that, like the Homeric gods, *thumos* can only act on man but is never acted upon in response. However, Homeric expressions rendering the idea of restraining one's *thumos*, such as *thumon*

---

[99] *Il.* 24. 41; *Od.* 9. 189. See further Dodds (1951), 16–17.

[100] Dodds (1951), 17.

[101] Dodds (1951), 16. Cf. Harrison (1960), 78: 'His θυμός . . . is felt to be an entity quite distinct from his ego, and even alien to it, "ordering" him and "impelling" him, like some external agent.' Heart (*ētor, kradiē*) or even 'stomach' (*gastēr*) may occasionally play the same role, see e.g. *Il.* 10. 220, 21. 571–2; *Od.* 1. 316, 6. 133, 7. 216–17, 220, 8. 204. At the same time, although Jahn (1987: 182–94) is certainly right to claim that in many cases 'spirit' (*thumos*) and 'mind' (*phrenes*) behave as functional synonyms, this does not affect the case under consideration. As Jahn's own table (p. 191) shows, though the function of command characteristic of *thumos* can also be ascribed to 'heart' (*ētor, kēr,* or *kradiē*), this function is never associated with *phrenes*: this is exactly where the functional distinction between *thumos* and *phrenes* should be drawn.

epischein, eretuein, damazein, and the like, although not numerous, surely point in the opposite direction.[102] Moreover, the much discussed pattern of self-deliberation, almost invariably opening with the formula 'and in distress he spoke to his large-hearted *thumos*', seems to have been cast especially for expressing the idea of man's interaction with his *thumos,* an interaction which usually results in man's taking control over the *thumos* rather than vice versa.[103] As far as man is able to constrain his *thumos* but not able to constrain a god, this must mean that while the latter was seen as an external agent the former was not. That is to say, the very fact that Homer takes into account the possibility of man's control over his *thumos* suggests that Homeric man was in fact much more integrated an entity than many are ready to admit.

Let us represent knowledge as a dividing line between the two models of Homeric man's behaviour, and let us try to outline the character of the relations between them. It is reasonable to suppose that, in so far as knowledge is seen as accumulated as a result of man's experience and practice, everything acquired by experience and practice would constitute the very nature of the self, its solid and inalienable core. As distinct from this, everything that has not undergone this process of accumulation would remain at the unconscious or semi-conscious periphery of the self, usually represented by man's *thumos.* Now, in view of the fact that everything entering man's knowledge becomes part of his consciousness, it is only natural that man should see himself as the cause of what derives from this conscious part of the self. On the other hand, in so far as things remaining beyond the limits of knowledge

---

[102] For the most part these are connected with Achilles and appear in *Iliad* 9, see 255-6 σὺ δὲ μεγαλήτορα θυμὸν | ἴσχειν ἐν στήθεσσι (Odysseus to Achilles); 496 δάμασον θυμὸν μέγαν (Phoenix to Achilles); 635-7 τοῦ δέ τ᾽ ἐρητύεται κραδίη καὶ θυμὸς ἀγήνωρ | ποινὴν δεξαμένῳ· σοὶ δ᾽ ἄλληκτόν τε κακόν τε | θυμὸν ἐνὶ στήθεσσι θεοὶ θέσαν εἵνεκα κούρης (Ajax to Achilles), cf. 462-3. Characteristically, the expression 'to yield to one's *thumos*' also appears mainly in this book, see 109-10 μεγαλήτορι θυμῷ | εἴξας (of Agamemnon); 598 εἴξας ᾧ θυμῷ (of Meleager); cf. *Il.* 24. 42-3; *Od.* 5. 126. Cf. Finkelberg (1995), 23 and n. 33. On these and related expressions see also Griffin's commentary on *Il.* 9. 109 f. in Griffin (1995), 88-9.

[103] ὀχθήσας δ᾽ ἄρα εἶπε πρός ὃν μεγαλήτορα θυμόν: *Il.* 11. 403, 17. 90, 18. 5, 20. 343, 21. 53, 552, 22. 98; *Od.* 5. 298, 355, 407, 464. As was pointed out by Hoekstra (1965: 68-70), the expression in question could only have been created after the disappearance of the digamma. This may well indicate that the situation described by Dodds could be relevant to some earlier stage in Greek thought; at the same time, the Homeric evidence shows that Homeric man is already far beyond this stage.

play no part in man's consciousness, it is, again, natural that man should not see himself as the cause of what derives from this non-conscious part of his self. The very fact that the two kinds of behaviour—of which one is characterized through knowledge and responsibility and the other through their opposites—coexist within one and the same person clearly indicates that man was not regarded by Homer as a simple entity.[104]

Note that the Homeric classification of human activities as described in this chapter clearly presupposes that whether or not one's behaviour is qualified in terms of individual responsibility is directly conditioned by the nature of the activity in which one is engaged at a given moment. Accordingly, there can be no conflict between these two sides of Homeric man's functioning, any more than there can be a conflict between, say, one's engaging in sports, in Homer a deliberate activity *par excellence*, and one's heroic valour, which is only manifested spontaneously. Now, given the strict specialization between what enters and what does not enter Homeric man's knowledge, it is manifest that the two parts of man's self would not intrude into each other's sphere because, in a sense, Homer's people a priori knew for what actions they were, or were not, to be held responsible. This is evidently the explanation for the apparent inconsistency between Agamemnon's claim in *Iliad* 19 that he is not to be held responsible for insulting Achilles, and his simultaneous proposal of fair compensation for the insulted party. In so far, indeed, as the action itself was ascribed to the *atē* thrown into Agamemnon's heart by the gods or stirred by his own *thumos* (see pp. 35–6 above), it could not be part of Agamemnon's self-consciousness; accordingly, he could not see himself as the real cause of this action and thus be held responsible for its consequences. In so far, on the other hand, as the action he performed was socially qualified as an insult, the situation thus produced fell under his knowledge of the norms of social behaviour shared by each member of the community.

That is to say, rather than being in conflict with each other, the two models of Homeric man's behaviour should be seen as mutually complementary. And although it cannot be excluded that

---

[104] Padel (1992: 45–6) aptly defines Homer's idea of self as 'unity in multiplicity'. On the interpretation of Homeric man's 'normal operating self' as characterized by reason and 'defined in opposition to the intervening organs and gods' see now Pelliccia (1995), 260.

Homeric man can be consistently described in categories of modern psychology such as 'self' and 'non-self', it seems to me that the coexistence of the two models of behaviour within one and the same person would find itself much more at home when rendered in terms of the partition of the soul like those used in Classical Greek philosophy.[105] The distinction between the rational and the irrational element in the soul shown in both cases certainly points to a similar configuration of parts. In view of this, I see no reason why the two opposite kinds of human behaviour that operate in Homer cannot be represented as corresponding to two mutually complementary parts of Homeric man's self.

As I have argued elsewhere, the principles on which man was recognized as either responsible or not for his actions did not differ greatly between Homer's times and those of Aristotle.[106] But this is not to say that the classification of human actions into voluntary and involuntary would be the same in both cases. The way in which Homer and Aristotle treat errors caused by the excessive consumption of wine provides a good example. In Homer, such errors are treated as deriving from *atē* ('infatuation') thrown into one's heart from outside and thus as actions for which the agent is not held responsible; in Aristotle, the same errors are treated as resulting from *akrasia* ('intemperance'), and, as with other acratic acts, they are deeds for which the agent *is* held responsible.[107] Moreover, to judge from Aristotle's examples of acts due to the agent's ignorance and therefore classed as involuntary, namely acts which Homer would ascribe to *atē*, only such misdeeds as unintentional homicide would continue to figure on Aristotle's list.[108] That is to say, although the division of human actions into voluntary and involuntary remained the same, the content of the list underwent some significant modifications after Homer. This allows us to conclude that the only invariable in the classification of man's activities is the very principle by which the two classes are distinguished from each other.

In view of this, it would be reasonable to suppose that the activities on the list may be subject to redistribution (that is,

[105] For a stimulating attempt at such an interpretation see Sharples (1983), 1–7. Cf. also Pelliccia (1995), 260–1.

[106] Finkelberg (1995), 26–8.

[107] *Od.* 11. 61, 21. 295–8; *Eth. Nic.* 1113ᵇ30–3. On the distribution of responsibility by Aristotle see *Eth. Nic.* 1110ᵃ1–1112ᵃ17; cf. *Rhet.* 1373ᵇ25–38, 1374ᵇ1–9.

[108] See *Eth. Nic.* 1111ᵃ8–21.

they may change their class membership) as a result of processes of cultural re-evaluation. Given the accumulative character of knowledge, it can be suggested that, if it takes place, such re-distribution would be centripetal, that is, it would proceed from the irrational periphery of the self to its rational centre rather than vice versa. In other words, conditions may arise under which additional activities would enter man's knowledge and be evaluated as subject to the individual's control. Judging by the new status it acquired from the fifth century BC, poetry was to be one of these activities.

3

The Song of the Muse

Song and Reality

At the beginning of this book, I suggested that inspiration and art are conceptions of creativity which imply typologically different poetics: a 'poetics of truth' which construes its object as a message of reality and a means to an end, and a 'poetics of fiction' which construes its object as a reality *sui generis* and an end in itself. The analysis of poetry among other activities of Homeric man led to the conclusion that in Homer 'singing', that is, poetry proper, was essentially connected with the idea of divine inspiration. Examination of the implications of this conclusion for the ontological and teleological status of the work of poetry in Homer will be my present task.

It has never been seriously challenged that, to the extent that he derived poetry from divine inspiration, Homer must have seen himself as a mouthpiece of the Muses.[1] The problem, however, is that the implications of this are not always taken into account, mainly because of a tendency to credit oral poets, and especially one as great as Homer, with a considerable degree of creative freedom. But the extent of the *conscious* creative freedom at the traditional poet's disposal is open to serious question. Proceeding from general considerations, it would appear to be valid to assume that the poet is free to treat his material as he wishes in those spheres where he is considered responsible for his activity. Excluding the playing of the lyre, which is of no relevance here, we have found the poet to be

[1] 'Der Gedanke, dass der Mensch mitnichten der Schöpfer des Werkes ist, dass da gesungen oder gesprochen oder aufgeschrieben wird, sondern dass er selbst, das Ich als solches, entweder scheinbar gar nicht vorhanden oder nur Empfangener oder nur Instrument einer höheren Gewalt ist—dieser Gedanke kann als der zentrale der ältesten hellenischen Literatur bezeichnet werden', Kranz (1967), 8. See also Falter (1934), 5; Sperduti (1950), 224–5; Dodds (1951), 81; Cornford (1952), 79, 100; Snell (1953), 136; Chadwick (1962), 14; Maehler (1963), 17; Barmeyer (1968), 102; Otto (1971), 31 ff.; Fuhrmann (1973), 73–4; Rösler (1980), 294–5; Puelma (1989), 66–73.

responsible for his activity in the following two areas: (i) the range of traditional subjects at his disposal, and (ii) the basic plot of each given subject. These, however, are precisely those areas in which any creative intervention on the poet's part is precluded. As we have seen, both the range of traditional subjects and their basic plots were a matter of common knowledge rather than the poet's exclusive prerogative. Clearly, no poet could offer his audience a song about heroes they did not believe to have existed or about events not believed to have taken place, and a song that substantially changed the main outline of a given story might well have left the poet open to the charge that he was either incompetent or deliberately lying. To quote Albert Lord, 'if the singer changes what he has heard in its essence, he falsifies truth'.[2]

Consequently, the Homeric poet's creative freedom must have commenced at the very point where the material predetermined by tradition ended. Here, indeed, the poet seems to be free to elaborate the traditional material handed down to him with new details, digressions, and interpretations of his own; to insert new episodes, and so on.[3] However, this is exactly the sphere over which the Muse presides. We have seen that it is not the poet but the Muse who was considered responsible for the improvisatory side of the poet's activity, so that each of the poet's *ad hoc* amplifications of a given subject must have automatically gained the status of divine truth by virtue of its origin in divine inspiration. Accordingly, the expansion of a traditional subject into a poem, the hallmark characteristic of oral composition, could not be viewed as the poet's creation either.[4] Thus, the poet could not be

[2] Lord (1960), 28. Cf. Page (1959), 253–4: 'The early Greek epic was designed for recitation to kings and noblemen, who took great interest in their pedigrees and in the deeds of ancestors near and remote: who can imagine a poet at the court of Mycenae reciting to the son or grandson of an earlier king the story of an expedition conducted by that king, when his audience knew very well that there was no such expedition and no king so named?'

[3] Cf. Latte (1946), 69: 'Der stofflichen "Erfindung" zieht die Sage, die ja als reales Geschehen gilt, enge Grenzen. Achill *hat* Hektor erschlangen, Troja *ist* von den Griechen erobert, daran kann der Sänger nichts andern. Die Einzelheiten mag er freilich aus der Kraft mitlebender Phantasie frei gestalten.'

[4] It should be kept in mind that the subject of our discussion is the theory and not the practice of poetry. From the point of view of practice, it is obvious that the traditional poet's creative individuality was expressed in the expansion of a traditional subject into a poem. It is, however, highly characteristic that the Greek epic tradition found it necessary to protect this very element in the poet's activity by the idiom of the Muses. Hence, paradoxically, the idea of the Muses allowed the Greek traditional poet a greater creative freedom than other epic traditions. In

considered responsible either for the traditional subject-matter of
his song or for the individual form it acquired in his performance.
No element in the song, therefore, would be construed by the
audience or the poet himself as the poet's 'creation'.

Can we, however, be sure that the song was thought to have no
'creator' at all? Since the Muse was held responsible for the song in
so far as it presented a poetic expansion of given historical and
mythological events, it would be plausible to regard the song as
created by the Muse herself. Obviously, whether the poet or the
Muse is considered the creator of the events related in the song,
what is created is not what really happened. Truth needs no
'creator' in order to be delivered. It seems that this was indeed
Hesiod's position as expressed in the Muses' words to the poet at the
beginning of the *Theogony*: 'We know to tell many lies which
resemble truth, but we know to utter true things when we will.'[5] It
is immaterial by whom, the poet or the Muse, the events related in
poetry are thought to be created: as soon as these events are conceived as created at all, they can no longer be considered true. We
shall return to Hesiod's statement later; yet, as far as Homer is concerned, there can be no doubt that the Muse who communicated
the song to the singer was not envisaged as its creator. Consider, for
instance, the words with which Telemachus rebukes Penelope for
having asked Phemius to change the subject of his song:

Mother, why grudge the sweet bard to please us in whatever way his mind
stirs itself? In all such things it is not the bards who are accountable
(*aitioi*); Zeus, it may be, is accountable, when he allots to toiling men to
each one as he will.

The Muse, who inspires the singer, is not even mentioned here as
a factor responsible for the content of the song. The real 'creator'
of Phemius' song is Zeus, who caused the events that the singer
sings of to occur.[6]

the South Slavic tradition, for example, where no provision is made for divine
inspiration, additions and amplifications of any kind are generally condemned as
deviating from the truth of the story. On this subject see Finkelberg (1990), 293–
303, and below, Ch. 5.

  [5] *Th.* 27–8; see also below, Ch. 5.
  [6] *Od.* 1. 346–50. Schadewaldt (1951), 81–2, comments ad loc.: 'Wenn hier der
Gott, der die Geschicke gibt und lenkt, nicht aber der Sänger für eine traurige
Geschichte verantwortlich erscheint, so ist es diesen Menschen ganz selbst-
verständlich, dass der Sänger mit seinem Liede nur treu dem Gange des Welt-
geschehens volgt.' *Il.* 6. 357–8 and *Od.* 8. 579–80, 24. 197–8 seem to converge on
the same idea.

But if the Muses do not create the song, what role do they play? Evidence regarding Homer's understanding of the Muses' role is supplied by the famous invocation introducing the Catalogue of Ships. Let us quote it again:

Tell me now, you Muses who have your homes on Olympus—you are gods, and attend all things and know all things, but we hear only the report and have no knowledge—tell me who were the leaders of the Danaans and their rulers.[7]

What the Muses communicate to the singer and, through his mediation, to other mortals, is information about events which they have personally witnessed. The Muses thus do not possess more creative freedom than the poet: the only relevant difference between the Muses and the poet lies in the scope of their knowledge.

Another passage which seems relevant in this connection is *Odyssey* 8, when Odysseus addresses Demodocus, who performs songs about the Trojan war:

Demodocus, I admire you beyond any man; either it was the Muse who taught you, the daughter of Zeus, or else it was Apollo, for perfectly in order you sing of the fortunes of the Achaeans—all they achieved and suffered and toiled over—as though you yourself were there or had heard from one who was.[8]

There is no way in which a blind bard residing in remote Phaeacia could have witnessed the events of which he sings; yet, a participant in the Trojan war vouches for the truthfulness of his account, naturally explaining this by the poet's divine inspiration.

Although the idiom of the Muses as such is unique to the Greek poetic tradition, it is characteristic that some other epic traditions also base their claim to truthfulness on the principle of firsthand evidence transmitted by superhuman means. Thus, the *Mahabharata* is cast as a recital by the bard Ugrasravas of the story told to him by another sage, Vaisampayana, who in turn was told it by Vyasa, the ancestor of all its protagonists; Vyasa outlived all his descendants and therefore is the only living eyewitness of the events recited.[9] In Fijian poetic tradition, the poet is inspired by the ancestors with whom he communes: 'This is believed to go further than mere inspiration: with the "true-songs" or epic songs the

---

[7] *Il.* 2. 484-7.   [8] *Od.* 8. 487-91.   [9] See Shulman (1991), 10-11.

ancestors themselves chant the songs as they teach them to the poet, and it is in their name that they are delivered.'[10] Consider also the following avowal of the nineteenth-century Kara-Kirghiz *akyn*, startlingly resembling Phemius' words in *Odyssey* 22: 'I can sing every song; for God has planted the gift of song in my heart. He gives me the word on my tongue without my having to seek it. I have not learned any of my songs; everything springs from my inner being, from myself.'[11] Although this epic singer does not say explicitly that his contact with the divine gives him access to knowledge of the past, the very fact that the songs he performed dealt with the heroic past allows one to suggest that the principle of firsthand evidence was considered relevant in his tradition as well.

That the privileged position of the Muses as eyewitnesses of past events was taken seriously by the Greeks can be seen from the fact that it was felt to be problematic as soon as the goddesses' theogonic status as daughters of Zeus and Mnemosyne was taken into account. In as much, indeed, as they were born at a late stage in the theogony, the Muses could not possibly have been eyewitnesses of events that took place before their birth. And although for heroic traditions such as those dealt with in Homer this point was of little relevance, it definitely constituted a difficulty when the Muses' authority was invoked to serve as a foundation for a theogony. This gave rise to attempts by some Greek poets, such as Alcman and Mimnermus, to solve the problem by creating an additional set of Muses, born from Uranos and Gaia at the earliest stage of the theogony.[12] Another attempt at coping with the same problem can be seen in the habit of Hesiod and other theogonic poets who begin their recital with the Muses and thus provide them with a privileged position in respect of the subsequent account; that is to say, they represent them as if they were the firstborn.[13] These attempts of Archaic age poets to base their

[10] Finnegan (1977), 171.

[11] See Bowra (1952), 41. Cf. Chadwick and Zhirmunsky (1969), 332–3.

[12] Alcman 5. 25–30 *PMG*; cf. Fränkel (1962), 254 n. 4. Mimnermus 13 West.

[13] Cf. e.g. a theogony (quoted below in Ch. 4) recited by Hermes in *H. Herm.* 428–33. Cf. also Heitsch (1966), 196–7. Belfiore (1985: 47–57) makes the interesting suggestion that the Hesiodic Muses' claim in *Th.* 27–8 that, besides truth, they can also deliver plausible lies, relates to events preceding the Muses' birth and of which, therefore, they are ignorant. Yet, the Muses' emphasis on the fact that their telling the truth depends on their will rather than on their knowledge makes this suggestion doubtful. Cf. Pratt (1993), 147 n. 26.

song on the Muses' authority at all costs, make it clear that the goddesses' position as eyewitnesses of past events was essential to their status.

Thus, Homer envisaged the song as deriving from the actual experience of an eyewitness, the Muse, and no element or part of the song as 'created', or invented, by either the poet or the Muse. Consequently, the concrete historical meaning of the ontological status of poetry as a product of inspiration would be, in the case of Homer, *a firsthand account of events that really happened*. Compare this with the following words of Aristotle in the *Poetics*.

And even if he [the poet] chances to be putting things that have happened into his poetry, he is none the less the poet; for there is no reason why some events that have actually happened should not conform to the law of plausible and possible, and in virtue of that quality in them he is their poet or maker.[14]

Nothing could illustrate the gap between Aristotle and Homer more clearly. As we have seen, no element in song is regarded by Homer as created by either the poet or the Muse. In contrast, according to Aristotle, no element in poetry should be regarded as not created by the poet. In other words, while for Homer everything in poetry is truth, for Aristotle everything in poetry is fiction. Aristotle's definition of history is thus more appropriate to Homer's idea of song than his definition of poetry.[15] With this in view, let us turn to the subject-matter of poetry and its objective.

'The Glories of Men'

Although the epic tradition was originally cast to preserve the memory of all past events of historical significance, for Homer, as also for generations of Greeks after him, the history of the past amounted to the history of the Heroic age, which ended with the Trojan war.[16] A justification of this approach can be found in the

[14] *Poet.* 1451^{b}29-32.

[15] Cf. Snell (1953), 90: 'Aristotle's assertions, regardless of the truth contained in them, at once prompt the question how the early Greeks understood the relationship between poetry and "the things which have happened". As regards Homeric epic, the answer is easily given; and, as was only to be expected, it does not conform with the Aristotelian proposition'.

[16] A slightly different treatment of this subject appeared in Finkelberg (1991-2), 22-37.

Cyclic *Cypria* and the Hesiodic corpus: the Trojan and Theban wars
were the two events that marked the low limit of the Heroic age,
in that both were especially designed by Zeus in order to destroy
the generation of heroes:

There was a time when the countless tribes of men, though wide-
dispersed, oppressed the surface of the deep-bosomed earth, and Zeus saw
it and had pity and in his wise heart resolved to relieve the all-nurturing
earth of men by causing the great struggle of the Ilian war, that the load
of death might empty the world. And so the heroes were slain in Troy,
and the plan of Zeus came to pass.[17]

In the epic tradition, the privileged status of the Trojan saga is
axiomatic. In the *Odyssey*, where the Trojan war as such is already
viewed as part of the heroic past, 'The Doom of the Achaeans and
Troy' engages everybody's attention, including that of the gods
themselves. The inhabitants of Ithaca, of Phaeacia, of the Island of
Aeolia, and even Odysseus himself, are eager to listen to songs and
stories about Troy (which, in fact, are the only songs and stories
they listen to), and this is the very subject that is included in the
Sirens' promise to bestow a knowledge greater than human—a
promise nobody can resist. That only a savage like Polyphemus can
remain ignorant of the Trojan war—as well, indeed, as of any
other mark of human civilization—shows clearly enough that
acquaintance with the Trojan saga was regarded as one of the
cultural codes that united the civilized world.[18] And the crowning
demonstration of the supreme significance of the Trojan saga is
found, of course, in the avowal of both Helen in the *Iliad* and
Alcinous in the *Odyssey* that the evil fate of all those involved in
the war was ultimately imposed by the gods only to supply a
subject for song for future generations.[19]

It is generally agreed that in everything concerning the subject-
matter of epic poetry the keyword is *kleos*—'rumour', 'fame',
'glory'. This is not to say, of course, that we are entitled to attach
the meaning 'fame' and, by implication, 'song', to all Homer's
usages of the term *kleos*. Although epic songs are twice designated
in Homer as 'glories of men',[20] it cannot be denied that, especially

[17] *Cypria* fr. 1 Allen, trans. H. G. Evelyn-White; cf. Hes. *Erga* 156–73 and fr. 204.
95–119 MW.
[18] *Od.* 9. 258–80. Cf. Clay (1988), 199.
[19] *Il.* 6. 354–8; *Od.* 8. 577–80. See also below, Ch. 5.
[20] κλέα ἀνδρῶν *Il.* 9. 189; *Od.* 8. 73; cf. Hes. *Th.* 100 κλεῖα προτέρων ἀνθρώπων.

when the term is applied to the present, its Homeric meaning may well be simply a 'rumour': 'we only hear *kleos* and know nothing', says the poet in the famous invocation of the Muses preceding the Catalogue of Ships. As this invocation clearly shows, the privileged realm of song begins where human witness ends. In other words, only where preservation of a given event is rendered in terms of longevity outreaching firsthand evidence, would poetry presumably be the means by which such an event would be perpetuated or immortalized.

Now, though it may be employed as a neutral term, *kleos* is never used in Homer in a negative sense. Hence, if we follow only such Homeric contexts concerning long-lasting memory of a certain event as employ the term *kleos*, we shall naturally arrive at the kind of generalization which gave rise to the widespread view that the sole objective of epic poetry in general and Homer's poetry in particular was to preserve for posterity the fame of glorious deeds on the battlefield.[21] Following T. B. L. Webster, I shall henceforth refer to this view as the 'monument theory' of epic poetry.[22] Yet *kleos* is not the only way to express such meanings in the Homeric poems. For example, the formula 'even men yet to be born shall hear of it' is even more favoured by Homer than expressions employing the term *kleos*.[23] Moreover, the only Homeric formula expressing the idea of preserving a given event in poetry, 'song for men yet unborn', obviously derives from this expression.[24]

When at *Iliad* 22. 304–5 Hector says that before he dies he will accomplish something great 'whereof even men yet to be born shall hear', it is clear that the same idea could be expressed just as well by the term *kleos*. But consider *Iliad* 2. 119–22, where Agamemnon says that 'even men yet to be born shall hear' of the shame of the Achaeans' retreat from Troy; or *Odyssey* 21. 253–5, where Eurymachus says that the suitors' inability to draw Odysseus' bow will bring disgrace upon them, of which 'even men

---

[21] As formulated, for example, in Schmitt (1967), 67–8: 'Der Ruhm, den sich der Held im Kampf erwirbt, wird ja im Verse des Dichters weiterleben.'

[22] Webster (1939), 166. To my knowledge, Webster was the first to question the relevance of the 'monument theory' to Homer's epics: he argued that the functions ascribed to poetry by this theory are fulfilled in Homer by the hero's tomb, and that the approach itself is relevant to post-Homeric poets rather than to Homer (p. 173).

[23] καὶ ἐσσομένοισι πυθέσθαι *Il.* 2. 119, 22. 305; *Od.* 11. 76, 21. 255, 24. 433; cf. also καὶ ἐσσομένῃσιν ὀπίσσω at *Od.* 11. 433.

[24] καὶ ἐσσομένοισι ἀοιδή *Od.* 3. 204 (v. l. καὶ ἐσσομένοισι πυθέσθαι), 8. 580. Cf. also ἀοίδιμοι ἐσσομένοισιν at *Il.* 6. 358.

yet to be born shall hear'. Although these two passages also express the idea of the preservation of a given event for posterity, their negative connotations preclude the term *kleos* from being employed in either of them. Other such passages are *Odyssey* 11. 432–3, 24. 433–5, and, in application to poetry, 24. 194–202:

> Then the soul of the son of Atreus answered: 'Happy son of Laertes, Odysseus of many devices, how virtuous was the wife you won! How single-hearted was your incomparable Penelope daughter of Icarius, how faithfully did she keep remembrance of the husband she has wedded! And therefore the fame (*kleos*) of her virtue will never perish, and the immortals will see to it that men on earth have a lovely song in honour of chaste Penelope. Not so will it be with the daughter of Tyndareus. She plotted evil, she slew her wedded husband, and the song of her among mankind will be one of loathing, she will bring an evil repute on all her sex, even on the virtuous.'

The latter passage makes the limitations on the usage of the term *kleos* especially clear: although both Penelope's and Clytaemnestra's story are said to supply the subject for a song, it is only in Penelope's case that the term *kleos* emerges.

This allows us to conclude that the expressions employing the term *kleos* account for only *some* of Homer's modes of declaring that certain events are worth preserving for posterity. Consequently, the 'monument theory' of epic poetry proves to be based on a generalization of only part of the relevant material in Homer. This difficulty was envisaged by Gregory Nagy, who proposed distinguishing between 'song of glorification', which alone preserves *kleos*, and song dealing with evil deeds, misfortune, or defeat: 'what you experienced may indeed be unforgettable (ἄλαστα), so that singers will always sing of it, but it is not κλέος ἄφθιτον . . .'.[25] Helpful as it is for delimiting the specific sphere of *kleos*, the distinction ceases to be relevant when one wishes to establish what is generally seen by Homer as worth preserving in poetry: actually, it only emphasizes the fact that glorious deeds are no more than a particular case of what is seen as worthy of preservation.

There is thus reason to suppose that if, in addition to the *kleos*-expressions, we consider those Homeric expressions of the idea of perpetuating a given event for posterity which do not employ the term *kleos*, the picture of what Homer regarded as worth

[25] Nagy (1974), 261.

perpetuation would become quite different from the one emerging from the 'monument theory'. What conception of epic poetry could in fact correspond to the idea that not only glorious and heroic deeds can be preserved in songs? As a possible answer, Werner Jaeger's educational theory can be considered. According to Jaeger, Homer's poetry 'chooses and presents its truth in accordance with a definitive ideal', and its objective is training of mind and character by means of exemplary life-patterns from the past.[26] It is evident that this explanation of what Homer regarded as worth preserving in poetry, accounting as it does not only for praiseworthy but also for reprehensible deeds, is indeed much more flexible than that proposed by the 'monument theory'. The problem, however, is that most Homeric utterances on the subject, especially those of the *Iliad*, are ethically neutral and therefore cannot be explained in terms of the educational theory.[27]

Another approach was proposed by Hermann Fränkel. Fränkel noticed that what is expected to be preserved in song is designated both by Helen in the *Iliad* and by Alcinous in the *Odyssey* as 'evil fate', 'doom', and 'ruin', and that these and similar characteristics are often applied by Homer to the major epic subjects like the Trojan war or the Return of the Achaeans.[28] Proceeding from these observations he came to the conclusion that 'what the Homeric singer aimed at was to arouse feelings of fear and pity through imagined participation in tragic events' and that, therefore, 'only what is sorrowful is worth preservation in song'.[29] Accounting as it does for ethically neutral as well as for praiseworthy and reprehensible deeds, the approach that derives song from human suffering fits in better with the complex and many-sided character of Homer's poetry than the 'monumental' and educational theories. Here, too, however, the question is whether this approach is comprehensive.

At *Iliad* 2. 324–9, Odysseus reminds the rest of the Achaeans of

[26] Jaeger (1947), 36, cf. also 40–1.

[27] Both Kraus (1955: 70) and Lanata (1963: 15) argue that the Penelope-Clytaemnestra opposition at *Od.* 24. 194–202 is the only passage regarding which the educational theory can be considered relevant. That this would be too rigid an approach has been shown by Verdenius (1983: 34) who also draws attention to other cases in Homer where 'the glorification of the past has an educational by-purpose'.

[28] *Il.* 6. 354–8; *Od.* 8. 577–80. Fränkel (1962), 14–15.

[29] Fränkel (1962), 15. See also Griffin (1980), 96–102; Macleod (1982), 1–8, and (1983), 11–12.

the great portent which they witnessed at Aulis at the very beginning of the Trojan expedition and adduces the words said on the occasion by Calchas the soothsayer:

This is a great sign revealed to us by Zeus the counsellor—a sign late-pointing, late-fulfilled, whose fame (*kleos*) will never perish. Just as this snake ate the sparrow's children and the sparrow herself, eight of them, and the mother who bore the brood made nine, so we shall battle there for that many years, and in the tenth year we shall take the broad streets of the city.

It can be seen that the statement that the portent's fame will never be lost accords with none of the principles purporting to account for Homer's idea of what is worth preserving in song. The portent at Aulis was not the act of a hero aiming at everlasting glory; it can serve neither as an authoritative example nor as a warning; nor can it be envisaged as an embodiment of human suffering. It is simply an event. Still, it is obviously regarded by Homer as worthy of the same everlasting fame as the glorious deeds and tragic fates of the most prominent of his heroes. Shall we infer from this that what Homer saw as worth preserving in song was merely what had happened? Obviously, such a principle would be the comprehensive one we are looking for. But if the totality of the epic songs amounted to the totality of events that had happened, that is, if the epic corpus was regarded, as A. W. Gomme put it, as 'chronicles',[30] this would mean that all the events of the Trojan war are supposed to be immortalized in song. That this is not so is clearly shown by Achilles' pondering of the possible alternatives before him in *Iliad* 9:

My mother, the silver-footed goddess Thetis, says that I have two fates that could carry me to the end of death. If I stay here and fight on round the Trojans' city, then gone is my homecoming, but my fame (*kleos*) will never perish: and if I come back to my dear native land, then gone is my great fame, but my life will stretch long and the end of death will not overtake me quickly.[31]

In showing that some of the events of the past will be preserved for posterity whereas the others will not, Achilles' case plainly indicates that Homer did have in mind a principle that determined which events of the past should be preserved. If what is preserved in song were simply what happened, Achilles' returning home

[30] Gomme (1951), 2-3.   [31] *Il.* 9. 410-16.

would be even more an 'event' than his remaining at Troy; still, in that case his fame would not have been preserved.

Thus far, in our attempts to arrive at a common denominator of the events which Homer says are worth preserving for posterity, we have obtained only negative results. Indeed, the only thing which can be said with certainty at this stage is that neither heroic deeds, nor moral examples, nor human sufferings, nor, finally, chronological documentation of past events can supply a basis for generalization. Perhaps the simplest way to arrive at the common denominator we are looking for is to assemble all the relevant instances and try to assess what they have in common. Apart from the events which Homer explicitly says will be preserved by poetry, we shall deal only with those whose future preservation is presented in terms of longevity beyond the reach of firsthand evidence, for, as we have seen, it is at this point that the privileged realm of song begins. Actually, the discussion will be confined to the expressions 'song for men yet unborn' and the like, 'even men yet to be born shall hear of it' and the like, 'fame will never perish', 'may the fame be inextinguishable', and those expressions employing the term 'late-born' in the sense relevant to our subject.[32]

Here, then, is the full list: (1) Helen and Paris; (2) Departure from Aulis; (3) Death of Hector; (4) Doom of the Achaeans and Troy; (5) Odysseus in Phaeacia; (6) Penelope's Virtue; (7) The Killing of the Suitors; (8) Clytaemnestra's Perfidy; (9) Orestes' Revenge; (10) Retreat of the Achaeans from Troy (unaccomplished); (11) Paris' death at Menelaus' hands (unaccomplished); (12) Achilles' Remaining at Troy (an alternative). The first conclusion to be drawn from this list is that, if these are indeed the events that were meant by Homer to be preserved by means of poetry, he conceived the poetry of the Trojan war as a collection of *oimai*, epic lays, each of which featured its own individual subject. It can also be concluded that the subjects he refers to as

---

[32] καὶ ἐσσομένοισι ἀοιδή *Il.* 6. 357–8, *Od.* 3. 204, 8. 580, 24. 194–202; καὶ ἐσσομένοισι πυθέσθαι see n. 23 above; κλέος οὔποτ' ὀλεῖται *Il.* 2. 325, *Od.* 24. 196, cf. *Il.* 7. 91; ἄσβεστον κλέος εἴη *Od.* 7. 331, cf. 4. 584; ὀψίγονος *Il.* 3. 353, 16. 31, *Od.* 1. 392, 3. 200. My criteria of selection rule out such passages as, for example, *Il.* 10. 212, Nestor's statement that he who volunteers to penetrate into the Trojan camp will get 'heaven-high' fame (ὑπουράνιον κλέος): when *kleos* is described by Homer in such 'spatial' terms, it usually means widespread reputation in the present, cf. *Il.* 8. 192; *Od.* 9. 264, 8. 74.

deserving perpetuation amount more or less to the main constituents of the Trojan saga, from the Cyclic *Cypria*, via the *Iliad*
and the *Odyssey*, to the Cyclic *Nosti*.

Now, if all the events referred to by Homer as worthy of preservation had been like these, we would have faced a real *aporia*: in
so far as the events which are treated as worth preserving for
posterity are the very ones that have actually been preserved, there
could be no way to define the principle according to which these
events were selected. Fortunately, however, among the events
regarded as deserving perpetuation Homer occasionally refers to
hypothetical situations, that is, things that could have happened
but in the end did not.

A good example of such a hypothetical situation is the episode
of the Diapeira in *Iliad* 2. Agamemnon intends to test his men by
proposing to return home without taking Troy. Contrary to his
expectations, the Achaeans rush to the ships, eager to depart
immediately. While trying to stop them, Agamemnon says, *inter
alia*, that the shame of their retreat will be known even to men yet
unborn.[33] It is significant in this connection that, although the *Iliad*
often refers to shameful behaviour in war, it is only in this instance
that such shame is expected to be perpetuated. What makes this
case different? To obtain the answer, we should take into account
what would have happened had the Achaeans indeed left Troy in
the tenth year of the war. Obviously, as is explicitly stated by the
poet himself, this premature withdrawal would have brought the
Trojan war to an end: 'Then the Argives would have made a
homecoming beyond what was fated, if Hera had not spoken to
Athene etc.'[34] Now, if a retreat that does not bring about a
dramatic turn in the course of events is not considered worth preserving for posterity, whereas one that does, or would, cause such
a dramatic turn is so considered, it can be suggested that only
events possessing far-reaching consequences were seen by Homer
as worthy to become the subjects of epic songs and thus to be
immortalized.

Thus, with the assistance of a hypothetical situation relating to
an event that never actually took place, we can distinguish
between the canonized repertoire of the episodes constituting the
Trojan saga and the poet's ideas that lie beyond this repertoire; for,
as a matter of fact, if we apply the conclusions obtained as a result

[33] *Il.* 2. 119 καὶ ἐσσομένοισι πυθέσθαι.   [34] *Il.* 2. 155-6.

of our analysis of a hypothetical situation to the other situations regarded as worthy of preservation, we shall see that the conclusion holds good in the real cases as well. Let us begin with the *Iliad*. The portent in Aulis, whose fame 'shall never perish', is said to be 'late-pointing' and 'late-fulfilled'.[35] It can be seen that these characteristics are also relevant to the Aulis episode as a whole: inasmuch as the Achaeans' departure for Troy will be brought to completion only with the end of the ten-year war, this event itself is also 'of late fulfilment'. In view of this, it seems reasonable to suggest, together with the scholiast, that the words 'whose fame will never perish' refer not only to the portent but also to the events for which it stands.[36] Furthermore, considering that no other portent in Homer is said to be destined to be remembered for ever, it is likely that it is not the portent's mere occurrence, but its occurrence simultaneously with so significant an event as the beginning of the Trojan war that guarantees that its fame will be remembered by posterity.

In *Iliad* 3, Menelaus says that if he overcomes Paris, this will prevent men in the future from repeating Paris' crime. Again, had the Menelaus–Paris single combat, which by agreement was to determine the outcome of the war, reached a decisive conclusion, the Trojan war would have ended; like the Retreat of the Achaeans, this combat, too, represents an 'historical option' which did not actually happen.[37] In view of this, it may reasonably be suggested that what was to make Paris' punishment by Menelaus so memorable was, above all, its association with so significant a prospect as the end of the war.

In *Iliad* 22, having realized the inevitability of his death at Achilles' hands, Hector intends to accomplish 'something great whereof men yet to be born shall hear'.[38] With these words he attacks Achilles with his sword, but Achilles strikes him first with his spear. This can hardly be defined as the greatest of Hector's feats. But Hector's death was indeed seen by Homer as one of the great events of the Trojan war. Hence, even if his behaviour at

[35] *Il.* 2. 325 ὄψιμον, ὀψιτέλεστον, ὅου κλέος οὔποτ' ὀλεῖται.

[36] Schol. BL to *Il.* 2. 325: τὸ τοῦ πολέμου κλέος ἢ τὸ τοῦ σημείου. Cf. also Maehler (1963), 11: 'Der Ruhm gilt nicht so sehr dem Zeichen als vielmehr dem Geschehen.'

[37] *Il.* 3. 353–4. Such introduction of unrealized options, termed by K. Reinhardt 'das "Fast"' and by B. Fenik 'the "almost" situation', is characteristic of Homer's technique of plot-making in general. See Reinhardt (1961), 107–20; Fenik (1978b), 80–1, and Ch. 5 below.　　　　　　　　　　　　　　　[38] *Il.* 22. 304–5.

such a moment had been shameful, it is very likely that posterity would still have heard about his fatal combat with Achilles. Hector's behaviour at the moment of his death could only determine how, not whether, he should enter into the memory of posterity.

The most illuminating case, however, is Helen. In *Iliad* 6 she says of Paris and herself: 'On us two Zeus has set a doom of misery, so that in time to come we can be themes of song for men of future generations.' Jasper Griffin comments on this: 'Helen sees herself as a character in history, whose sin has produced suffering for everyone.'[39] At the same time, it seems unlikely to me that Helen's (and Homer's) confidence about the perpetuation of Helen's story issued, as is argued by Griffin, from the tragic character of her fate,[40]—and not only because the same kind of immortality is promised on the same occasion to so untragic a character as Homer's Paris. After all, Helen's fate can hardly be considered more unhappy than, say, that of Andromache. Nevertheless, as the latter ponders what will happen to her after Hector's death and the fall of Troy, she envisages no prospect that her suffering will make her famous in posterity.[41] Rather, it is Helen's being, together with Paris, the cause of the Trojan war that guarantees that her personal fate shall supply a subject for future song.

Thus all the cases of the preservation of a given event for posterity mentioned in the *Iliad* (apart from the case of Achilles, which will be treated separately) seem to be closely associated with crucial stages in the history of the Trojan war. Helen and Paris as persons embody the very reason for this war; the Aulis episode signifies its actual beginning just as Hector's death stands for its logical end, so to speak; finally, the Achaeans' intention to abandon Troy and the Menelaus–Paris combat represent, each in its own way, unrealized options for the war's solution.

Let us turn now to the *Odyssey*. It may seem that, as distinct from the *Iliad*, the setting of this poem is hardly suited to any sort of 'historical' explanation. Indeed, Clytaemnestra's perfidy, Orestes'

---

[39] *Il.* 6. 357–8; Griffin (1980), 96.

[40] See Griffin (1980), 97–8: 'And Helen is a legendary figure not for her great achievements, not even for her womanly virtue, like Penelope, but for her guilt and suffering.' Cf. also ibid. 80.

[41] *Il.* 24. 725–45, cf. also 22. 477–507 and 6. 447–65. If Andromache's fate was a matter of interest, this was due to her being Hector's wife rather than to her suffering.

revenge, Alcinous' hospitality, the constancy of Penelope—all referred to as worth perpetuating—seem to fall short of the standards of historical significance set in the *Iliad*. We can hardly expect, however, that Homer's criteria of historical significance would be identical to ours: it is sufficient for our purpose that the aftermath of the Trojan war, the Returns, was clearly seen in Greek tradition as a no less integral part of the Trojan saga than the events of the war itself. If we take this into account, we shall see that in the *Odyssey*, too, everything expected to be preserved for posterity is inseparable from great events, which in that poem are significant developments in the homeland at the time of the Achaean heroes' return, rather than the crucial stages of the Trojan war.

Thus, just as Clytaemnestra's perfidy, crowned as it was with Agamemnon's murder, cannot be separated from the palace revolution and the dethronement of the ruling dynasty in Argos, so also Orestes' virtue is an integral part of the restoration.[42] Penelope's constancy, too, in that it represents the necessary condition for the restoration of Odysseus' rule over Ithaca,[43] is a factor 'of late fulfilment' in the poem's plot rather than simply a demonstration of didactic virtue. The same is true of the suitors. Their behaviour is characterized as blameworthy throughout the poem; still, it is only at *Odyssey* 21. 253-5, in the bow episode, that the suitors' disrepute is expected to be preserved for posterity. Now, the bow episode, already referred to as 'the beginning of the killing' in the opening verses of the book,[44] leads directly to the killing of the suitors by Odysseus and is thus inseparable from the restoration of the latter's reign over Ithaca: that is to say, a great event catches the suitors at the moment of their inability to draw Odysseus' bow, and it is in conjunction with this disgrace that they are to be remembered by posterity. This is also true of the unaccomplished revenge of the suitors' kinsmen, the shame of which is referred to at *Odyssey* 24. 433 as something expected to become known to posterity. Odysseus' restoration of his rule directly depends on whether or not this revenge will be success-

---

[42] *Od.* 3. 204, 24. 194-202, cf. also 1. 302, 3. 200, 11. 432-4.

[43] Inasmuch as the marriage with Odysseus' widow is generally seen in the poem as legitimizing accession to the kingship of Ithaca; see Finley (1978), 88-91; Finkelberg (1991), 306-7.

[44] *Od.* 21. 4 φόνου ἀρχή.

ful,[45] and thus its preservation, whether in the form of honour or of shame, is guaranteed.

Two other cases concern Odysseus' sojourn in Phaeacia. In *Odyssey* 7, Odysseus says that if Alcinous' promise to give him an escort is fulfilled, not only will he himself return home but Alcinous' fame will be imperishable.[46] This is one of the clearest examples of how participation in a significant event can condition perpetuation of one's fame. Indeed, the syntax makes it perfectly clear that Alcinous' fame and Odysseus' return reciprocate one another: 'his fame, on the one hand . . . I, on the other hand . . .'. Alcinous and his Phaeacians certainly do not owe their existence to the *Odyssey*; yet their 'inextinguishable fame' is conditioned by their assistance in the return of the great Odysseus.[47] And finally, at *Odyssey* 8. 579-80, in a remark to which we shall return later, Alcinous says that the doom and ruin of the Achaeans and Troy have been wrought by the gods 'that there might be a song in the ears of men yet unborn': these words show that, according to Homer, all the participants in the Trojan war, and not only its protagonists, would receive a share in the future song.

We have now examined all the episodes about which Homer explicitly says that they are to be preserved for posterity. In every case, these have proved to be associated with events that are of great significance in the Trojan saga and thus structurally essential to the larger story. The question now is whether such a pattern is in itself sufficient to justify the inference that participation in a significant event is the sole guarantee that one's fame will be perpetuated. To argue that this is so, we must have proof that in Homer's eyes the memory of all the episodes in question would otherwise have perished. It seems to me that the case of Achilles' choice provides such a demonstration.

By all standards, Achilles was the greatest of the Achaean heroes of the generation of the Trojan war. Still, as reported in *Iliad* 9, had he left Troy and returned home, his fame would have been lost. Note that it is the very fact that of all the Achaean heroes it was

---

[45] Cf. Finley (1978), 77.

[46] *Od.* 7. 332-3 τοῦ μέν κεν ἐπὶ ζείδωρον ἄρουραν | ἄσβεστον κλέος εἴη, ἐγὼ δέ κε πατρίδ᾽ ἱκοίμην.

[47] Cf. Diod. Sic. 4. 72. 4: 'To Phaeax was born Alcinous, who brought about the return of Odysseus to Ithaca.' The only other case where someone's *kleos* is expected to be 'inextinguishable' is the *kleos* of Agamemnon which is to be preserved by his tomb, see *Od.* 4. 584 and n. 50 below.

Achilles whose fame might have fallen into oblivion that casts doubt on the validity of the widespread view which we have called, after Webster, the 'monument theory'—i.e. that heroic deeds on the battlefield guarantee everlasting glory. Indeed, up to the moment that Achilles pronounced his speech, his warlike exploits surpassed by far those of any other Achaean hero, and he was unanimously recognized as the greatest of the heroes who fought at Troy. Still, had he left the siege in the tenth year of the war, his fame would have been lost.

Note also that, like the unaccomplished retreat of the Achaeans, Achilles' choice is again an option that is ultimately not taken, but this time the alternative is not preservation but the deletion of fame from the memory of posterity. Let us, then, imagine again what would have happened had Achilles indeed left the Trojan campaign in the tenth year of the war. The most obvious answer is that he would not have killed Hector and, consequently, would not have influenced the war's course in the way he actually did. Now, an Achilles who did not kill Hector may be compared to a Helen who did not elope with Paris. It is doubtful indeed whether Helen's position as queen of Sparta and the most beautiful of the Achaean women would have sufficed to give her a more prominent representation in poetry than something like 'she surpassed all girls of her age in beauty and handcraft and sense', a remark made of Anchises' daughter Hippodameia when her husband is killed by Idomeneus.[48] That the same could have been true of Achilles can be inferred from Patroclus' words to Achilles in *Iliad* 16: 'What other men born hereafter shall be advantaged unless you beat aside from the Argives this shameful destruction?'[49] Patroclus' words clearly imply that, by abstaining from participation in war, Achilles is losing his *raison d'être* from the point of view of others, including posterity.

At *Odyssey* 8. 579-80, Homer has Alcinous say that the doom and ruin of the Achaeans and Troy were wrought by the gods in order to provide song for future generations. One can infer from these words that it was Homer's contention that everyone involved

[48] *Il.* 13. 431-2.
[49] *Il.* 16. 31-2. τί σευ ἄλλος ὀνήσεται ὀψίγονός περ | αἴ κε μὴ Ἀργείοισιν ἀεικέα λοιγὸν ἀμύνῃς; (trans. R. Lattimore). Ebeling, s.v. ὀψίγονος, proposes 'quid juvabis posteros?' as an equivalent for this rather puzzling remark; the rendering given in LSJ, s.v. ὀνίνημι, is 'what good will others have of thee?, i.e. what good will you have done them?'

in the war would receive his or her share in the future song of it. This is not to say, however, that every participant would be treated equally. There is, indeed, a great difference between those who remained hardly more than names in the catalogues and those few protagonists who exerted a decisive influence on the course of the war. After all, 'song' (*aoidē*), promised to all, is a far weaker term than the 'everlasting fame' individually promised to Achilles. Given the difference, discussed in Chapter 2, between *aoidē* as referring to epic poetry as a whole and *oimē* as referring to a single lay, and considering that the poetry of the Trojan war, as shown above, was conceived of by Homer as consisting of just such single lays, it can be conjectured that the perspective of 'everlasting fame' actually amounted to the prospect of one's becoming the principal subject of an individual epic lay.

Consider now that the conception of our *Iliad* is based on the presumption that the death of Hector would amount to the fall of Troy (see also Chapter 5). The *Iliad* thus places Achilles at a strategic position within the Trojan saga: as long as Hector lived Troy would not fall, and it was Achilles who killed Hector. But Troy was destined to fall. This means that if Achilles had not been there Hector would have had to be killed by someone else. That is to say, had Achilles returned home, the history of the Trojan war would have been remembered differently, without Achilles as its key figure. It can be assumed that, living peacefully in Phthia, Achilles would still not have been lost to the rumour of his contemporaries; and his fame would not have been lost either, in the sense that it would have been preserved by his tomb. But this is also true of such a minor character as Odysseus' companion Elpenor.[50] It can also be assumed that Achilles' warlike record up to the moment of his departure from the conflict would have sufficed to guarantee him some minor part in the poetic account of the Trojan saga, and his name, like the names of other minor warriors, would certainly have emerged in the battle scenes and catalogues. But he would not have obtained everlasting fame, that is, there would not have been a song dedicated to Achilles. If I am correct, the reason for this would be that, had Achilles left Troy, he would have missed his chance to become a significant figure in Greek historical

---

[50] *Od.* 11. 75-6, cf. 10. 552-3. Apart from song, the hero's tomb is the only other means of perpetuating fame, see e.g. *Il.* 7. 91; *Od.* 4. 584, 11. 75-76, 24. 80-94.

memory. Compare, for example, the case of Philoctetes, who did not even participate in the ten-year war, but whose place in the war's history was guaranteed by the simple fact that, if he had not joined the Achaeans at the last moment, Troy would not have fallen.[51]

Note that the Trojan saga abounds in heroes without whose participation Troy would not have fallen. It would not have fallen without Achilles, who killed Hector; without Philoctetes, who killed Paris; without the participation of Neoptolemus; without Odysseus and Diomedes, who stole the Palladium; and, above all, without the Wooden Horse, which was devised by Odysseus and was conveniently made big enough to harbour all the leading characters in the saga. Yet, as has been pointed out by Martin West, Achilles does not fulfil two essential requirements of a Trojan war hero—he was not one of Helen's suitors and he did not take part in the sack of Troy;[52] Diomedes' real connections lie with the Theban cycle; Philoctetes did not even participate in the ten-year war; Neoptolemus would have been only ten years old by the time of the sack of Troy, and so on. It is, indeed, a well-known peculiarity of heroic poetry to telescope history by concentrating around the same event personages belonging to different historical periods. This peculiarity evidently originated in that tendency to economy which caused the traditional poets to concentrate all the prominent figures of broadly the same historical period around one prominent event associated with the period in question. That is to say, instead of recycling a mass of unconnected events, each of which would feature its own hero, the heroic tradition preferred to link its canonical list of heroes by one all-inclusive event of pre-eminent historical significance. That the Greek heroic tradition found it necessary to treat each of its prominent heroes as an indispensable link in the general course of the Trojan war shows that, in spite of the lack of historicity in the modern sense of the word, the primary motives of this tradition were nevertheless historical.[53]

[51] In that he kills Paris, Philoctetes seems to play the central part in the *Ilias parva*, see Allen, V. 106. 23–7.

[52] West (1985), 137 n. 30.

[53] It would be anachronistic to approach epic tradition with modern criteria of historicity and on the basis of this to deny it all historical basis. The following invective by Finley (1978: 170–1) is characteristic of such an attitude: 'Not every tradition is as distorted as that of the *Nibelungenlied*, which manages to combine into a single complex of events the Ostrogoth Theoderic, who ruled most of the western Empire from 493 to 526, Attila the Hun, who invaded Italy in 452 and died in 453,

There can be little doubt that the Homeric epics originated in heroic lays whose main object was to praise the military exploits of the Greek chieftains; however, not only in their structure and ethos but also, as I hope I have shown, in their subject-matter, they are far removed from songs of military prowess, which properly belong to a much earlier stage in the epic tradition. To treat them on the same plane would do little justice to either form of heroic poetry. To quote Jasper Griffin, 'in the Homeric poems glory is not a simple and straightforward thing, won by heroic deeds', and 'we are far from the unreflective heroism of the Germanic lays'.[54] This is not to say, of course, that military exploits were of no interest to the poet. Yet heroic deeds, tragic fates, and praiseworthy or reprehensible acts were regarded by him as preserved in song not in their own right but by virtue of their being part of events that determined the course of history. Without fulfilling this condition, they would, like Achilles' fame, have been lost to posterity.

A Means to an End

Although it is almost generally agreed that Homer intended to tell the truth, not everyone draws the conclusion which ensues, namely, that belief in the 'truthfulness' of songs entails their 'usefulness' in the eyes of both the singer and his audience.[55] There is no doubt that the emphasis which Homer placed on the pleasure aroused by the singer's performance is the cause of this misapprehension. However, careful examination of Homer's references to pleasure in connection with poetry reveals that these references apply as a rule to both the song and its musical accompaniment which, as we have seen, is not intrinsically related to 'singing' proper.[56]

forty years before the accession of Theoderic, and a certain Pilgrim, who was bishop of Passow from 971 to 979. But for the historian a 100-year error is not significantly less vicious than a 400-year error.' That Finley's argument does not undermine the historicity of large-scale historical events such as the Trojan war has been convincingly argued by Hainsworth (1984: 112–13) and Kirk (1990: 43–4).

[54] Griffin (1980), 96. On Homer's concept of heroism as compared to other heroic traditions see Renehan (1987), 99–116.

[55] Cf. Finkelberg (1988a), 1–10.

[56] For pleasure resulting from the performance as a whole see *Od.* 1. 347, 8.

In approaching Homer's poetics it is of the utmost importance to keep in mind that the effects of poetry as described in the epics are in fact effects of *performance*, which involved not only recitation, or 'singing' proper, but also music and dancing. Performance, with its surrounding social context, was the sole form in which the oral poem, or the 'song', could be actualized in oral societies. This is not to say, however, that the whole of the oral poem resided in performance and that outside the context of performance the oral poem had no identity of its own. The importance of distinguishing between performance and the text of the oral poem was recognized by J. B. Hainsworth and Ruth Finnegan. Hainsworth, though he admits that 'the oral poem properly speaking is knowable only through its performances', proposes that the performance be separated from the poem and 'set . . . apart for its own special criticism'; Finnegan, while saying that 'an oral poem is an essentially ephemeral work of art, and has no existence or continuity apart from its performance', at the same time warns against the reduction of oral poetry to its performance, arguing that 'the linguistic content—the text—provides the frame and focus of the piece [of oral poetry], whatever the surrounding circumstances'.[57] A possible implication of this distinction is that in oral societies each of the two aspects, performance and the song as a 'text', has a separate function.

In Homer, the social occasion for the singer's performance is afforded by the feast. In the mansions of Olympus and in the palaces of earthly kings, singing is inseparably linked with feasting. Singing and dancing, and singing and playing the lyre are both referred to as 'offerings of the feast', and the lyre is described as 'the mate of the rich banquet', which 'the gods have made to be the companion of the feast'.[58] Now, the essential feature of Homeric feasting is its ceremonial character. Everything at the feast takes place in accordance with firmly established rules: the social

---

44–5, 368, 17. 385; from dance and song, *Od.* 1. 421–2, 17. 605–6, 18. 304–5. Musical accompaniment as a source of pleasure is explicitly mentioned only at *ll.* 9. 186 and 189, but cf. also *ll.* 18. 569–70 and φόρμιγγα λίγειαν *Od.* 8. 67, 105, 254, 261, 537, 22. 332, 23. 133. On the song's words as a source of pleasure see ἐπεὶ τέρποντ᾽ ἐπέεσσιν at *Od.* 8. 91 and ἔπεα ἱμερόεντα at *Od.* 17. 519.

[57] Hainsworth (1970), 98; Finnegan (1977), 28–9.

[58] *Od.* 1. 152 μολπή τ᾽ ὀρχηστύς τε· τὰ γάρ τ᾽ ἀναθήματα δαιτός; 21. 430 μολπῇ καὶ φόρμιγγι· τὰ γάρ τ᾽ ἀναθήματα δαιτός; 8. 99, φόρμιγγός θ᾽, ἣ δαιτὶ συνήορός ἐστι θαλείῃ; 17. 270–1 φόρμιγξ . . . ἣν ἄρα δαιτὶ θεοὶ ποίησαν ἑταίρην.

part of the feast, whether business or entertainment, can begin
only after the meal proper is over, the formula 'after they have
been satisfied by their food and drink' serving as a clear line of
demarcation between these two stages.[59] Entertainment at the feast
is also governed by such conventions. When Demodocus' songs
cause Odysseus to weep, his host Alcinous twice stops the performance, the second time justifying his interference as follows:

Listen, Phaeacian chiefs and princes, and now let Demodocus hush his
ringing lyre, for in what he sings he is far from pleasing all of us. Ever
since the divine bard was moved to sing as our meal began, ever since
then our guest has not ceased from mourning and lamenting; sorrow has
filled his heart indeed. Let the bard therefore make an end, so that hosts
and guest may enjoy themselves together; surely it is far more proper (*polu
kallion*) so.[60]

That Alcinous' stopping of the performance is supported with a
guest-friendship argument clearly indicates that the situation
involves the moral rather than the aesthetic values of Homeric
society. What is *kalon* is not simply listening to the singer but,
rather, listening that gives pleasure to all those present at the
feast.[61]

Note that, quite apart from the singer's performance, the feast
itself is generally regarded in Homer as a pleasurable occasion.[62]
The formulaic line 'they enjoyed themselves, and among them the
divine singer performed',[63] in which the audience's enjoyment does
not, as might be expected, follow the performance, but precedes it,
is especially characteristic in this connection. Enjoyment on the
part of those at the feast is represented here as a self-contained
state of mind that makes them receptive to the singer's performance—not a sensation that derives from that performance.
Pleasure thus proves to be both the specific effect of the performance and its social pre-condition. In the list of *dēmioergoi*,

---

[59] αὐτὰρ ἐπεὶ πόσιος καὶ ἐδητύος ἐξ ἔρον ἔντο: see. e.g. *Il*. 9. 222, 24. 628 (a business conversation); *Od*. 3. 67, 4. 68 (questioning a visitor), 1. 150, 8. 72, 485 (the
singer's performance).

[60] *Od*. 8. 536-43, cf. also ibid. 139-40.

[61] Cf. Walsh (1984), 3-4, 5-6; Goldhill (1991), 59. Listening to the singer is
characterized as *kalon* in the formula καλὸν ἀκουέμεν ἐστὶν ἀοιδοῦ (*Od*. 1. 370, 9. 3),
and constitutes an inseparable attribute of the ideal of peacetime life as formulated
by Odysseus in Phaeacia, see *Od*. 9. 5-11. On the ethics of Homeric feasting see
Finley (1978), 124-6.   [62] *Od*. 1. 26, 369, 4. 15-17.

[63] τερπόμενοι· μετὰ δέ σφιν ἐμέλπετο θεῖος ἀοιδός *Il*. 18. 604, *Od*. 4. 17, 13. 27.
Cf. also *Od*. 8. 429 δαιτί τε τέρπεται καὶ ἀοιδῆς ὕμνον ἀκούων.

'those who work for the people', the singer is characterized as one who 'ever delights with his singing':[64] just as the physician is professionally committed to curing diseases, the seer to practising divination, and the carpenter to building houses, so also the Homeric singer is committed to entertaining the community in its hours of leisure. In other words, adding to the pleasure of those who partake of the feast is the social function of the singer's performance in Homer. This must, however, be distinguished from the question of whether this is also the function of the song itself.

Let us consider the following description of the effect of Odysseus' narration given by Eumaeus the swineherd:

It was just as when one keeps gazing at a bard whom the gods have taught to give joy to mortals with his song, and whenever he begins to sing, men have a ceaseless desire to hear him, so long as he will sing—so did this man enchant me as he sat beside me in the halls.[65]

The effect of poetry introduced in these lines is not pleasure but *enchantment*. The fact that a singer's song consisted of words, music, and sometimes also dance, might allow us to attribute the enchantment created by his song to any one of these. However, the enchantment adduced in Eumaeus' description is a *tertium comparationis* to singing and story-telling, which seems to indicate that in Homer's view a song's enchantment was produced by no feature other than its words. That enchantment was not seen by Homer as an effect of music also follows from the fact that it is often depicted as produced by persuasive speech.[66] Furthermore, Eumaeus' comparison also contains, so to speak, an inner translation of the term *thelgein*, 'to enchant': the enchantment he experienced actually amounts to a 'ceaseless desire to hear'.[67] Consequently, the meaning of *thelgein*, as this term is applied to poetry, can tentatively be assumed to be *a ceaseless desire to hear directed towards the content of song*.[68]

[64] ὅ κεν τέρπῃσιν ἀείδων *Od*. 17. 385, cf. 8. 45.

[65] *Od*. 17. 518-21.

[66] *Od*. 1. 57, 3. 264, 14. 387, 18. 282-3.

[67] *Od*. 17. 520 τοῦ δ' ἄμοτον μεμάασιν ἀκουέμεν. This is also clear from Odysseus' reaction to the Sirens' song in *Od*. 12. 192-3: αὐτὰρ ἐμὸν κῆρ | ἤθελ' ἀκουέμεναι.

[68] In his 'Early Orphism and Kindred Religious Movements' (1935: 191), M. P. Nilsson came to a similar conclusion about the source of Orpheus' power: 'I am afraid that a warning is needed against the common misconception that Orpheus was primarily a musician and that the tunes of his lyre had the power of enchantment. It was his song.'

Now, the remarkable feature of enchantment in Homer is that,
though songs are once referred to as 'spells of mortals' and the
singer is described as one who 'ever' enchants his audience,[69]
except for the song of the Sirens, no specific song sung by an individual singer is ever explicitly described as having produced
enchantment. On several occasions the *Odyssey* gives a detailed
description of a singer's performance at a feast; however, the effect
created in such cases is invariably that of pleasure. Moreover, not
only are normal performances of Homeric singers not described as
enchanting the audience, but the characteristic feature of such performances is that the singer is obliged to hold himself, as Milman
Parry put it, 'at the convenience of his hearers'.[70] Thus, when
Demodocus' songs cause Odysseus to weep, his host Alcinous twice
arrests the performance: had Demodocus' songs indeed enchanted
the audience one would have expected Alcinous at the least not to
have stopped the singer, and not even to have noticed that his
guest was weeping. This is not to say, however, that a singer
enchanting his audience corresponded to no real experience of
Homeric man. Odysseus' audience in Phaeacia, left 'spellbound' by
his narration, and Eumaeus' reacting in a similar fashion in
Ithaca[71] show that enchantment in Homer can indeed represent a
concrete feeling aroused by a concrete person. The question therefore is this: why is enchantment, though explicitly described as the
effect of poetry, not the effect of any given song sung in the
Homeric poems?

If our interpretation of enchantment as a 'ceaseless desire to hear
directed toward the content of song' is correct, it would be very
much a typical effect of story-telling, whether or not the word
thelgein is used. As a matter of fact, on many occasions in the
Odyssey a narrated story arouses such enthusiasm that the
audience cannot stop listening to it. Thus Penelope was so
delighted with Odysseus' stories that 'sleep fell not upon her eye-
lids'; Alcinous was ready to listen to Odysseus 'even till the bright
dawn'; Eumaeus was so charmed with Odysseus' tales that he
detained him in his cabin for three nights and three days; Aeolus
kept Odysseus as his guest for a whole month, 'and questioned

[69] *Od.* I. 337, 17. 520-1.
[70] M. Parry (1971), 457; see also Notopoulos (1949), 1–23, and (1951),
81–102; Hainsworth (1991), 16.
[71] κηληθμῷ δ' ἔσχοντο *Od.* 11. 334, 13. 2; θέλγειν 17. 514, 521.

about each thing, about Ilios, and the ships of the Argives, and the return of the Achaeans'; Telemachus was ready to listen to Menelaus' account of his travels 'even for a year'.[72] The reason why singing and story-telling differ from each other in this regard will become clear if we take into account that stories told by Homer's narrators generally inform the listeners of things of which they have not yet heard. Thus, in Phaeacia, though Alcinous praises Odysseus for the shapeliness of his words, the nobility of his mind, and the masterly way in which he has delivered his story, he expresses no wish to hear the same story again, but urges Odysseus to proceed with his account of his adventures; and when the narration reaches the point from which it started, Odysseus himself stops with the following words: 'Why prolong the tale? Yesterday in this very place I recounted the rest to you and your noble queen, and it irks me to tell a second time a story already plainly told.'[73]

But if Homeric man sees no point in listening to the same story twice, this is by no means so where songs are concerned. However rich a singer's repertoire may be, it is not inexhaustible, and though in principle the singers are seen as moving from one community to another,[74] the fact is that both in Ithaca and in Phaeacia there is a resident singer. Accordingly, Homer's audiences must have been used to listening to songs with which they were familiar. Consider the following description of Demodocus' performance: 'and the Phaeacian nobles stirred him to sing, because they enjoyed the words'. The song whose words the Phaeacians enjoyed was that concerning the quarrel between Odysseus and Achilles, a song whose popularity is stressed a few lines earlier: 'the lay (*oimē*) whose fame then reached the broad heaven itself'.[75] Now, since listening to a familiar song produces pleasure, while listening to a new story effects enchantment, it appears that enchantment would emerge in the context of poetry only when a new song was sung. The song of 'the pitiful return of the Achaeans', sung by Phemius in *Odyssey* 1, affords an opportunity to test this hypothesis.

When Penelope weeps on hearing the song and asks the singer

[72] Penelope, *Od.* 19. 589-90, 23. 308-9; Alcinous, 11. 370-6; Eumaeus, 17. 515-21; Aeolus, 10. 14-15; Telemachus, 4. 595-8.

[73] *Od.* 11. 367-72, 12. 450-3. Cf. Goldhill (1991), 48.

[74] *Od.* 17. 382-5.

[75] *Od.* 8. 90-1 and 74.

to change the subject, Telemachus objects, arguing as follows: 'men praise that song the most which comes the newest to their ears'.[76] As we saw above, a similar sorrowful reaction on the part of Odysseus twice gave Alcinous sufficient reason to interrupt Demodocus' performance. Telemachus' words in *Odyssey* I clearly deviate from this pattern. But that Telemachus did not wish the Song of the Return to be interrupted is not the only peculiar thing about it. It is in reference to this song that Penelope calls songs in general 'other spells of mortals', plainly implying that the song had actually enchanted the audience. It is to this song, once again, that even the suitors listened in silence.[77] Finally, Telemachus calls this song 'the newest', a clear indication that, like the stories of Homeric narrators, it informed the listeners of things that they had not heard before.[78] Note also that in another similar situation, in the Intermezzo, when Odysseus interrupts his narration, arguing that 'it is now time to sleep', Alcinous, like Telemachus in our passage, objects to the interruption, because of his eagerness to hear the continuation of Odysseus' story.[79] Considering all these points, it seems reasonable to infer that Homer means to tell us that the song of Phemius effected enchantment just like a narrated story.

If our hypothesis is correct, enchantment aroused by a song differs from pleasure in a song much as the fascination of a first acquaintance with a subject differs from the enjoyment of an old favourite.[80] Accordingly, we should not regard enchantment as a

---

[76] *Od.* I. 351-2 ἥ τις νεωτάτη ἀμφιπέλεται (my translation).

[77] *Od.* I. 337 πολλὰ γὰρ ἄλλα βροτῶν θελκτήρια οἶδας; 325-6 οἱ δὲ σιωπῇ | ἥατ' ἀκούοντες, cf. also II. 333, 13. I. Rüter (1969: 205) remarks on *Od.* I. 325-6: 'im Schweigen der Zuhörer wird der Zauber des Gesangs spürbar.' Cf. also Page (1950), 60.

[78] Cf. Maehler (1963), 31. As to the argument by Sealey (1957: 315), that Phemius' subject in his song could not be considered new because 'it was probably on every poet's lips', one must keep in mind that the plot of the *Odyssey* begins just when the last of the Achaeans have returned home. Thus, Menelaus has returned only recently, and in both Ithaca and Pylos he is thought to have the most up-to-date information (*Od.* I. 286, 3. 317-18). Even Nestor's story of his and the other Greeks' return nearly ten years before is still news to Telemachus (upon his visit to Pylos in *Odyssey* 3) and, consequently, to the other inhabitants of Ithaca.

[79] *Od.* II. 330-1, 373-6, 380-1.

[80] This does not necessarily mean that enchantment could not be conceived by Homer as, to use Macleod's definition (1983: 7), 'an intenser term' for pleasure. Thus, for example, Telemachus' fascination with Menelaus' tale is described in *Od.* 4. 597-8 as just such a more intense pleasure: αἰνῶς γὰρ μύθοισιν ἔπεσσί τε σοῖσιν ἀκούων | τέρπομαι, cf. also 19. 590, 23. 308. The relevant distinction between

sine qua non of Homeric song—otherwise, we would have to conclude that the singer was obliged to present new songs to his audience over and over again. Indeed, the words with which Alcinous stops Demodocus' performance, 'let the bard make an end, so that hosts and guest may enjoy themselves together', demonstrate that for Homer pleasure is just such a *sine qua non*. It follows that the singer fulfils his function in so far as his performance gives pleasure to those who partake of the feast, whether or not he also enchants them. It would be wrong, therefore, to see in enchantment an effect of song representative of the normal experience of Homeric audiences. Rather, enchantment may be an incidental effect of song, like tears flowing in one who remembers his personal involvement in the events recounted.[81] However, the fact that Homer calls songs 'spells of mortals' and says of the singer that he 'ever' arouses a 'ceaseless desire to hear' indicates that this effect of song does somehow belong to his basic conception of poetry.

It seems to me that we cannot solve the problem of Homer's viewing enchantment as both the incidental effect of song and its essential feature unless we look beyond specific occasions like singers' performances at feasts: to find the answer, we must investigate not so much what reaction the performance of a given song calls forth under given circumstances as what song in general signifies for Homeric man. The Sirens episode seems to be especially pertinent to this undertaking.

The Sirens of the *Odyssey* share two fundamental features with Homer's Muses—they know 'all things', and they pass their knowledge on to men by means of song.[82] But while the song inspired by the Muses is sung in the social context of a singer's performance at a feast, the song of the Sirens is subject to no such limitation: unlike singers, the Sirens are not committed to entertaining their listeners. Hence, in the case of the Sirens the pure effects of song enchantment and pleasure may lie more in their respective aetiologies than in the character of the emotions involved.

[81] See *Od.* 1. 336, 8. 83-6, 90-3, 521-31, cf. 4. 113-16.

[82] Cf. *Od.* 12. 189-91 as against *Il.* 2. 485. On the Sirens and their relation to the Muses see Buschor (1944); Otto (1971), 57-8; Koller (1963), 45-8; Pucci (1979), 121-32. The question of whether or not the Muses and the Sirens should be considered mythologically allied (as Pollard (1952: 60-3) and Gresseth (1970: 203-18) would have it) is not relevant to the present discussion. It is sufficient for our argument that both the Sirens and the Muses are, as Schadewaldt (1951: 85) put it, 'epische Sängerinnen'.

are much clearer. Thus, the first time they appear in Circe's instructions to Odysseus regarding his future voyage, we learn that their song has a twofold effect—it both delights and enchants:

You will come to the Sirens first of all; they enchant any mortal who approaches them. If a man in ignorance draws too close and hears the sound of the Sirens' voice, he will never return to find wife and little children near him and to see their joy at his homecoming; the Sirens will enchant him with their clear song. They sit in a meadow; men's corpses lie heaped up all round them, mouldering upon the bones as the skin decays. . . . But if you yourself are bent on hearing, then give them orders to bind you both hand and foot as you stand upright against the mast-stay . . . thus with delight you may hear the two Sirens' voices.[83]

It is also clear from this passage that the pleasure produced by the Sirens derives from their voices ('thus with delight you may hear the two Sirens' voices'), while their song causes enchantment ('the Sirens will enchant him with their clear song'). The distinction is not accidental. If Odysseus follows Circe's instructions, he will not stay to listen to the Sirens' song and so will not, like other travellers, be enchanted by it; the only consequence of his giving ear safely but briefly to the Sirens will be enjoyment derived from their pleasurable voices.[84]

When Odysseus' ship approaches the island of the Sirens, the Sirens catch sight of it:

and they raised their clear-toned song: 'Come hither, renowned Odysseus, great glory of the Achaeans! Pause with your ship; listen to our voice. Never has any man passed this way in his dark vessel and left unheard the honey-sweet voice from our lips; he has had pleasure in it and gone on his way knowing more things. We know all the sorrows in the wide land of Troy that the Argives and Trojans bore because the gods would needs have it so; we know of all things that come to pass on the fruitful earth.' So they sang with their lovely voices, and my heart was eager to listen still.[85]

Though the resources at the Sirens' disposal are the same as in the first passage, namely 'voice' and 'song', here the Sirens are

[83] *Od.* 12. 39–52.
[84] Note that not only the Sirens, but Calypso and Circe too are represented as having beautiful voices (*Od.* 5. 61, 10. 221, 227); yet, though the last two also practise magic, that has nothing to do with their voices, see *Od.* 1. 56–7, 10. 213, 235–7, 290–1, 316–20, 326.
[85] *Od.* 12. 183–93; note esp. 'he has had pleasure in it and gone on his way knowing more things' ἀλλ᾽ ὅ γε τερψάμενος νεῖται καὶ πλείονα εἰδώς.

described as giving delight and imparting knowledge rather than as delighting and enchanting: 'he has had pleasure in it and gone on his way knowing more things'. Now, the knowledge imparted by the Sirens can derive only from the content of their song, and not from their voices, and it is reasonable to assume that the Sirens' 'sweet' and 'beautiful' voices cause the pleasure created by their song.[86]

Hence, the two passages prove to be completely parallel: the effect of the content of the Sirens' song, as distinct from the pleasure of hearing their voices, is called 'enchantment' by Circe and 'acquiring knowledge' by the Sirens themselves. In other words, enchantment and acquiring knowledge are one and the same effect of the Sirens' singing. This conclusion accords with our previous observation that only hearing a new story or song produces enchantment in the listener. Indeed, if an audience is eager to listen to a traveller who has seen 'cities of many men' 'till the bright dawn' or 'even for a year', it is not surprising that Homeric man is irresistibly tempted to listen to the omniscient Sirens for ever and ever.[87] Significantly, the enchantment produced by a human narrator ends when his subject is exhausted: Penelope did not go to sleep till Odysseus had told her the whole story, and Alcinous was eager to listen to Odysseus until the narration had returned to its starting-point.[88] However, the subject-matter of the Sirens, who know 'all things', cannot be exhausted: hence the enchantment produced by them never ceases.

As Bruno Snell put it, 'the uncomplicated views which he [Homer] holds concerning knowledge always apply in the same stable ratio: the wider the experience the greater the knowledge.'[89] It is owing to this ratio that, as we have seen, the eyewitness possesses greater knowledge than the recipient of hearsay, that the older man has the same advantage over the younger and that, in general, mortals can never compare in knowledge with the omnipresent and omniscient gods. Like the difference between human

---

[86] This is not to say, of course, that the distinction is always clear-cut: 'voice' and 'song' (that is, the verbal content of a poem) are distinct in that only the latter is regarded as bearing the Sirens' message, but they overlap in that both are seen as possessing aesthetic qualities, see λιγυρὴ ἀοιδή at 12. 44 and 183, cf. Verdenius (1983), 16 n. 3.

[87] Cf. Maehler (1963), 30-1.

[88] Penelope, *Od.* 23. 308-9; Alcinous, 12. 450-3.

[89] Snell (1953), 136-52; cf. Heitsch (1966), 196. On Homer's view of knowledge see also above, p. 62.

knowledge and divine knowledge, the difference between the
enchantment produced by men and the Sirens' enchantment is
only one of degree. This is why the comparison by W. B. Stanford
of the temptation of the Sirens with that of the fruit of the Tree of
Knowledge in Genesis seems pertinent in this connection.[90]

In the everyday context of the singer's performance, the recital
of a song whose content was already known to the audience would
have been the norm. Consequently, the function of song as a
means of entertainment would have come to the fore. The song of
the Sirens restores the balance of functions inherent in Homer's
conception of epic song. This song both delights and enchants: it
delights, because listening to the Sirens' voices affords pleasure,
just as do the singer's melodies, and his words,[91] and it enchants,
because in their song they impart knowledge of everything that
happens in the world—just as the Muses' song is divine evidence
of events of the past. Accordingly, enchantment is that effect of
song which results directly from this essential function. That is
why—though only on rare occasions is a specific song said to have
produced enchantment—ideally, the singer ever arouses the 'ceaseless desire to hear', and songs in general are 'spells of mortals'.

True, the Homeric singer, professionally committed as he is to
satisfying the community's need for entertainment, was one of the
dēmioergoi, 'workers for the people'; but his song was also the song
of the Muses, deriving from the goddesses' knowledge of everything
that happens on earth: this is why the singer is called 'divine', and
his song 'inspired'. That is to say, though the song of the Muses is
employed as a means of entertainment, the Muses are not *dēmioergoi*, and their song is not meant for entertainment alone. The
Muses' song is also the vehicle through which men have access
to things not given to them in their immediate experience. As
E. R. Dodds put it, 'But in an age which possessed no written
documents, where should firsthand evidence be found? Just as the
truth about the future would be attained only if man were in touch

[90] Stanford (1967), 412. Cf. Padel (1992), 65: 'Their song is dangerous, not
false. To modern imagination, its temptation might seem to lie in its beauty. In
Greece this was inseparable from its intellectual content. The fact that the Sirens
offer knowledge is the essence of their sensuous magnetism.' See also S. H. Butcher,
'The Greek Love for Knowledge', in Butcher (1904), 97; Verdenius (1983), 32 and
n. 87; Goldhill (1991), 65.

[91] See φόρμιγγα λίγειαν (n. 56 above); ἱμερόεσσαν ἀοιδήν *Od.* 1. 421, 18. 304;
ἡδεῖαν ἀοιδήν 8. 64; ἔπε' ἱμερόεντα 17. 519.

with a knowledge wider than his own, so the truth about the past could be preserved only on a like condition.'[92] Though knowledge acquired by means of song does not always come to the fore at the time of performance, it is present virtually whenever Homeric man demonstrates his acquaintance with events of the past. In oral societies like that described by Homer, nothing else can fulfil this function.

'If poetry is derived from divine inspiration, the poem is conceived as a message and a means to an end, whereas if poetry derives from art, the poem is conceived as a reality *sui generis* and an end in itself'—this is the definition of the ontological and teleological status of poetry in the 'poetics of truth' and the 'poetics of fiction' adopted in Chapter 1. We can see now that Homer—for whom poetry was derived from inspiration sent by the Muses —approached it as a firsthand account of events that really happened, and saw its objective as preserving information about the most historically important of these events.

[92] Dodds (1951), 81. Cf. Rösler (1980), 293-5.

4

Song and Artefact

Creation by Craftsmanship

Although we have seen that only the 'poetics of truth' was relevant to the traditional Greek view of poetry, this does not necessarily mean that the 'poetics of fiction' was altogether alien to the Greek tradition. The very fact that Homeric man, as our discussion has shown, was held to be either responsible or not responsible for his activities, makes the poetics of fiction possible. Whether or not this possibility would also be actualized depends on whether or not the class of activities for which Homeric man is held individually responsible makes provision for an activity which can act as a typological counterpart to poetry. There is no difficulty in seeing that the activity in question is represented by *handicrafts*.

Proceeding from their position within the classification of Homeric man's activities discussed in Chapter 2, handicrafts can be defined as an activity of Homeric man belonging to the class of activities (constituted by practical wisdom, skills, and sports) which possess the semantic characteristics 'teaching' and 'knowledge' and for which, therefore, man is held individually responsible; it is thus opposed to the class of activities (constituted by instincts, emotions, insight, heroic valour, and singing) which possesses the semantic characteristics 'giving' and 'ignorance' and for which, therefore, man is not held individually responsible. At the same time, handicrafts and poetry, or 'singing', are not only set against each other as members of the opposed classes of Homeric man's activities: their relationship is determined by the fact that they are seen as the only productive activities in their respective classes. That is to say, within the general opposition between the two classes of human activity, handicrafts and singing form a particular opposition relevant to these two activities alone, that between the author's being, and not being, responsible for his work. This allows one to suggest that the two typological variants of poetics, the 'poetics of truth' and the 'poetics of fiction', are both present in Homer.

The fact that, in contrast to the Classical view, the early Greeks saw poetry and handicrafts as based on mutually exclusive foundations, is often overlooked.[1] Yet, characteristically, not only does Homer never treat poetry in terms of crafts, but even the term *technē* itself is never associated with the activity of the poet in Homer. The only occasion on which the poet and the artisan are described by a common term is *Odyssey* 17, where the singer, the carpenter, the physician, and the seer are referred to as *dēmioergoi*: 'No man of his own accord goes out to bring in a stranger from elsewhere, unless that stranger be one of the *dēmioergoi*, a prophet or one who cures diseases, a worker in wood, or again an inspired bard, delighting men with his song.'[2] Both the term itself, which in Homer still possessed its original sense 'those who work for the people' (*dēmiourgos* as a word for 'artisan' being a later development), and the context in which it appears make it clear that these four professionals are brought together on the basis of their common social status as travelling specialists in the service of the community, not on the grounds of the common source of their creative ability.[3]

While Homer displays no noticeable tendency to use a specific term for designating handicrafts as a whole, it is possible nevertheless to subsume the craftsman's activities under two major categories: those dealing with solid materials (the field of competence of a carpenter, *tektōn*) and those employing metals (the field of a (copper)smith, *chalkeus*). Other handicrafts tend to fall into one of these two categories: those dealing with solid materials are

---

[1] B. Schweitzer (1963: i. 45) being an honourable exception: 'Der Dichter war ein von göttlichen Geist beseeltes Instrument der die Welt lenkenden und ordnenden Mächte, der Künstler nur der Bewahrer eines ursprünglich göttlichen Erbes von Kenntnissen, nichts anders als der Bauer, der Tischer, der Schmied, der Schiffbauer, ohne dass man ein schöpferliche Vermögen in ihm suchte.' See also Svenbro (1976), 193-212; Ford (1992), 31-9; Scheid and Svenbro (1996), 111-22.

[2] *Od.* 17. 383-6; at 19. 135, its only other occurrence in Homer, the term *dēmioergoi* is applied to the heralds.

[3] Ford (1992), 36-7. Cf. Finley (1978), 55: 'Others were specialists, carpenters and metal workers, soothsayers, bards and physicians. Because they supplied certain essential needs in a way that neither the lords nor the non-specialists among their followers could match, these men, a handful in numbers, floated in mid-air in the social hierarchy.' For a different interpretation see Schadewaldt (1951), 70; Nagy (1989), 19; Pratt (1993), 68; Murray (1996), 8.

usually described in terms similar to the ones used for carpentry;
while those dealing with molten or soft substances are modelled on
the language of (copper)smithing.[4] If there is a term that links all
the handicrafts without at the same time being used to designate
any specific variety, it is without doubt *technē*. While it is true that
the explicit use of *technē* as a generic term for crafts is found only
after Homer,[5] the fact that *technē* is the only term equally applicable to both metalworking and carpentry indicates that it was perceived as a generic characteristic of handicrafts as early as Homer.
True, the term *technē* itself is applied to carpentry only once, but its
etymological affinities with *tektōn*, 'carpenter', should also be taken
into account here.[6] The tendency to use *technē* as an inclusive
term, as follows first of all from the expression '*technē* of various
kinds',[7] seems to point in the same direction. To a certain extent,
the same can also be said of the term *sophiē* ('craft', 'wisdom')
which, judging by the expression 'all kinds of *sophiē*', could also be
used inclusively. But *sophiē* occurs in Homer only once, which prevents us from using it as a basis for comprehensive conclusions.[8]

That Homer saw the craftsman as responsible for his activity is
clear from the fact that the product of this activity, the artefact, is
invariably treated as the craftsman's own creation. 'It was I who
made it, no one else'—these words of Odysseus, referring to his
bride-bed,[9] establish between the maker and the thing made a relationship which is totally different from that observed in the case of
poetry. To outline the conditions under which creation by craftsmanship could take place, we should take into account that (a) the
Greeks made no provision for creation out of nothing; and (b) the

---

[4] See κεραοξόος τέκτων at *Il.* 4. 110; see also *Od.* 3. 425 and 432, where the
terms *chrusochoos* ('one who melts gold') and *chalkeus* ('smith') are used inter-
changeably.

[5] In Homer τέχνη is 'skill' or 'cunning of hand' rather than 'art' or 'craft', see
LSJ s.v. τέχνη.

[6] Metalworking, *Od.* 3. 433, 6. 234, 11. 614, 23. 161; carpentry, *Il.* 3. 61. The
derivative verb τεχνάομαι is applied to both carpentry and metalwork, see *Od.* 5.
259, 11. 613.

[7] *Od.* 6. 234 τέχνην παντοίην.

[8] *Il.* 15. 411-12 πάσης σοφίης. Havelock (1963: 155-6 and 162 n. 27) mis-
interprets Snell's study 1924: 1 ff.) of the early Greek usage of *sophiē* and its
cognates, projecting Snell's results onto Homer's concept of poetry (see also above,
Ch. 2). As we shall see in Ch. 6, application of this and similar terms to poetry by
post-Homeric poets simply indicates their deviation from the traditional idiom (the
first time that the term *sophiē* is found applied to poetry is Solon 13. 52 West).

[9] *Od.* 23. 189 τὸ δ' ἐγὼ κάμον οὐδέ τις ἄλλος.

craftsman was considered an ordinary man not endowed with supernatural abilities.

In so far as creation by craftsmanship was not creation out of nothing, an artefact's coming into being could only be made possible as a result of the transformation of things that already existed. That Homer is not unaware of this side of handicraft production is made clear from his frequent references to the artefact's former existence as a natural object. Thus, the staff by which Achilles swears 'will never again put out leaves and branches, from the moment it parted from its stump in the mountains, and it will sprout no more, since the bronze stripped it of its leaves and bark all round'; Pandarus' bow had once been the horns of a wild goat 'that he himself had once shot under the chest as it sprang down from a rock'; an oak, a pine-tree, a poplar-tree 'which grows smooth in the grassy flat of a great water-meadow, smooth-trunked, with branches springing at its very top' become a chariot or a ship; Odysseus' bed was fashioned of a bush of olive 'long of leaf', and so on.[10]

Again, in so far as creation by craftsmanship was not creation out of nothing, the only way in which the transformation in question could proceed was the gradual fashioning of a given natural object into an entirely new form. As a result of this, both the process and the final outcome of handicraft production were seen as substantially dependent on the kind of material employed. In effect, the natural object the craftsman proceeds from can be either amorphous or heteromorphous in respect of the final form assumed by the artefact. The remarkable fact is, however, that the kinds of craftsmanship dealing with molten or plastic materials are either not treated by Homer in tectonic categories (so metalworking) or not dealt with at all (so pottery). Metalworking is usually described in special terms such as *koptein, elaunein, chalkeuein*, etc., while the technology of pottery is mentioned only once in the Homeric poems.[11] This makes the kinds of craftsmanship that deal with solid materials, and above all carpentry, the model for handicrafts production in general.[12]

[10] *Il.* 1. 234-7, 4. 105-8, 482-6, 13. 389-91; *Od.* 23. 190-2.

[11] For metalworking see the description of Hephaestus at work in *Il.* 18. 372-9. For pottery see *Il.* 18. 601.

[12] At the same time, Frontisi-Ducroux (1975: 60) is probably right to argue that since Homer's acquaintance with the technique of metalworking is restricted to a number of simpler operations, the tectonic procedures in metalworking and

Accordingly, creation by craftsmanship was seen by Homer not so much in terms of moulding amorphous matter into a new form but, rather, as a gradual transformation of the original form of a given natural object. Thus, wood is cut, hewed, and carved, stone hewed, leather cut—this is how a ship, a chariot, a bed, building-bricks, a belt, a pair of sandals are made;[13] everything unnecessary is removed;[14] timber is bent or made straight;[15] single pieces of the same or two different materials are joined together or adjusted to each other;[16] additional details are attached as a finish;[17] the surface is planed, smoothed, polished, and ornamented.[18] Cutting off and joining together seem to present the two basic tectonic operations of the Homeric craftsman;[19] the result is a new thing whose shape is entirely different from that of the natural object out of which it has been fashioned.

Finally, in so far as the craftsman was not seen as endowed with supernatural abilities, the artefact could only come into being with the assistance of implements which enabled him to surpass the

carpentry must have been conceived as basically the same: 'Le bronze est martelé, mais il est aussi taillé et découpé, comme les matériaux qui lui sont associés, le cuir et le bois.'

[13] τάμνω *Il.* 11. 88, 13. 180, 21. 38, 23. 119; *Od.* 5. 243, 12. 11, 14. 24, 17. 195; ἐκτάμνω *Il.* 3. 62, 4. 486, 12. 149, 13. 391 (cf. also εὔτμητος, 'well-cut', applied to the objects made of leather in *Il.* 7. 304 and 10. 567); πελεκάω *Od.* 5. 244; ξέω *Od.* 23. 199 (cf. also ξεστός, 'hewn', applied to the objects made of wood and stone in *Il.* 6. 243, 248, 18. 504, 20. 11; *Od.* 3. 406, 4. 272).

[14] See e.g. ἀπέκοψα κόμην τανυφύλλου ἐλαίης, | κόρμον δ' ἐκ ῥίζης προταμών in Odysseus' description of his making of the bed in *Od.* 23. 195-6.

[15] κάμπτω *Il.* 4. 486 (cf. also εὐκαμπής, 'well-bent', *Od.* 18. 368, 21. 6); ἰθύνω *Od.* 5. 245, 17. 341, 21. 44, 23. 197; ἐξιθύνω *Il.* 15. 410.

[16] ἀραρίσκω *Il.* 4. 410, 16. 212, 23. 712; *Od.* 3. 248, 5. 361; ἐναραρίσκω *Od.* 21. 45; ἐπαραρίσκω *Il.* 14. 167, 339; ἁρμόζω *Od.* 3. 247, 5. 162, 247; κολλάω (cf. κολλήεις and κολλητός, 'glued together', 'closely joined', in *Il.* 4. 366, 15. 389, 678, 19. 395; *Od.* 21. 164, 23. 194); ἐπελαύνω (of metals only) *Il.* 7. 223, 13. 804, 17. 493.

[17] See ἐπιτίθημι *Il.* 4. 111; *Od.* 21. 45, 23. 194; ὑποτίθημι *Il.* 18. 375; ὑφίημι *Il.* 14. 240; *Od.* 19. 57; cf. also ἔπειμι *Od.* 21. 7 and πρόσκειμαι *Il.* 18. 379.

[18] ξέω *Od.* 5. 245, 17. 341, 21. 44; ἀμφιξέω *Od.* 23. 196 (cf. also εὔξεστος and εὔξοος, 'well-planed', 'well-polished', in *Il.* 2. 390, 10. 373, 24. 271, 275, 280; *Od.* 4. 590, 5. 237, 13. 10, 14. 225, 15. 333, 17. 602, etc.); λεαίνω *Il.* 4. 111; δαιδάλλω *Il.* 18. 479; *Od.* 23. 200.

[19] Cf. Frontisi-Ducroux (1975), 61: 'Les diverses techniques mises en œuvre pour la réalisation du *daidalon* paraissent pensées selon un même modèle intellectuel. L'accent y est mis, semble-t-il, sur la relation entre l'ensemble et les parties. Découpage et assemblage en constituent les axes privilégiés. Ces deux opérations qui, nous l'avons vu, correspondent aux phases majeures du travail tant du charpentier que du métallurgiste dominent aussi l'ouvrage des artisans du textile.' Cf. ibid. 56, 60, 78.

physical limitations of an ordinary man. These are, first of all, various tools (*hopla*) employed by the craftsman in his work.[20] Thanks to these, the craftsman is able to change the original form of the material with which he works, imparting to it any form he wants. At the same time, it is clear that without professional knowledge all the tools in the world would be of no use to the craftsman. After all, the tools are only 'implements of art', and it is more 'by cunning' (*mētis*) than simply with his axe that the woodcutter fells trees.[21] In a Homeric simile, it is said that the axe assists the man's strength, but not before it has been pointed out that it is due to the carpenter's skill (*technē*) that the ship's timber on which he is working is being shaped.[22] Although the tools are indispensable, it is nevertheless the professional skill, *technē* and the cunning of hand, *mētis* that employ these tools and thus, eventually, produce things. These limitations being taken into account, creation by craftsmanship as seen by the Greeks can be preliminarily determined as *the ability to produce things by means of an orderly transformation of natural objects*.

It has often been held against the Greeks that they lacked a concept of artistic creativity comparable to the one that first came to the fore with the emergence of the Romantic movement at the end of the eighteenth and beginning of the nineteenth century. The concept in question amounts to endowing the artist with a creative power analogous to the creative power of God, allowing him to create *ex nihilo* an imaginative world of his own.[23] However, it is only too rarely taken into account in this connection that the

---

[20] Actually, the term is applied to the smith's tools only, see *Il.* 18. 409, 412; *Od.* 3. 433. Among the latter, Homer mentions bellows (φῦσαι *Il.* 18. 372), anvil and anvil-block (ἄκμων, ἀκμόθετον ibid. 476, 410; *Od.* 3. 434, 8. 274), firetongs (πυράγρα *Il.* 18. 477), melting-pot (χιανός ibid. 470), and two kinds of hammer—ῥαιστήρ and σφῦρα (*Il.* 18. 477; *Od.* 3. 434). The tools used by the carpenter include two kinds of axe, πέλεκυς for felling trees (*Il.* 13. 391, 23. 114; *Od.* 5. 234, 9. 391; cf. also πελεκάω at *Od.* 5. 244) and σκέπαρνον for hewing and smoothing (*Od.* 5. 237, 9. 391)—although the axe can also be designated by the materials from which it is made, see χαλκός *Il.* 1. 236; *Od.* 23. 196; σίδηρος *Il.* 4. 485); the rule (στάθμη *Il.* 15. 410; *Od.* 5. 245, 23. 197); the borer (τέρετρον *Od.* 5. 246, 23. 198); the tool for drawing circles (τόρνος, the use of which is implied in τορνόομαι at *Od.* 5. 249); other terms connected with carpentry are: the bolts (γόμφοι *Od.* 5. 248) and the joints (ἁρμονίαι ibid. 248, 361).

[21] *Od.* 3. 432 πείρατα τέχνης; *Il.* 23. 315 μήτι.

[22] *Il.* 3. 61-2 [πέλεκυς] ὅς τ᾽ εἶσιν διὰ δουρὸς ὑπ᾽ ἀνέρος, ὅς ῥά τε τέχνῃ | νήϊον ἐκτάμνῃσιν, ὀφέλλει δ᾽ ἀνδρὸς ἐρωήν.

[23] On the Romantic concept of creativity see e.g. Abrams (1953), 272-85; Lieberg (1982), 159-73; Halliwell (1986), 60-1 and 82 n. 1.

modern idea of artistic creativity derives directly from the Judaeo-
Christian notion of the creator God and thus, naturally, could not
have been available to the Greeks.[24] Like most other pagans, the
Greeks saw the cosmological process as proceeding in accordance
with the biological pattern or, as M. P. Nilsson put it, 'automatically'.[25] Rather than having been 'created', the world was
conceived of as having been 'born', or 'developed', from a limited
number of primary elements in what can be seen as a quasi-
evolutionary process. None of the stages of this development,
represented as a series of births issuing from perpetual interaction
between the male and the female principles, was accompanied by
the intervention of a transcendent force. The Greek gods, who did
not create the world but were themselves 'born' in the process of
its development, were conceived of as immanent to the universe
and thus subject to its laws. The idea of a creator god was alien to
Greek religion and Greek thought in general.

Accordingly, creation by craftsmanship was the only pattern
available to the Greeks which made provision for the idea of
creation. This is obviously why, whenever such an idea emerged
in Greek thought, it was always modelled after the pattern of
craftsmanship. This is true of Hesiod's myth of Pandora, the first
woman, created by the gods by means of the handicraft technology; of Plato's myth of the Demiurge, in which the entire universe
is envisaged as having been produced in the manner of an artefact;
of the concept of nature in the Aristotelian and the Stoic doctrines,
and so on.[26] That is to say, whereas in the Judaeo-Christian
tradition the creative ability of the artist is modelled on the creative
ability of God, in the Greek tradition the creative ability of God
would be modelled on that of the artisan. This naturally rules out
any idea of a creator, divine or otherwise, who knows no limits to
his power and is free to create whatever he wishes. The first Greek
myth of divine creation, introduced by Plato in the *Timaeus*, can
serve as an illustration.

According to Plato, the activity of the Divine Craftsman, the
Demiurge, who has created the visible world, is subject to two
important limitations. First, the Demiurge is limited in that he

[24] This fact has been paid due attention in Curtius (1953), 146; Sperduti (1950),
220-1; Lieberg (1982), 161-3.

[25] Nilsson (1949), 73; cf. Snell (1953), 29.

[26] See further Cornford (1937), 37; Wehrli (1957), 41-2; Solmsen (1963),
473-96; Lloyd (1966), 207-8.

chooses to create the world in accordance with the eternal and ideal pattern: being himself good, he naturally would not create a world which would not be as good as possible. Secondly, the Demiurge is limited in that he is not able to execute in full his intention to create the perfect world. Like an ordinary craftsman, he has to cope with the restrictions imposed on him by the medium in which he works. Thus, the Demiurge is not omnipotent, and the world created by him is not perfect:

for the creation of this world is the combined work of necessity and mind. Mind, the ruling power, persuaded necessity to bring the greater part of created things to perfection, and thus and after this manner in the beginning, through necessity made subject to reason, the universe was created.[27]

Note that it is not all created things but only 'the greater part' of them that have been brought to perfection by the Demiurge; as a result, the created world is as good as possible rather than perfect in all respects. It is little wonder, then, that when the Greeks came to be exposed to the biblical version of creation, it struck them as irrational and arbitrary. The following, often quoted passage from Galen is especially illuminating in this connection:

The doctrine of Moses differed from that of Plato and of all the Greeks who have correctly approached the study of Nature. For Moses, God has only to will to bring matter into order, and matter is ordered immediately. . . . We do not think in that way; we say that certain things are impossible by nature and these God does not even attempt; he only chooses the best among the things that come about.[28]

In the Western tradition, which inherited both the Greek and the biblical patterns of creation, the two often clashed, to produce a conflict. This is true, for example, of the dispute in medieval theology between the view of God as an absolutely free agent and the view of God as necessarily restricted by his own goodness. And this would be equally true of the opposition which became popular with the Romantics between the view of the artist as freely creating from his imagination an entirely new world of his own, and the view of the artist as a mere 'imitator', confined by limita-

---

[27] *Tim.* 48a, trans. B. Jowett.
[28] Galen, *de U. Part.* 11. 14, trans. F. M. Cornford. Cf. Cornford (1937), 36; Dihle (1982), I, 159–60.

tions imposed on him by the world of actuality.[29] Thus, as a result
of being taken on a par with the biblical Creator, the Greek artisan
has been pushed into the narrow niche of a slavish imitator of
nature—an interpretation which is as anachronistic as it is
factually incorrect.

To understand the traditional Greek view of *technē* in its
proper cultural context we should turn to situations in which
Homeric man executes a trick. While a trick may occasionally be
represented as the result of a brilliant idea 'put' into someone's
mind by a god,[30] more often than not Homeric man uses his own
resources in situations of this kind. This is true when Antilochus
wins his chariot-race against Menelaus, when Odysseus brings the
Wooden Horse into Troy and when he blinds the Cyclops, when
Aegisthus slays Agamemnon, and so on. The resources which
Homer's people use to cope with these and like situations are
usually described by a group of semantically allied terms such as
mētis, *technē*, *kerdea*, *dolos*, the common semantic denominator of
which is 'cunning'.[31] Two of these terms, namely *mētis* and *technē*,
also designate the resources employed by craftsmen in their work.
To understand why Homer uses the same terms to designate both
fraud and carpentry, we must examine the contexts in which these
terms occur.

Taken together, the contexts containing epic terms for 'cunning'
reveal that all these terms have the same semantic opposite,
which may be designated 'natural advantage'. The opposition
between 'cunning' and 'natural advantage' is manifested whenever
physical or social superiority is overcome by an inferior but more
inventive rival.

In every confrontation or competitive situation—whether the adversary be
a man, an animal or a natural force—success can be won by two means,
either thanks to a superiority in 'power' in the particular sphere in which
the contest is taking place, with the stronger gaining the victory; or by the
use of methods of a different order whose effect is, precisely, to reverse the
natural outcome of the encounter and to allow victory to fall to the party
whose defeat has appeared inevitable.[32]

[29] See Lovejoy (1936), 67-98; Abrams (1953), 21-6, 272-85.
[30] As, for example, at *Od.* 19. 138.
[31] On cunning in Homer see Detienne and Vernant (1978), 11-26; on the
artisan's cunning see Frontisi-Ducroux (1975), 79-82, 90-4, 157-9, 162-7,
181-93; for cunning and deception see Pratt (1993), 70.
[32] Detienne and Vernant (1978), 13.

Thus, it is 'by cunning', and not 'by strength', that Odysseus gains the upper hand over the mighty Cyclops, and Lycurgus the Arcadian slays Ereuthalion, champion of the Pylians;[33] it is 'by cunning', and not 'by quickness', that Antilochus wins the race against the speedier horses of Menelaus, and the lame Hephaestus catches Ares, 'the swiftest of the gods',[34] and it is 'by cunning' that Antilochus and Aegisthus, in quite different circumstances, overcome the 'far more noble' Menelaus and Agamemnon.[35]

Skill, whether that of the craftsman or of any other specialist, is another opposite of natural advantage.[36] What underlies Homer's evenly balanced attitude to trickery and skills becomes clear from Nestor's advice to Antilochus before the race:

> The others have faster horses, but their drivers know no more tricks than you do yourself. So then, my friend, put into your mind all manner of cunning, so that the prizes do not slip past you. It is cunning (*mētis*), you know, that makes the good woodcutter, much more than strength. By cunning again the helmsman keeps his quick ship running straight over the sparkling sea, though the winds are buffeting. And it is by cunning that charioteer beats charioteer.[37]

On the surface of it, it looks as if Nestor's use of a woodcutter and a helmsman to illustrate his point is inappropriate. Even if the stratagems of cunning provide a charioteer with the means to beat a superior rival, with whom do the woodcutter and helmsman compete? The only answer that makes sense of Nestor's example is that the superiority overcome in these two cases is that of nature itself. Indeed, if his bodily resources were the only means available to man to overcome the might of a tree or the strength of the winds, he would never have a chance against nature. Only armed

[33] *Od.* 9. 408 δόλῳ, οὐδὲ βίηφιν; *Il.* 7. 142 δόλῳ, οὔ τι κράτεΐ γε. Cf. also *Il.* 23. 725.

[34] The horses of Antilochus are βάρδιστοι, ἥσσονες, and πολὺ χείρονες than the horses of Menelaus (*Il.* 23. 310, 322, 572, 577), and he wins κέρδεσιν, οὔτι τάχει γε (515). Ares is ὠκύτατος, Hephaestus βραδύς and χωλός, and he wins τέχνῃσι (*Od.* 8. 329-32).

[35] In comparison with Antilochus, Menelaus is κρείσσων ἀρετῇ τε βίῃ τε, πρότερος καὶ ἀρείων, and ἀμείνων (*Il.* 23. 578, 588, 605), and it is said of Aegisthus that he killed πολλὸν ἀρείω (*Od.* 3. 250, cf. 235). Generally speaking, cunning is the only means by which Homeric men can get the better of their social superiors. Projected into theogony, the tension between superiority and cunning is seen in the Hesiodic gods' struggle for sovereignty with their predecessors, see *Th.* 496 and Detienne and Vernant (1978), 55-130.

[36] Cf. *Il.* 7. 197-8, 23. 315, 713.

[37] *Il.* 23. 311-18, cf. also 713.

with the stratagems of cunning can man compete with nature and overcome it.[38] This gives the craftsman's cunning precedence over all the other varieties of cunning. Obviously, this is also the reason why a neutral term like 'knowledge' (*idreiē*) can enter into an opposition with 'might' (*biē*) in exactly the same way as such terms of cunning as *kerdea, dolos, mētis*, etc. do.[39]

It would not be an exaggeration to say that at bottom craftsmanship was always perceived by the Greeks as a violation of the natural order of things. This point was made especially clear by J.-P. Vernant, who showed that the Greek attitude to agriculture, an activity carried out within the limits set by nature, differed fundamentally from the attitude to craftsmanship: 'Le travail de la terre ne prend donc pas la forme d'une mise en œuvre de procédés efficaces, de règles de succès. Il n'est pas une action sur la nature, pour la transformer ou l'adapter à des fins humaines. Cette transformation, si même elle était possible, constituerait une impiété.'[40] All this seems to indicate that in Greek thought, art was endowed with the special status of a competitor of nature. Of course, art's ability to produce things is but another aspect of its ability to compete with nature. Just as by its ability to neutralize the forces of nature art offers an alternative to these forces, so also by its ability to produce things it offers an alternative to nature's creative power. In view of this, creation by craftsmanship as it is presented in Homer can be defined more specifically as *the ability to produce things by means of an orderly transformation of natural objects which is alternative to the productive ability of nature*.

It is reasonable to expect that, as soon as poetry begins to be treated as deriving from art, the productive ability of the poet will be conceived along the same lines. Aristotle's concept of the organic form that transforms the events which form the subject-matter of poetry according to the rules of art, just as Homeric craftsmen transform the natural objects which serve as raw material for their art, immediately comes to mind in this connection. Furthermore, the inherited attitude to production by art may possibly throw light on the much discussed question as to why, up to a fairly late date, Greek writers preferred to use ready-

[38] Cf., again, *Il.* 3. 60–2 (see n. 22 above).
[39] See the opposition βίη : ἰδρείη at *Il.* 7. 197–8.
[40] Vernant (1965), ii. 24. On the subject see also Finley (1970), 599, and Frontisi-Ducroux (1975), 81–2.

made subjects rather than invent new ones. Again, it would be anachronistic to ascribe this phenomenon to a lack of artistic creativity in the modern sense of the word. The following observation by Stephen Halliwell seems to be pertinent in this connection: ' "Creativity" is strictly inappropriate as a historical concept in the Greek context. Aristotle himself holds that everything which comes into being must do so out of something pre-existent. Moreover, the artist must know in advance the form of that which he intends to produce.'[41]

To recapitulate: in so far as art constituted the productive force that competed with the productive force of nature rather than derived from it, objects of art could by no means be regarded as deriving from objects of nature. Things created 'by art' confronted the world of nature as, in a sense, another world which derived its *raison d'être* from its own sources. We can expect, therefore, that the artefact's relation to reality would be construed differently from the relation we saw in the case of the song.

Artefact and Reality

Whatever the functional purpose of a given artefact, Homer's standard rendering of the effect of a well-wrought piece of craftsmanship is by means of the formula 'a marvel to behold'.[42] Obviously, this emphasis on the beauty of the artefact rather than its usefulness, fitting as it does the teleological status of the work of art in the 'poetics of fiction', forms a clear contrast to the specific kind of 'usefulness' which is enshrined in Homer's idea of song. At the same time, in view of the general truth, made especially clear by Plato, that a real couch and a picture of a couch do not exist on the same plane of reality, there is good reason to doubt whether the artefact, taken indiscriminately, can in any case serve as a legitimate counterpart to the song. After all, poetry, at least

---

[41] Halliwell (1986: 82 n. 1), quoting *Metaph.* 1032ᵃ14, ᵇ30–2, 1033ᵇ11, and 1032ᵇ6 ff. As already mentioned (Ch. 1 above), the first narrative genre in Greek literature to use invented rather than traditional subjects was the Hellenistic novel.

[42] θαῦμα ἰδέσθαι: applied in the *Iliad* to the tyres of Hera's chariot-wheels (5. 725), to the armour of Rhesus (10. 439) and Achilles (18. 83), and to the automated golden statues of Hephaestus (18. 377). See also *Il.* 18. 549, where the term 'marvel' is applied to one of the images of the shield of Achilles (n. 62 below), and *Od.* 19. 229, where the hunting scene on Odysseus' brooch is described as producing a similar reaction (n. 66 below). Cf. Philipp (1968), 8–9.

the kind of poetry meant by Homer, is about something, which means that it forms a relationship with reality that cannot be automatically transferred to all artefacts. So that the comparison between poem and artefact will be a really balanced one, we must turn from artefacts as a whole to the specific class of representational artefacts.

To be sure, Homer's descriptions of works of craftsmanship by no means lack figurative motives. The golden cup of Nestor with pecking doves on each of its four handles; the hunting scene on Odysseus' golden brooch; the belt of Heracles with 'bears and wild boars and lions with gleaming eyes, struggles and battles, men slain and men murdered'; the armour of Agamemnon—the corselet and the belt with snakes and the shield with the 'terribly glaring' Gorgon, Dread, and Terror upon it; and, above all, the shield of Achilles are examples.[43] The sculptural images, such as the golden handmaidens in Hephaestus' house, the dogs of gold and silver and the golden youths in the palace of Alcinous, form another group of artefacts dealing with representation.[44] Now, it is a well-known fact that Homer's descriptions of representational artefacts often allow for effects which could hardly be achieved by means of actual craftsmanship. To illustrate the point, let us try to reduce such a major work of Homeric art as the shield of Achilles to a real piece of craftsmanship.[45]

Even if the black colour of the ploughed field or the grapes, which suddenly emerges on a shield of gold, could possibly have been produced by the Minoan use of niello on gold,[46] a similar explanation would consequently be required for the rest of the colour and light effects mentioned in the description of the shield— the dark colour of blood, the whiteness of sheep, the youths' tunics glittering with oil, the blaze of torches, and so on.[47] Furthermore, even if these and similar effects can be accounted for by certain techniques of combining metals that result in 'painting in metal',[48] one would still have to explain the remarkable fact that the figures

---

[43] The cup of Nestor, *Il.* 11. 632-5; the belt of Heracles, *Od.* 11. 609-14; Odysseus' brooch, *Od.* 19. 227-31; the armour of Agamemnon, *Il.* 11. 24-8, 32-40; the shield of Achilles, *Il.* 18. 478-608.

[44] Hephaestus' handmaidens, *Il.* 18. 417-20; the golden statues in the palace of Alcinous, *Od.* 7. 91-4, 100-2.

[45] Cf. Finkelberg (1994), 1-6.

[46] *Il.* 18. 548, 561-2, see Webster (1939), 177 n. 14; Gray (1954), 1-15.

[47] *Il.* 18. 538, 583, 529, 588, 596, 492.

[48] Gray (1954), 3.

on the shield are described not as stationary, as would naturally be expected of reliefs on gold, but as moving. Thus, in what is supposed to represent a siege scene, the besieged, who at the beginning of the episode are depicted as arming themselves for an ambush, then proceed, as it were, to leave the city, to arrive at the site of the ambush, to attack a herd and its herdsmen, and join battle; the besiegers, in turn, originally pictured as taking counsel together near the wall, proceed, as it were, to ride towards the enemy and join battle; finally, the herdsmen, playing pipes at their first appearance, are attacked and slain by the besieged.[49] Again, even if a plausible interpretation of this scene along the lines of primitive art cannot be ruled out (one might think, for example, of a series of scenes rather than a single scene),[50] there is no explanation for the fact that the figures on the shield are described not only as moving but also as making sounds—the flutes and lyres utter a 'loud sound', the boy sings his song 'with delicate voice', the river murmurs, the cattle bellow, the dogs bark.[51] The result is an impossible blend of colours, movements, and sounds which can hardly be thought of in terms of a real piece of craftsmanship.[52]

Accordingly, the manner in which Homer's artistic images appropriate the functions and properties of their prototypes has given rise to the suggestion that there must have been a magic connection between the image and its prototype, a connection that caused the image to behave as a magical substitute.[53] Yet interpretation of Homeric images of art in terms of magic, attrac-

---

[49] *Il.* 18. 509-40, cf. also 503-6, 573-86. According to Frontisi-Ducroux (1975: 74), the succession of events on the shield is 'plus temporelle que spatiale'. Cf. also Edwards (1987a), 207-8.

[50] Cf. Boas (1955), 73-5, and the examples adduced in Webster (1939), 176.

[51] *Il.* 18. 495, 569-71, 576, 575, 580; cf. Frontisi-Ducroux (1975), 74-5.

[52] Cf. Schrade (1952), 80: 'Es ist wie gesagt möglich . . . dass der Dichter bestimmte Kunstwerke vor Augen gehabt hat; es ist auch denkbar, dass diese Werke in einem für die Zeit sehr bemerkenswerten Illusionismus gebildet gewesen sind. Aber es bleibt unvorstellbar, dass der Illusionismus der Beschreibung und der Illusionismus der vorauszusetzenden Kunstwerke übereingestimmt haben'; Philipp (1968), 7: 'Das Ganze ist ein Komplizierter vorgang, den man zwar erzähler kann, aber niemals in seinem Ablauf in der bildenden Kunst daszustellen vermag.' Frontisi-Ducroux (1975: 74), though admitting that 'il est certes possible de confronter l'œuvre d'Héphaistos à des modèles réels', says at the same time that 'la convention de description . . . est constamment rompue au cours de l'évocation du chant xviii'.

[53] Webster (1939), 176-8; Schrade (1952), 81-3; Frontisi-Ducroux (1975), 101-2.

tive as it may seem at first sight, proves unwarranted. Consider, for
example, the following description of the golden handmaidens in
the house of Hephaestus: 'his maids ran to help their master. They
are made of gold, looking like living girls: they have understanding in their hearts, and voice too and strength, and have learnt
their handiwork from the immortal gods.' Hephaestus' handmaidens not only possess general human characteristics such as
voice and strength, they are also endowed with what can be called
the standard womanly virtues, namely understanding and knowledge of domestic skills.[54] And yet, if we try to substitute any one
of them for a real woman, it will become clear that no such
substitution is feasible. This is because these statues, as well as all
other images of art in Homer, are *anonymous*.[55] It goes without saying that this anonymity is sharply at variance with the very idea
of magical substitution: anonymous images simply have no prototype for which they can be substituted. In this, they fail to fulfil the
essential condition that makes magical substitution possible.

It has also been suggested that Homer drew no distinction
between art and reality.[56] Yet a closer examination of the manner
in which he describes the shield disproves this suggestion.
Although the siege scene which transforms itself into the battle
scene is explicitly described in terms of movement, the same scene
has among its figures the gods Ares and Athene, of whom the
poet does not forget to say that they were 'both wrought in gold,
and dressed in golden clothing'.[57] In another scene a boy appears
in a vineyard playing a pleasant melody on the lyre and singing a
sweet Linos-song with delicate voice—but the vineyard itself is 'a
beautiful thing wrought in gold', its vines hang on silver poles and
it is surrounded by a ditch of cyanus and a fence of tin. The herd
which hurries to the pasture with lowing is made of gold and tin
and is followed by golden shepherds, and the dancing scene with
the youths whose tunics are glittering with oil is compared to a

[54] *Il.* 18. 417-20. Cf. *Il.* 9. 390, 13. 432; *Od.* 2. 117, 7. 11, 13. 289, 15. 418,
16. 158, 20. 72. That the golden statues owe their human properties to their
anthropomorphic character rather than to the fact that they are self-moving
automatons becomes clear when they are compared with the self-moving tripods in
the same episode (*Il.* 18. 373-7): though both groups of artefacts are self-moving,
the tripods are totally devoid of the human properties with which the statues are
endowed.

[55] This fact has been paid due attention in Himmelmann (1969), 22.

[56] Schrade (1952), 79-85.

[57] *Il.* 18. 516-18.

piece of craftsmanship wrought by Daedalus.[58] In a similar vein, the moving figures of men are only 'like living mortals', and the black field of gold is only 'similar' to the real field.[59] These and similar remarks leave no room for doubt that Homer was fully aware of the artificial character of the images on Achilles' shield.

Thus, there is no reason to suggest that Homer drew no distinction between art and reality or that he treated images of art in terms of magic. Since, nevertheless, the likeness of the artistic images to natural objects is envisaged as encompassing the functions and properties of their actual prototypes, the only way to account for the peculiar behaviour of these images is to admit that, according to Homer's conception of representation in art, images of art were, in a sense, seen as alive.[60] To be sure, the idea of the 'living artefact' is quite compatible with the primitive view of representation in art as expressed, for example, in the following passage by C. Lévi-Strauss:

> Thus, the chests of Northwest Coast art are not merely containers embellished with a painted or carved animal. They are the animal itself, keeping an active watch over the ceremonial ornaments which have been entrusted to its care . . . . The final product is a whole: utensil-ornament, object-animal, box-that-speaks. The 'living boats' of the Northwest Coast have their exact counterparts in the New Zealand correspondences between boat and woman, woman and spoon, utensils and organs.[61]

Even more significantly, it is quite compatible with the Archaic Greek tradition—the living statues of Daedalus immediately come to mind in this connection.

Homer's description of the ploughing scene on the shield of Achilles makes my point especially clear:

> And he made on it a field of soft fallow, rich ploughland, broad and triple-tilled. There were many ploughmen on it, wheeling their teams and driving this way and that . . . And the field was black behind them, and

---

[58] *Il.* 18. 509-40, 561-72, 573-86, 590-8.

[59] *Il.* 18. 539 ὡμίλευν δ' ὥς τε ζωοὶ βροτοὶ ἠδ' ἐμάχοντο, 548 ἡ δὲ μελαίνετ' ὄπισθεν, ἀρηρομένη δὲ ἐῴκει.

[60] This is, in fact, the conclusion reached in the majority of studies dealing with Homer's attitude to the fine arts, see e.g. Webster (1939), 176-8; Schrade (1952), 81-2; Himmelmann (1969), 17-23; Frontisi-Ducroux (1975), 75; Morris (1992), 227-9.

[61] Lévi-Strauss (1963), 260-1. Cf. Frontisi-Ducroux (1975), 109.

looked like earth that is ploughed, though it was made of gold. This was the great marvel of his work.[62]

Note that the 'likeness' of the field of gold to a real ploughed field includes its blackness, an effect which, as we have seen, almost certainly surpasses what could be achieved by the artisan's technique. In view of this, it is hard not to agree with J. W. Atkins, to whom this passage represents the earliest extant judgement on the fine arts:

the poet comments on the workmanship of Hephaestus in depicting a freshly ploughed field on the shield of Achilles. He notes that the upturned soil seemed black, though the shield was made of gold; and this he describes as the 'marvel' (*thauma*) of the work. It was an implicit recognition of the illusion of art; a passing glimpse of an artistic truth which was to be developed later in more reasoned terms.[63]

Although the majority of the artefacts spoken of by Homer as in some sense 'alive'—as indeed were most of the representational artefacts he mentions—were made by Hephaestus, this does not mean that the attitude would be different in the case of 'man-made' artefacts, and not only because the gods, as we have seen, possessed no special status in the matter of creation. Note in particular that the statues of Daedalus, human though he was, were treated in the Archaic Greek tradition in the same vein as Hephaestus' artefacts are treated in Homer.[64] What matters here is the idea of the representational artefact as such rather than its divine or human origins. It is true of course that as it is described in *Odyssey* 19, the hunting scene on Odysseus' brooch, where 'a hound had a dappled fawn between his forepaws, holding it firm as it struggled', though admitting of a degree of illusion unparalleled in the material evidence of the time, is much more conceivable as a real work of craftsmanship than the moving and audible images on Achilles' shield, just as the golden youths with torches in their hands illuminating the palace of Alcinous in *Odyssey* 7 are much more like real statues than the golden hand-maidens of Hephaestus in *Iliad* 18, endowed as they are with understanding, voice, strength, and even competence in women's

[62] *Il.* 18. 541–9; note esp. 549, 'this was the great marvel of his work' τὸ δὴ περὶ θαῦμα τέτυκτο.

[63] Atkins (1934), 13.

[64] Cf. Webster (1939), 177–8; Panofsky (1968), 14–15; Pollitt (1974), 63–4. On Daedalus see esp. Frontisi-Ducroux (1975), 95–117; Morris (1992), 215–37.

work.[65] Note, however, that the golden dogs of Alcinous do guard the house as if they were real dogs, and the description of the hunting scene on Odysseus' brooch not only follows the same pattern as that of the ploughing scene on the shield of Achilles but also provokes the same kind of admiration: 'Everyone was amazed to see how the hound and the fawn both were gold, yet the one was gripping and throttling the fawn, and the other striving to break away and writhing with its feet.'[66]

This compares well with the description of the shield of Heracles found in a late traditional poem of this name ascribed to Hesiod. The poet of the *Shield of Heracles* resembles Homer in that he not only describes such effects as the black colour of snakes' jaws, of blood, and of grapes on the vine, the noise of teeth gnashing, the sound of an echo, and the like,[67] but also emphasizes more than once that the figures on the shield of Heracles are like living beings.[68] It is true, of course, that 'Hesiod' differs from Homer in that his figures are sometimes represented as frozen for ever and therefore much less 'alive' than those in Homer. Consider, for instance, the following description of a chariot-race:

The charioteers standing on their well-woven cars urged on their swift horses with loose rein; the joined cars flew along chattering and the naves of the wheels shrieked loudly. So they were engaged in an unending toil, and the end with victory came never to them, and the contest was ever unwon.[69]

The fact is, however, that this description goes well with other passages indicating that 'Hesiod', like Homer, also tries to maintain a distance that would not allow the images on the shield to overstep the limits of artistic representation. Thus, the snakes only look '*as though* there were spots' upon them, the Muses who are beginning a song are only '*like* clear-voiced singers', the dolphins only '*seem* to be swimming', and the men who were 'reaping with sharp hooks the stalks which bended with the weight of the ears' are

---

[65] *Od.* 19. 228–9; 7. 100; *Il.* 18. 417–20.

[66] *Od.* 19. 229–31 τὸ δὲ θαυμάζεσκον ἅπαντες, | ὡς οἱ χρύσεοι ἐόντες ὁ μὲν λάε νεβρὸν ἀπάγχων, | αὐτὰρ ὁ ἐκφυγέειν μεμαὼς ἤσπαιρε πόδεσσι, cf. nn. 59, 62 above. Cf. Morris (1992), 227: 'although less explicit a metaphor for art come alive, this artifact inspires the same sense of wonder at the conflict between its artifice and its life.' The golden dogs of Alcinous, *Od.* 7. 91–4.

[67] The black colour, *Aspis* 167, 173–4, 300; the sound, 235, 279.

[68] See *Aspis* 189 ὡς εἰ ζωοί περ ἐόντες; 244 ζωῆσιν ἴκελαι.

[69] *Aspis* 306–11, trans. H. G. Evelyn-White. Cf. Edwards (1987a), 208.

described by the poet only '*as if* they were reaping Demeter's grain'.[70] All this demonstrates beyond doubt that the practice of treating objects of art as artificial and real at one and the same time is not characteristic of *Iliad* 18 only.

There can be no doubt that the view of the representational artefact as 'living' afforded images of art a special status with respect to reality. Given the anonymous character of these 'living' images, it is reasonable to suppose that the representation of 'a man' would always, in a sense, be envisaged as an actual man, whose existence does not depend on the existence of any real person whatsoever. Indeed, by virtue of the fact that there is no concrete person through correlation with whom the representation of 'a man' can be identified, the 'living' artefact can never be judged as either true or false in respect of reality. A man of gold is no more 'true' or 'false' than a man of flesh and blood: the only thing that can be said of such a man is that he simply exists side by side with real people, just as Pandora, the woman-artefact, is simply a woman whose autonomous existence extends even to her receiving a singular name of her own.[71] That is to say, just as the *technē* by means of which it is produced offers a full-scale alternative to the productive force of nature, so also the representational artefact offers a full-scale alternative to reality.

Let us turn for a moment to the distinction drawn by Panofsky for Greek art, between the work of art that is 'inferior to nature, insofar as it merely imitates nature, at best to the point of deception' and the work of art that is 'superior to nature because, improving upon the deficiencies of nature's individual products, art independently confronts nature with a newly created image of beauty'.[72] It goes without saying that the concept of the 'living artefact' as outlined above could only emerge if art was seen as creating products which, as in Panofsky's formulation, 'independently confronted nature with a newly created image of beauty'. Indeed, the only concept of representation in art that would correspond to the idea of the 'living artefact' without at the same time exceeding the limits of art proper, is the treatment of images of art as typical and generic rather than as individual and

---

[70] See *Aspis* 166 στίγματα δ' ὡς ἐπέφαντο ἰδεῖν; 206 λιγὺ μελπομένης ἐϊκυῖαι; 211 νηχομένοις ἴκελοι; 290 ὡς εἰ Δημήτερος ἀκτήν, *sc.* ἤμων.

[71] On Pandora see Morris (1992), 31-2, 230.

[72] Panofsky (1968), 14. Quoted in full in Ch. 1, p. 24.

specific. Only an image that concentrates within itself the most permanent and essential characteristics of its prototype, while at the same time eliminating everything momentary and accidental, can independently confront its prototype with no danger of becoming its double.[73] This attitude to representation in art probably accounts for so characteristic a feature of Archaic Greek art as representation of the specific in the light of the generic, rendered by J. J. Pollitt as follows: 'Greek artists tended to look for the typical and essential forms which expressed the essential nature of classes of phenomena in the same way that Platonic "forms" or "ideas" expressed essential realities underlying the multiplicity of sense perception. A geometric statue of a horse is an attempt to get at the "horseness" which lies behind all particular horses.'[74] The late development of the portrait genre in Greek art seems also to be explicable along these lines.[75]

The same would also be true of Homer's description of the shield of Achilles itself. It is, indeed, generally agreed that in this description Homer, as Mark Edwards put it, 'does not intend to present a particular occurrence, but paradigms of ever-continuing human social activities'.[76] This can clearly be seen from the sequence and the arrangement of the scenes. After the heavenly bodies in the first band around the boss, there appear in the second band two cities—one at peace, in which both a homicide trial and a wedding ceremony are taking place, the other at war, in fact, under siege; in the third band, there are agricultural scenes arranged in the order of the seasons of the farmer's year—ploughing, reaping, and the vintage; in the fourth, two pasture-land scenes, the one peaceful and the other violent, with the herd being devoured by lions; in the fifth, a festival accompanied by music and dance, the whole surrounded by the river of Ocean. It has become customary to see in this picture a contrast to the realistic and prosaic account of peasant life given by Hesiod in the *Works and Days*, and accordingly to interpret it as an idealized picture of human life. Yet, it

[73] Characteristically, the 'phantoms' (*eidōla*) of living men created from time to time by the Homeric gods (see e.g. *Il.* 5. 449; *Od.* 4. 796) are in fact only insubstantial forms with no option for materialization and thus, in contrast to the artefacts, with no chance of becoming 'doubles' existing side by side with their originals.

[74] Pollitt (1972), 6.

[75] On this subject see especially Schweitzer (1963), ii. 121–58.

[76] Edwards (1991), 208. My interpretation of the arrangement of the scenes on the shield follows in essentials Edwards's analysis, as in op. cit. 206–32.

seems to me that for Homer it is rather descriptions of life on Olympus or in Phaeacia, whose inhabitants know nothing about loss and danger, that would pass for such idealized pictures. The shield of Achilles is far removed both from these descriptions of blessed and careless life and from those of the harsh realities of everyday existence supplied by Hesiod. Indeed, in that it represents war and death alongside peace and prosperity, loss and crime alongside gain and justice, the shield of Achilles provides, rather, a representative model of real life, which would inevitably include war, death, and loss. Without being reducible to any particular situation of a concrete human society, the shield of Achilles can account for all of them. In that, it does not differ from any other representational artefact described by Homer.

To be sure, no explicit references to the 'living artefact' can be found in the Greek sources relating to the 'poetics of fiction'. Instead, from the fifth century BC, representation in art, both in fine arts and in poetry, comes to be labelled by the term *mimēsis*. What is of paramount importance in understanding the Greek concept of mimesis is that, 'imitation' though it is, rather more often than not mimesis presupposes the imitation of things that do not exist in reality. This is true of both the popular and the philosophic view of mimesis. When a chorus of Pindar wants to 'imitate' the song of the Sirens, when Plato speaks in terms of mimesis about sculptors and painters who deform the natural proportions of the human body, or reproaches poets for falling short in 'imitating' things which are beyond the scope of their experience, when Aristotle says that art 'imitates' those things that nature is unable to produce or that the purpose of art is 'to imitate nature by making her deficiences good'—in all these cases 'imitation' is understood, to put it in Butcher's words, as a creative act.[77] Juxtaposition of the concept of mimesis with that of the 'living artefact', which can justifiably be seen as its Archaic predecessor, gives us reason to believe that in Greek thought the representation that 'independently confronted nature with a newly created image of beauty' had both historical and semantic priority over the more narrow sense of 'making copies' by which the Greek idea of representation has often been interpreted.

[77] Pind. *Parth.* 2. 14-15; Pl. *Soph.* 235e-236a; *Tim.* 19d; Arist. *Phys.* 199ª15; Pol. 1337ª2-3. Cf. Butcher (1951), 154; Vicaire (1960), 219-20; Verdenius (1983), 54-7; Halliwell (1986), 124-5. On mimesis see also below, Ch. 6.

Thus, Homer derived poetry from inspiration and saw its product as a message whose existence was justified by the reality of which it was a message. On the other hand, he derived handicrafts from art and saw their product as a reality *sui generis*, whose existence was justified by nothing outside this product itself. With this in view, let us turn again to the *Poetics*. According to Aristotle, history relates 'what has happened' while poetry relates 'what may happen'; history deals with the particular, or 'what Alcibiades did or suffered', whereas poetry deals with the universal, or 'how a person of a certain type will on occasion speak or act, according to the law of probability and necessity'.[78] We saw above that it is Aristotle's definition of history that fits in better with Homer's idea of song. We can see now that Aristotle's definition of poetry is in accordance with Homer's idea of representation in the arts.

The Form of Truth and the Form of Fiction

One of the implications of the opposition between the 'poetics of truth' and the 'poetics of fiction' is that each of the two poetics suggests a different concept of form. That *parataxis* as the concept of form embodied in oral poetry and the Aristotelian concept of form as organic unity are polarly opposed to each other has been argued by J. A. Notopoulos: on the basis of this distinction, he sought to create a new 'oral' poetics, based on principles other than those of the *Poetics* of Aristotle.[79] Notopoulos proceeded from the general premiss that 'technique is at the basis of any poetics'; to support it, he drew attention to the inventory of formal devices at the oral poet's disposal and the conditions of performance influencing the form of the song.[80] Yet the accumulation of empirical data concerning the oral poet's practice, though important in itself, has not led to a new synthesis to challenge the *Poetics* of Aristotle, and J. B. Hainsworth was certainly right to conclude that 'Notopoulos . . . did not clearly explain what were the special non-Aristotelian virtues the traditional poet displayed. . . . Instead he described certain aspects of craftsmanship. . . .'[81]

In view of this, we can ask whether it is methodologically valid

[78] *Poet.* 1451[a]37–[b]11.
[79] Notopoulos (1964), 46–65, see also Notopoulos (1949), 1–23, and (1951), 81–102. Cf. M. Parry (1971), 439–64.   [80] Notopoulos (1964), 46.
[81] Hainsworth (1970), 91. Cf. also Finnegan (1977), 2, 130; Griffin (1980) pp. xiii–xiv.

to draw inferences about the system of general principles accounting for the mode of existence of the work of art (for this is what a
poetics ultimately is) from the form in which the work of art is
realized. It seems more likely that it is the principles according to
which the work of art is conceived that condition its form. Thus,
Aristotle's idea of organic form was logically subordinated to his
conceiving art in general and the art of poetry in particular
as essentially fiction. Indeed, it is only on the premiss that art
moulds reality in accordance with its own laws that the very idea
of organic form is possible, for the events of real life are all too
rarely arranged so as to exhibit organic unities.[82] Thus the concept
of organic form is generated by a poetics in which 'not to know
that a hind has no horns is a less serious matter than to paint it
inartistically',[83] that is, the kind of poetics that I have defined as
the 'poetics of fiction'. To see how *parataxis* can similarly derive
from the 'poetics of truth', we should turn to the references to
poetry found in the epics.

'Sing, goddess, the wrath of Achilles, Peleus' son' are the opening words of the *Iliad*; characteristically enough, however, the
beginning of the *Iliad* is the only instance in both Homeric poems
when an invocation of the Muse is introduced by the verb 'to sing'.
In the other invocations found throughout the *Iliad* and in the
proem of the *Odyssey*, the poet asks the Muse(s) not to 'sing' but
to 'tell' him of a given subject.[84] It can be inferred from this that
song was understood by Homer as narration;[85] the examination of
Homeric invocations provides a fuller understanding of the kind of
narration involved.

The characteristic features of Homeric invocations have been set
out in W. W. Minton's important article as follows: 'First, all the
invocations are essentially *questions*, appeals to the Muse for
specific information for which the poet clearly expects an *answer*.
Secondly, the information for which the poet asks and which is
reflected, however vestigially, in the following "answer" is that of
an *ordered enumeration* or catalogue' (Minton's italics).[86] At the

---

[82] This point receives due emphasis in Lucas (1968), 118.

[83] *Poet.* 1460ᵇ32–3.

[84] ἔσπετε *Il.* 2. 484, 11. 218, 14. 508, 16. 112; ἔννεπε *Il.* 2. 761; *Od.* 1. 1; εἰπέ
Od. 1. 10.   [85] Cf discussion in West (1981), 113–29, esp. 115.

[86] Minton (1960), 292–3, cf. Minton (1962), 188–212. On the catalogue form
as a basis for Homeric narrative see Krischer (1971), 131–58, and Edwards (1980),
81–103.

same time, the only real catalogue following a Homeric invocation is the Catalogue of Ships in *Iliad* 2. In the other cases, formulaic questions of the type 'Tell me, O Muse . . ., who first . . .?', rather than introducing catalogues, precede dramatic turns in the story.[87] That the invocation thus proves to be a conventional device used to introduce forthcoming events shows that it was important for Homer to present his narrative as constituting a catalogue-like sequence. What could have been his reasons for this?

It is important to emphasize in this connection that the epic narrative is never described by the poet as consisting of single words. As was shown by Albert Lord, the lack of consciousness as regards the single word as a unit of speech is one of the characteristic features of oral poetries and probably of oral societies in general.

The singers themselves . . . do not think in terms of form as we think of it. . . . Man without writing thinks in terms of sound groups and not in words, and the two do not necessarily coincide. When asked what a word is, he will reply that he does not know, or he will give a sound group which may vary in length from what we call a word to an entire line of poetry, or even an entire song.[88]

Even when claiming that he has repeated his own or another singer's song 'word for word', the oral singer, without even being conscious of this, is never able to be exact in following his prototype. He would repeat it 'point by point' rather than 'word by word'. This clearly indicates that he analyses his song in units of narrative rather than in verbal units such as words. The Homeric evidence makes it clear that this must also have been true of the traditional poetry of the Greeks.

Although the very name of epic poetry immediately evokes the term *epos* ('word'), this in fact has never been its conscious self-identification: actually, the collective term *epea* ('words', 'speech') is indiscriminately applied in Homer to both sung and spoken narrative.[89] When used in such a sense, the word *epos* is employed almost exclusively in the plural—as, for example, in the formula 'the winged words', designating human speech in general.[90] Both

[87] Calhoun (1938), 157–66; Minton (1960), 292–309, and (1962), 201–4; Verdenius (1983), 26. [88] Lord (1960), 25.

[89] See e.g. *Od.* 4. 597–8 μύθοισιν ἔπεσσι τε . . . | τέρπομαι, of narrative, as against *Od.* 8. 91 ἐπεὶ τέρποντ' ἐπέεσσιν and 11. 561 ἔπος καὶ μῦθος, of song; or, again, *Il.* 20. 204 πρόκλυτα ἔπεα, of narrative, as against *Od.* 17. 519 ἔπε' ἱμερόεντα, of song.

[90] But see *Od.* 11. 561 ἔπος καὶ μῦθον and 14. 131 αἶψά κε καὶ σύ, γέραιε, ἔπος παρατεκτήναιο.

this formula and the famous description of Odysseus' speech in *Iliad* 3, 'he uttered . . . words like the snowflakes of winter',[91] the only two descriptions of human speech found in Homer, suggest that Homer was far from regarding human speech analytically, that is, as a succession of single words. Into what units, then, if any, did he analyse his narrative?

During the feast that is held in his honour in Phaeacia, Odysseus asks the Phaeacian singer Demodocus to sing the song of the Wooden Horse. He makes his request as follows:

Demodocus, I admire you beyond any man; either it was the Muse who taught you, the daughter of Zeus, or else it was Apollo, for perfectly in order (*kata kosmon*) you sing of the fortunes of the Achaeans—all they achieved and suffered and toiled over—as though you yourself were there or had heard from one who was. Come now, change your theme, and sing the order (*kosmon*) of the Wooden Horse; Epeius made it, Athene helped him, noble Odysseus planned its cunning climb to the citadel; inside the horse he had housed his warriors, and the warriors achieved the sack of Troy. If you recount all this for me according to the portion (*kata moiran*), then I will tell the world forthwith how the god has blessed you ungrudgingly with the gift of inspired song.[92]

Odysseus says that the Phaeacian singer sings of all that the Achaeans suffered at Troy 'according to the order' (*kata kosmon*); later on in the same speech the sense of the phrase *kata kosmon* is conveyed more specifically as follows: 'as though you yourself were there or had heard from one who was'. From this we can infer that the 'order' of Demodocus' song is the order of the events as they took place.[93] The following passage from the Homeric *Hymn to Hermes*, describing Hermes' singing to the accompaniment of the lyre he has just invented, throws additional light on the issue:

He sang the story of the deathless gods and of the dark earth, how at the first they came to be, and how each one received his portion. First among the gods he honoured Mnemosyne, mother of the Muses, in his song; for the son of Maia was of her following. And next the goodly son of Zeus hymned the rest of the immortals according to their order in age, and told how each was born, recounting all according to the order (*kata kosmon*) as he struck the lyre upon his arm.[94]

---

[91] *Il.* 3. 222 ἔπεα νιφάδεσσιν ἐοικότα χειμερίῃσιν.

[92] *Od.* 8. 487–98. On the expression *kata moiran* see pp. 126–9 below.

[93] Cf. Webster (1939), 175; Lanata (1963), 12–13; Maehler (1963), 32; Krischer (1965), 171; Adkins (1972), 16–17; Verdenius (1983), 53; Macleod (1983), 5; Walsh (1984), 8; Goldhill (1991), 57.   [94] *H. Herm.* 428–33.

Like Demodocus in the *Odyssey*, Hermes sings or, to be more precise, recounts[95] 'according to the order'. But the song he performs is a theogony, so that there can be little doubt that the order according to which he sings is identical to the catalogue-like sequence of divine genealogies.

The same must also be true of the expression 'the order of song', *kosmon aoidēs*, found in a hexametric line of an Orphic theogony quoted by Plato in the *Philebus*: 'but at the sixth generation cease the order of song'.[96] The context of the quotation is strictly enumerative, and it is obvious that the theogonic poem to which it originally belonged was also arranged as an enumerative sequence. The meaning of the verb *kosmein* and its cognates as attested in Homer and other traditional poetry points in the same direction.[97] The action to which this verb is almost exclusively applied in Homer is the marshalling of troops by their leaders,[98] whereas in Herodotus 'in order' and 'one after another' are used as synonyms.[99]

It is true, of course, that the verb *kosmein* is never directly applied to poetry in Homer. But in the concluding lines of the Homeric *Hymn to Dionysus* we find: 'Hail, child of fair-faced Semele! He who forgets you can in no wise order sweet song', whereas in the Platonic *Ion* another traditional singer testifies about himself that he 'has ordered Homer well', and a similar sense can be suggested for a passage from the *Phaedrus*, where inspired poetry like that produced by Ion is described as 'ordering the countless deeds of the ancients'.[100] Thus far, no attention seems to have been paid to the fact that Ion's words evoke similar expressions in

[95] ἐνέπων, the word used in the Homeric invocations.

[96] Orpheus, B 1 DK = *Phileb.* 66c ἕκτῃ δ' ἐν γενεᾷ καταπαύσατε κόσμον ἀοιδῆς.

[97] On *kosmos* and *kosmein* in early poetry see esp. Kranz (1967), 197-8; Kerschensteiner (1962), 5-10.

[98] κοσμεῖν *Il.* 2. 554, 704, 727, 806, 3. 1, 11. 51, 12. 87, 14. 378, 388; this usage is supplemented by the formula κοσμήτορε λαῶν, 'the two marshals of troops', relating to the leaders themselves (primarily Agamemnon and Menelaus), see *Il.* 1. 16, 375, 3. 236; cf. *Od.* 18. 152. At the single occurrence of the verb which does not belong in the military sphere, Nausikaa's maid Eurymedousa is described as preparing supper in the inner chamber; this action is described by means of the verb *kosmein*, see *Od.* 7. 13.

[99] Hdt. 7. 36. 4 κορμοὺς ξύλων . . . κόσμῳ ἐπετίθεσαν κατύπερθε τῶν ὅπλων τοῦ τόνου, θέντες δὲ ἐπεξῆς ἐνθαῦτα αὐτὶς ἐπεζεύγνυον.

[100] *H. Hom.* 7. 58-9 γλυκερὴν κοσμῆσαι ἀοιδήν; *Ion* 530d εὖ κεκόσμηκα τὸν Ὅμηρον, cf. *Phdr.* 245a ἀπὸ Μουσῶν κατοκοχή τε καὶ μανία . . . μυρία τῶν παλαιῶν ἔργα κοσμοῦσα κτλ.

the Orphic theogony and the Homeric *Hymn to Dionysus*, in both of which the poet's work with his material is also designated by means of the terms *kosmos* and *kosmein*. Yet, this coincidence may well indicate that 'to order the song' was the oral poets' professional designation of their method of arranging the material at their disposal.[101]

This conclusion throws light on the phrase 'sing me the order (*kosmon*) of the Wooden Horse' addressed by Odysseus to Demodocus. The usual interpretation of this phrase as relating to the actual process of constructing the horse would not agree with Homer's terminology relating to the technology of carpentry as described earlier in this chapter. At the same time, the metrical position of *kosmon aeison* ('sing the order') of *Odyssey* 8 is identical to that of *kosmon aoidēs* ('the order of song') in the Orphic poem, and differs by only one syllable from the related expression *kosmēsai aoidēn* ('to order the song') in the Homeric *Hymn to Dionysus*. This seems to indicate that what we have here is a formulaic system for expressing the basic idea of 'ordering the song' in two principal metrical breaks at the verse-end, after the bucolic diaeresis and the hephthemimeral caesura, respectively.[102] If this conclusion is correct, then the poet's view of his narrative as an ordered sequence of events should be regarded as belonging to the traditional stock of epic ideas. This would allow (*a*) the expression *kosmon aeison* in *Odyssey* 8 to be interpreted as a formulaic variation of the basic idea in question, and (*b*) the word *kosmos*, as used in the expression 'sing the order of the Wooden Horse', to be taken as standing for the song of the Wooden Horse itself.[103]

Odysseus also says to Demodocus: 'If you recount all this for me according to the portion (*kata moiran*), then I will tell the world forthwith how the god has blessed you ungrudgingly with the gift of inspired song.' The poet's narrative is designated here by the word *katalegein*, 'to recount'. The verb is applied once more to poetry, though indirectly, in Alcinous' praise of Odysseus' narra-

[101] On the use of this expression in later Greek poetry and prose, in accordance with the later meaning of *kosmos* as 'ornamentation', see Kerschensteiner (1962), 10–11.

[102] Cf. M. Parry (1971), 40–54. On formulaic systems see Finkelberg (1989), 179–97; on *Odyssey* 8 as containing a unique constellation of technical terms 'relating to the rhapsodic representation of piece after piece of heroic poetry' see Ford (1992), 111–13.

[103] A similar interpretation of this expression is adopted in Kirk (1962), 312.

tion of his adventures: 'you recounted your story expertly, like a singer.'[104] Now, *katalegein* is not an ordinary verb of speaking. It is an enumerative verb that joined the *verba dicendi* as a result of semantic evolution, and it still possesses clear enumerative associations in all the contexts in which it occurs.[105] In his study of *katalegein*, Tilman Krischer has shown that this verb in Homer designates concrete and exact accounts that relate the subject 'point by point', and is applied only to the conveying of information; moreover, Krischer provides what seems to be conclusive proof that the limitations on the meaning and usage of *katalegein* as described above are the limitations inherent in the early Greek understanding of truth as conveyed by the terms *alēthēs* and *alētheiē*.[106] This seems to indicate that Homer applied the verb *katalegein* to poetry because he conceived the epic narrative as just such a truthful and 'point-by-point' account of facts.

As I have argued elsewhere, the formulae *alētheiēn katalexai* ('to recount the truth') and *kata moiran katalexai* ('to recount according to the portion') are used by Homer at the end of the verse as two variants suited to different metrical conditions.[107] Metrically, it is convenient for the poet to reserve two metrically equivalent expressions that convey the same idea but differ in their initial sounds: the expression beginning with a vowel is suited to metrical conditions under which the one beginning with a consonant cannot be employed, and vice versa. Clearly, this could only be possible if he thought that 'the truth' and 'according to the portion' were closely associated in their meanings. This calls for a closer examination of the semantic content of *kata moiran* ('according to the portion') in Homer.

In fact, *kata moiran* is metrically isomorphic with *alētheiēn* ('truth') only when it occurs in combination with the verb 'to recount' (*katalegein*) in the aorist form *katalexai* at the verse-end. Characteristically, in this combination alone does the word *moira* ('portion') appear in its ancient form, **mmoira* (*mm-* from *sm-*), thus giving the expression *kata moiran* the metrical shape

---

[104] *Od.* 8. 496–8 αἴ κεν δή μοι ταῦτὰ μοῖραν καταλέξῃς . . .; 11. 368 μῦθον δ᾿ ὡς ὅτ᾿ ἀοιδὸς ἐπισταμένως κατέλεξας.   [105] Fournier (1946), 58.

[106] Krischer (1965), 167–70.

[107] Other expressions belonging to this group are ἀτρεκέως καταλέξαι ('to recount precisely') and ἐπισταμένως καταλέξαι ('to recount expertly'); see further Finkelberg (1987a), 135–8.

∪–––.[108] In all other contexts *kata moiran* is shaped ∪∪–∪ and thus is not commensurable with *alētheiē*. Examination of the two metrical shapes of *kata moiran* in the *Iliad* and the *Odyssey* shows that they differ from each other not only metrically but also semantically. In its ancient form, *kata *mmoiran*, the expression is applied to actions that have as their common semantic denominator the ordered sequence in which they are performed: outfitting a ship, milking sheep, cutting up a sacrificial animal, the advance of troops.[109] The only cases in which *kata *mmoiran* is applied to human speech are those in which it is combined with the verb *katalegein*.[110] No ordered sequence, however, is implied in the formula 'you have spoken according to the portion' and related expressions, which as a rule refer to single utterances (or, sometimes, acts) not subject to further differentiation and are usually rendered as 'you have said it rightly' (or, 'not rightly'); none of these expressions preserves *kata moiran* in its ancient form.[111] In view of this, it is reasonable to suggest that the meaning of *kata moiran*, which originally connoted an ordered sequence, evolved to connote 'rightly', and that only the phrase *kata *mmoiran*, shaped ∪–––, preserves the original meaning of the expression together with the ancient metrical shape.[112]

Thus, the two meanings of *kata moiran*, 'in order' and 'rightly', correspond to the expression's two metrical shapes: the phrase *kata moiran* shaped ∪∪–∪ means 'rightly' and the phrase *kata moiran* shaped ∪––– means 'in order', 'in turn'; for the kind of enumerative account implied by the verb *katalegein*, 'to recount point by point' seems to be the most appropriate rendering of 'to recount according to the portion' in Homer. That is to say, when varying the two expressions *kata moiran* and *alētheiēn*, before *katalegein* at the verse-end, Homer had to choose whether he wished to say 'to recount point by point' or 'to recount the truth'. We have seen that his choice was actually determined by

[108] See Chantraine (1968), 679, s.v. μείρομαι; Monro (1891), 275–8; M. Parry (1971), 232.

[109] *Od.* 4. 783, 8. 54; *Od.* 9. 245, 309, 342; *Od.* 3. 457; *Il.* 16. 367.

[110] *Od.* 3. 331, 8. 496, 10. 16, 12. 35.

[111] κατὰ μοῖραν ἔειπες *Il.* 1. 286, 8. 146, 9. 59, 10. 169, 15. 206, 23. 626, 24. 379; *Od.* 2. 251, 7. 227, 8. 141, 397, 13. 385, 18. 170, 20. 37, 21. 278, 22. 486; μυθεῖται κατὰ μοῖραν *Od.* 17. 580; κατὰ μοῖραν ὑποκρίναιτο *Od.* 15. 170. Cf. also the expressions ἔρεξας, τελέσειεν (οὐ) κατὰ μοῖραν at *Od.* 9. 352, 15. 203.

[112] Note that the expression κατὰ κόσμον ('in order', 'duly') underwent a similar semantic development; see Kerschensteiner (1962), 6.

metrical conditions. In view of this, and considering that the verb *katalegein* itself connotes both an ordered sequence and truth, we should conclude that these two meanings were seen by Homer as mutually interchangeable. That is to say, the ordered sequence was regarded as the correct form for a truthful narration, and the truth as the content of a 'point-by-point' narrative sequence.

Characteristically, the expression *kata moiran* is never applied by Homer to the lying stories told by Odysseus in the second part of the *Odyssey*, and the same holds true of the expression *kata kosmon*. When related to human speech, *kata kosmon* is applied to Demodocus' song of the Wooden Horse, whereas *kata moiran* is applied to Nestor's account of the events in the royal house of Argos, to Odysseus' accounts of his adventures to Aeolus and to Circe, and to Demodocus' song of the Wooden Horse again—all of which are set as truthful narrations relating events that really happened.[113] This should be an important caveat against the recent tendency that unconditionally treats the lying Odysseus as a paradigm of the Homeric singer.[114] And although, as we shall see later, there are indeed some points on which Odysseus' lies and Homer's poetry concur, they give no support to an overall generalization of the kind (see Chapter 5). Alcinous' praise of Odysseus' narrative, 'you recounted your story expertly, like a singer', clearly implies that Homer not only thought of the epic song as a 'point-by-point' narrative succession but even found in this feature of epic song the pattern of all veracious narrative.[115]

Alcinous also says to Odysseus, 'there is shapeliness (*morphē*) on your words'.[116] In Homer, however, the term *morphē* does not imply the idea of structure: it is *on* Odysseus' words, and not *in*

---

[113] *Od.* 3. 331 (Nestor), 10. 16 and 12. 35 (Odysseus), 8. 489 and 496 (Demodocus).

[114] Pratt (1993: 85–93) goes as far as to claim that, according to Homer, the lying of Odysseus is *kata kosmon* and *kata moiran*. This, however, is a gross misrepresentation of the evidence at our disposal: there is no single occasion in either of the Homeric poems on which either of these expressions can be shown to apply to lies. On criticism of this approach in general see Gill (1993), 70–1.

[115] ἐπισταμένως κατέλεξας *Od.* 11. 368. Cf. Macleod (1983), 5: 'The word "cunningly" (ἐπισταμένως), like "well" (κατὰ κόσμον) in Odysseus' praise of Demodocus . . . refers to the truth rather than artistry of what is told, or at least not to the artistry in isolation from the truth.' Cf. further Krischer (1965), 170–1; Verdenius (1983), 25; Walsh (1984), 7. On ἐπισταμένως of this passage as relating to the sphere of the poet's professional competence and thus not covered by divine inspiration see Ch. 2 above.

[116] *Od.* 11. 367 σοὶ δ' ἔπι μὲν μορφὴ ἐπέων (my translation).

them that *morphē* is found,[117] while at *Odyssey* 8. 170, the only
other case where *morphē* appears in Homer, it 'crowns' the words
exactly as does *charis* ('charm') in the same passage a few lines
later.[118] Moreover, indirect evidence allows us to infer that Homer
considered any arrangement of events which deviated from their
succession in reality as the equivalent of a lie. Thus, in his praise
of Odysseus' ordered and therefore truthful narration, Alcinous
compares it to the stories of the vagabonds who arrange lies about
things that nobody would ever see; the verb *artunein* ('to arrange'),
used by Alcinous in this connection, also describes Hephaestus'
fashioning of the handles of the self-moving tripods.[119] Likewise,
Homer applies *paratektainesthai* ('to work into another form', from
tektainesthai, 'to frame') to the false story Eumaeus is prepared to
hear from the disguised Odysseus; this word, however, is the one
used to describe the process of building Paris' ships in the *Iliad*.[120]
This indicates that tectonic terms were seen by Homer as appropriate for false narratives. The expression 'carpenters of lies' used
by Heraclitus in one of his philosophical invectives also comes to
mind in this connection.[121]

Since Homer meant poetry to deliver truth, and since Homer's
truth consisted of properly ordered items, he would naturally have
grasped the 'point-by-point' progression as the only form appropriate for the epic narrative. The conclusion sheds light on the
catalogue-like nature of Homer's invocations. By asking the Muse
for an ordered enumeration of facts, the poet imparts a 'documentary' touch to his song and assures the audience that the subsequent narration is veracious. Consequently, the idea of the transformation of the material in accordance with the rules of art as
known to us from Aristotle's *Poetics* would not be applicable to the
poetics of Homer. *Parataxis*, therefore, would be the only form of
narrative admissible in the 'poetics of truth'.

---

[117] Cf. Stanford's commentary ad loc. in Stanford (1967), 395.

[118] *Od.* 8. 170 θεὸς μορφὴν ἔπεσι στέφει, 175 οὐ οἱ χάρις ἀμφιπεριστέφεται ἐπέεσσιν.
According to Page (1955: 35), *morphē* is a 'modern' term and 'an intruder upon
the Homeric vocabulary'. Cf. also Shipp (1972), 335; Goldhill (1991), 48.

[119] *Od.* 11. 366 ψεύδεά τ' ἀρτύνοντας, ὅθεν κέ τις οὐδὲ ἴδοιτο; *Il.* 18. 379 τά [sc.
οὔατα] ῥ' ἤρτυε, κόπτε δὲ δεσμούς.

[120] *Od.* 14. 131 αἶψά κε καὶ σύ, γεραιέ, ἔπος παρατεκτήναιο, with 14. 125; cf. *Il.*
5. 62 τεκτήνατο νῆας ἐΐσας.

[121] DK 22 B 28 καὶ μέντοι καὶ Δίκη καταλήψεται ψευδῶν τέκτονας καὶ μάρτυρας. See
further Ch. 6 below.

5

'Lies Resembling Truth'

Homer's Poetics and the Homeric Poems

In so far as the song is understood as a truthful account of events that really happened, and in so far as a catalogue-like sequence seems to be the form in which Homer conceived of a truthful account, any arrangement of events differing from the point-by-point sequence would be precluded in the 'poetics of truth'. At the same time, it is not difficult to discern that the *Iliad* and the *Odyssey* themselves can hardly be envisaged as forming the point-by-point narrative sequence presupposed by Homer's own poetics. Both compositional unity and narrative diversity, the two signal characteristics of the Homeric epics, would make it impossible to account for them in such terms.

The compositional unity of both the *Iliad* and the *Odyssey* emerges clearly from even a cursory survey of their plots. The *Iliad* begins *in medias res* and relates only one event of 'historical' significance—the death of the Trojan leader Hector at the hands of Achilles in the tenth year of the Trojan war. But it also absorbs within itself a vast quantity of material relating to the preceding stages of the war and to other personages of the Trojan saga. Why does such enlargement of the scope of the poem not interfere with the unity of its main plot? The answer lies in the effectiveness with which Homer exploits the motif of the hero's wrath, a typical motif emerging in other heroic traditions and in the *Iliad* itself, in the story of the wrath of Meleager related by Phoenix in book 9. Homer's use of the wrath motif allows him to postpone to the end of the poem the decisive intervention of Achilles that leads to Hector's death and, accordingly, to the solution of the plot; to introduce, as a result of this delay, many additional episodes enlarging the scope of the poem; and to account for Achilles' absence in books 2–8 and 12–15, in which these other episodes are introduced. Above all, however, the use of the wrath motif allows Homer to place in direct causal connection with Achilles' absence the heavy losses suffered by the Achaeans in most of the books which do not feature the poem's main hero. That this was a deliberate effect on the part of the poet is clear from the opening lines of the poem: 'Sing, goddess, the wrath of Achilles, son of Peleus, the ruinous wrath which brought uncounted anguish on the Achaeans and hurled down to Hades many mighty souls of heroes, making their bodies the prey to dogs and the birds' feasting.'[1] By subordinating the events described in the *Iliad* to the theme of the wrath, Homer turns these events, whether or not they are directly related to the main action, into an integral part of his poetic edifice.[2]

The organization of the subject-matter is not the only level on which the motif of Achilles' wrath acts as a unifying factor. The direct cause of the wrath is Achilles' quarrel with Agamemnon, which is described in book 1. Yet, although Achilles and Agamemnon are already reconciled by book 19, this does not put an end to the wrath. The death of Patroclus, the very event that brought Achilles to set aside his wrath against Agamemnon, channels this wrath, now more violent than ever, against Hector, Patroclus' slayer. Hector dies in book 22; but the *Iliad* does not end until his body has been ransomed by his father Priam in book 24. In order to appreciate correctly the structural function of the concluding book of the *Iliad*, we must turn again to the poem's opening words, in which the poet asks the Muse to sing of 'the ruinous wrath of Achilles', thus proclaiming the wrath of Achilles as the main theme of his poem. That is to say, it is not the 'historical' issue of Hector's death but the human issue of Achilles and his wrath that is after all the poet's main interest. Note now that Achilles is the only hero who is dealt with in the poem in terms of the development of character. The egocentric and wild youth of books 1, 9, and 16 begins to be transformed after the death of Patroclus, and already in book 18 he is represented as turning to a re-evaluation of his former behaviour. But only book 24 brings forth what Paul Mazon called 'the death of the Wrath', which means not only Achilles' reconciliation with Priam but first and

---

[1] *Il.* 1. 1–5.

[2] Cf. Kakridis (1949), 92: 'the *Iliad*, which weaves its material around a single motif governing the narrative from the beginning to the end, requires an uninterrupted view of the piece as a whole in order to be comprehended as a unit.' Cf. also Bethe (1914), 11–68; Schadewaldt (1966), 22–8.

foremost the essential humanization of his character. 'What we are told in the last book', Alfred Heubeck wrote, 'is no loose or inorganic appendage: without the description of the Lytra, the picture of Homer's hero would be incomplete; one could even go so far as to say that the portrayal of Achilles is aimed at this *telos* from the very beginning.'[3] In that it presents a mirror image of the birth of the wrath in book 1, book 24 superimposes upon the historical framework of the *Iliad* what can be justly defined as the first study of character in European literature, thus endowing the poem with a perfect structural harmony unparalleled in most traditional poetry.

In many respects, the arrangement of the material in the *Odyssey* is similar. The *Odyssey* too opens *in medias res*, only a short time before Odysseus' return home, and in the course of the development of its plot introduces episodes giving the poem a large-scale historical perspective. As in the *Iliad*, these episodes possess no independent status but are subordinated to the main plot. Thus, in books 3 and 4 the reminiscences of Nestor and Menelaus, which supply information on what happened to other Achaean heroes in the time between the fall of Troy and the beginning of the *Odyssey*, are inseparable from Telemachus' quest for his missing father, whereas the reminiscences of Odysseus himself in Books 9–12, in that they emerge in the course of the poet's description of Odysseus' sojourn in Phaeacia, are made part of the last year of his wanderings. The *Odyssey* also uses the traditional motif of the absent hero: as with the absence of Achilles in the *Iliad*, so also Odysseus' absence from Ithaca allows the poet to build his story around one central axis and to lead it to an extreme situation which is resolved at the last moment. All the strings of the plot lead to one central event entailing Odysseus' re-establishing himself in his kingdom and his own home—the killing of the suitors, described in book 22. This sort of arrangement allows the poet to preserve the unity of action in spite of the diversified and many-faceted plot of the *Odyssey*.

At the same time, the plot of the *Odyssey* is much more complex than that of the *Iliad*. Up to book 15, the poem develops simultaneously on two parallel planes. The bifurcation begins at the very beginning of book 1, when Zeus announces before the assembly of

---

[3] Heubeck (1978), 14; 'the death of the Wrath', Mazon (1943), 230.

the gods his decision to send Hermes to Ogygia and Athena to Ithaca. Up to the beginning of book 5, the story follows out the fulfilment of the second part of Zeus' decision: Athena arrives in Ithaca, and Telemachus, accepting her advice, embarks on his journey to Pylos and Sparta. While he is still being entertained by Menelaus at Sparta and the suitors are plotting against him at home, the story switches to Odysseus who is still with Calypso on Ogygia. In the second assembly of the gods, which opens book 5, Zeus repeats his decision to send Hermes to Ogygia, and this time we see this decision being executed. From now on, the separate story of Odysseus begins; yet the chronological sequence is broken once more by Odysseus' lavish reminiscences in books 9-12, which relate everything that happened to him from the fall of Troy to his arrival in Phaeacia. Only in book 15, after Odysseus has departed from Phaeacia and arrived safely in Ithaca, does the poet turn back to Telemachus, who is still in Sparta with Menelaus and Helen. Telemachus leaves Sparta and arrives in Ithaca; only at that point, in the cabin of Eumaeus the swineherd, do father and son meet, and the two strands of the plot eventually come together. It goes without saying that this, again, is not a narrative arrangement easily reconcilable with the 'point-by-point' sequence of events demanded of a truthful account.

Likewise, there is good reason to doubt whether the richly digressive style that is characteristic of the Homeric poems would answer the criterion of the 'point-by-point' narrative sequence demanded in the 'poetics of truth'. Both the *Iliad* and the *Odyssey* abound in extended descriptions, catalogues, similes, paradigms, reminiscences, and above all speeches, which are mainly responsible for the extraordinary length of both poems. Another kind of digression, one that contributes even more to the wide diversification of both epics, is the insertion of episodes which enlarge the scope of the poem by going beyond its main plot. The most salient examples are, of course, the complete abandoning of the main plot and the main hero in books 2-7 of the *Iliad* and the retrospective of Odysseus' wanderings in books 9-12 of the *Odyssey*. In that they only expand the story without changing its basic 'facts', all such episodes serve the same purpose as, say, the extended simile; but their distinctive characteristic is that they are interwoven with the main story, developing and enriching it with an effectiveness which could never have been achieved by means of similes.

It would be wrong to see in the digressive character of Homer's narrative a factor acting against the unity of his plots. As was demonstrated by Norman Austin in an important paper first published in 1966, both the length and the location of the Homeric digressions are directly related to the significance of the episode to which they belong: the more important the situation, the more expansive the digressions anticipating it.[4] Thus, the first encounter of the Achaean and Trojan armies in *Iliad* 3 is introduced in the second part of *Iliad* 2 by a series of five similes (455–83), an invocation of the Muses (484–93), and two extended catalogues (494–877); the importance of Patroclus' first intervention in the course of events, which is the turning-point in the poem's plot, is emphasized by an especially long reminiscence by Nestor (11. 642–805); the extended description of the shield of Achilles in *Iliad* 18 introduces Achilles' return to the battlefield and anticipates the central event of the *Iliad*, the duel with Hector, and so on.[5] Rather than interfering with the unity of the plot, all these digressions serve to emphasize the strategic points in the story and thus prove to be a functional part of Homeric composition.

The same would also be true of the inserted episodes. Take, for example, such major single combats of the *Iliad* as the Menelaus–Paris and Hector–Ajax duels, described in books 3 and 7. Two protagonists meet on the battlefield; in the subsequent fight one of them gains the upper hand, but at the last moment the death of the defeated hero is prevented, mainly thanks to divine intervention. Note that both duels could only be left unresolved: for, according to the saga, Hector will be killed by Achilles, Paris by Philoctetes, Ajax will commit suicide shortly before the capture of Troy, and Menelaus will return home safely.[6] It follows, then, that

[4] Austin (1966), 295–312.

[5] To claim, as Heath (1989: 120) does, that in the case of Nestor's reminiscence in *Iliad* 11 'Austin has exaggerated the urgency of the situation' is to lose one's way in the train of Homer's narrative. The significance of this episode for the poem's plot (emphasized by Homer himself in the phrase κακοῦ δ' ἄρα οἱ πέλεν ἀρχή at *Il.* 11. 604) has been correctly brought out in Edwards (1987b), 48: 'So we may conclude that the prolixity of Nestor in recounting nearly a hundred lines of his reminiscences at xi. 670–761, while the agitated Patroclus stands fidgeting miserably in the doorway, in an enormous hurry to get back to his demanding friend Achilles, is not intended to depict senile garrulity . . . but because he is leading up to the most important suggestion that Patroclus borrow Achilles' armour and lead the troops into the battle in his stead. The importance of his advice is conveyed by the expansions of the conversation.'

[6] Cf. Kirk (1978), 23.

by their very nature the unresolved duels are prevented from out-
weighing the main plot. This is obviously the reason why, in spite
of the huge amount of military activity described in the *Iliad*, the
poem contains only three major deaths, all connected with each
other and with the main action—Sarpedon is slain by Patroclus,
Patroclus by Hector, and Hector by Achilles. Or consider, for
example, the so-called 'almost' motif, consisting in the poet's introduction of an extreme situation leading to a decisive turn in the
course of events, such as the untimely end of the Trojan war or
the premature return of Odysseus; at the last moment, however,
the gods interfere to prevent what would have been at variance
with destiny or, for that matter, with the course of the poem's
plot.[7] In that they cannot develop into full-scale narratives com-
peting in interest and significance with the main narrative of the
poem, the inserted episodes remain subordinated to the main
action and to the unity of the plot. But by introducing such
episodes the poet is enabled to put all the protagonists into action,
to enlarge the scope of his narrative, and thus to raise it to the
scale of a monumental composition.

All this shows that the poems of Homer can be characterized as
complex unities in which each part possesses its own narrative
function subordinated to the purposes of the whole. It is exactly this
kind of tight functional organization that allows for the effective
development of the hierarchic compositional structure characteristic of a large-scale narrative. It is not only that the 'poetics of truth'
makes no provision for unities of this kind: suggesting as they do
artificial fashioning of the traditional material at their disposal, the
Homeric poems prove to be closer to Homer's concept of artefact
than to his concept of song. In view of this, it is not surprising that
some scholars, notably J. H. Myres and C. H. Whitman, have found
it possible to interpret the structure of the Homeric poems in terms
of artistic harmony, comparable to the harmony of geometric vase-
painting or the pediments of Greek temples.[8] Needless to say, this
harmony can hardly be interpreted as a kind of arrangement stipulated by the 'poetics of truth'.

But this is not to say that there were no traditional poems for

[7] This motif has been identified in Reinhardt (1961), 107-20. See also Fenik
(1968), 153-4, and (1978*b*), 80-1, and above, Ch. 3, pp. 80-1.

[8] Myres (1952), 11; Whitman (1958), 87 ff., 249. For recent bibliography and
critical discussion of this approach see Stanley (1993), 29-32.

which the 'poetics of truth' could effectively account. Hesiod's *Theogony*, for one, beginning as it does *ab ovo* and arranging its material along the lines of genealogical succession, is obviously such a poem,[9] and the same would be true of the poems of the Epic Cycle. There is, indeed, good reason to suppose that it was especially the latter that represented the kind of epic poetry for which 'poetics of truth' was appropriate. Judging by the evidence of Proclus' summary, the poems of the Epic Cycle consisted of a number of self-contained episodes arranged in plain chronological succession. The following passage from the *Cypria* will illustrate this point:

Next they sail as far as Tenedos: and while they are feasting, Philoctetes is bitten by a snake and is left behind in Lemnos because of the stench of his sore. Here, too, Achilles quarrels with Agamemnon because he is invited late. *Then* the Greeks tried to land at Ilium, but the Trojans prevent them, and Protesilaus is killed by Hector. Achilles *then* kills Cycnus, the son of Poseidon, and drives the Trojans back. The Greeks take up their dead and send envoys to the Trojans demanding the surrender of Helen and the treasure with her. The Trojans refusing, they assault the city, and *then* go out and lay waste the country and cities round about. *After this* Achilles, etc.[10]

As distinct from what we observed in the case of Homer, all the episodes of the *Cypria* are equal in status: they are simply juxtaposed to one another with nothing to unite them into a single narrative whole. Note in particular the lack of connection between the episodes of Protesilaus being killed by Hector and Cycnus being killed by Achilles, which follow each other directly. Although the two episodes are clearly represented as constituting two subsequent stages of the Greek landing in the Troad, it is obvious that no attempt was made by the poet to create even a superficial causal connection between them. That the author of the *Cypria* did not envisage his poem as delivering a single coherent plot is the natural conclusion from this situation. As is well known to every

[9] This does not mean that paratactic composition, including that employed by Hesiod in the *Theogony*, is devoid of sophisticated organizational techniques. However, these techniques differ from those of organic composition. On the techniques of paratactic composition in general see Notopoulos (1964), 46; on the specific methods of the arrangement of material in both the *Theogony* and the pseudo-Hesiodic *Catalogue of Women*, which belongs to the same genre, see West (1966), 37–9, and (1985), 46–50.

[10] Allen, v. 104. 21–105. 7, trans. H. G. Evelyn-White (my italics).

student of Homer, this is an attitude which would be inconceivable in the Homeric narrative.[11]

The essential difference between the narrative techniques of the Homeric epics, on the one hand, and the Cyclic epics, on the other, was paid due attention by Aristotle. In chapter 8 of the *Poetics* he praises Homer for the unity of the plot of his poems:

But Homer, as in all else he is of surpassing merit, here too—whether from art or natural genius—seems to have happily discerned the truth. In composing the *Odyssey* he did not include all the adventures of Odysseus—such as his wound on Parnassus, or his feigned madness at the mustering of the host—incidents between which there was no necessary or probable connection: but he made the *Odyssey*, and likewise the *Iliad*, to centre round an action that in our sense of the word is one.

And he further elaborates on this idea in chapter 23:

Here again, then, as has been already observed, the transcendent excellence of Homer is manifest. He never attempts to make the whole war of Troy the subject of his poem, though that war had a beginning and an end. It would have been too vast a theme, and not easily embraced in a single view. . . . As it is, he detaches a single portion, and admits as episodes many events from the general story of the war—such as the Catalogue of the ships and others—thus diversifying the poem. All other poets take a single hero, a single period, or an action single indeed, but with a multiplicity of parts. Thus did the author of the *Cypria* and of the *Little Iliad*. For this reason the *Iliad* and the *Odyssey* each furnish the subject of one tragedy, or, at most, of two; while the *Cypria* supplies materials for many, and the *Little Iliad* for eight. . . .[12]

It is not difficult to see that Aristotle's characterization of the Cyclic poems as recounting their subjects in a point-by-point succession supports our conclusion that these poems must have conformed to Homer's view of epic narrative as described in Chapter 4. This is not so in the case of the Homeric poems themselves, which Aristotle contrasts sharply with the poems of the Cycle. Not only does he interpret the Homeric poems as fully conforming to his own concept of organic unity, but he even cites

[11] Cf. e.g. Jaeger (1965), 51: 'Homer sees life as governed by universal laws; and for that reason he is a supreme artist in the craft of motivation. He does not passively accept tradition: he does not relate a simple succession of events. He presents a plot which develops by its own compulsion from stage to stage, governed by an unbreakable connexion of cause and effect.'

[12] *Poet.* 1451ᵃ23–30; 1459ᵃ30–ᵇ7.

them as normative examples of such organic unities. There is, then, good reason to infer that the Cyclic epics applied a narrative style which sharply differed from that of Homer in that it lacked both the diversification and the structural unity so characteristic of the Homeric poems. This allows us to suggest that, rather than simply reflecting a difference in artistic quality, the opposition between Homer and the Cycle was due to a typological distinction within Greek epic tradition itself.

South Slavic heroic poetry provides an example of another epic tradition explicable in terms of the 'poetics of truth'. 'There are some people', the Yugoslav singer Đemail Zogić says, 'who add and ornament a song and say: "This is the way it was", but it would be better, brother, if he were to sing as he heard it and as things happened' (sic). Another singer, Sulejman Makić, says: 'What's the good of adding things that didn't happen. One must sing what one has heard and exactly as it happened. . . .'[13] And even Avdo Međedović, whose distinctive style was characterized by lavish expansion, allowing for the composition of songs much longer than those of other Yugoslav singers, accounts for his art in similar terms. Thus, he holds a singer who does not ornament his songs very much to be just as good as himself, because 'his song would go straight along, smoothly and cleanly, so no one could say of it: "There's a bit of a lie in this one!" ', while on another occasion he reveals that he is, in fact, not even certain whether his own individual practice of rich ornamentation is 'good' or 'bad'.[14] Clearly, as J. B. Hainsworth put it, this is 'not aesthetic criticism'.[15]

The South Slavic evidence is important, because it comes from a living oral tradition. We can see, then, that although the 'poetics of truth' expounded by Homer cannot account for the practice of Homer himself, it effectively accounts not only for Hesiod and the Cycle but also for the practice of oral poetry.[16] On the whole, there is ample evidence to the effect that Homer's descriptions of poetic performances, invariably referring as they do to the practice of oral poetry, are not always compatible with our *Iliad* and *Odyssey*. Take, for example, Homer's view of the Trojan saga as a collection of

[13] Lord (1954), 239, 266. Cf. Finkelberg (1990), 295–6.
[14] Lord (1974), 71–2, 74.
[15] Hainsworth (1970), 96.
[16] Cf. Hainsworth (1970), 96. That the complex structural organization of the Homeric poems prevents them from being accounted for by 'oral poetics' has recently been argued in Stanley (1993), 268–79.

oimai, short lays, each featuring a single subject, which was discussed in Chapter 3. It goes without saying that this view, which again agrees well with the practice of the Cyclic epics, cannot account for monumental epics on the scale of the *Iliad* or the *Odyssey*. However, it is exactly such short lays, each of them comparable to one of the episodes in the Cyclic epics, that are performed by the *Odyssey* bards Phemius and Demodocus. That no trace of the form of the monumental epic is found in the references to poetry made by Homer himself indicates that this form was not stipulated by traditional poetics.

'Self-references in Archaic Greek poetry', Gregory Nagy writes, 'may be diachronically valid without being synchronically "true". For example, the epic poetry of Homer refers to epic poetry as a medium that was performed in the context of an evening's feast. And yet, we know that the two epic poems of Homer, by virtue of their sheer length alone, defy this context.'[17] According to J. Th. Kakridis, we should distinguish between the earlier 'chronographical' epic, which is represented by the poems of the Cycle, and the later 'dramatic' epic, of which the *Iliad* is the most prominent representative. The chronographical epic cannot be both long and united: '*It belongs to the nature of a long epic that it lacks the unity which we find in the Iliad*. Therefore the contention that the chronographical epic is a decadent and deteriorated form of the dramatic epic is fundamentally mistaken' (Kakridis' italics).[18] Homer's failure to make explicit the principles on which his own practice is based also suggests that this practice signified a radical break within Greek epic tradition. It is not out of the question, therefore, that what we have in the case of the Homeric tradition is a relatively late development within the epic tradition itself, a development which, probably as a result of the codification of the Homeric poems in the sixth century BC, simply had not had enough time to become fully aware of the new practice it was applying and to create an articulated poetics of its own.

As far as I can see, the conclusion that Homer's theory, even though it accounts for the practice of oral poetry, does not account for his own practice, may bear in more than one way on the much-vexed issue of the Homeric Question, especially in the form

---

[17] Nagy (1989), 6. Cf. Stanley (1993), 259.
[18] Kakridis (1949), 92. Cf. Bethe (1914), 12–13; Heubeck (1978), 13–17; Herington (1985), 135; Hainsworth (1991), 17, 24–8.

it acquired in this century after the emergence of the Parry–Lord formulaic theory.[19] Indeed, in the debate over whether the Homeric poems should be regarded as composed orally or in writing, the conclusion that, even though these poems refer to what can be called a highly developed oral poetics, the latter is not reflected in their own structure, may have considerable impact. For example, this conclusion could lead to the supposition that, although deeply rooted in the oral tradition, the Homeric poems themselves emerged in a written form; or to the revival of the hypothesis formulated by F. A. Wolf, the founder of the Analytic School, in his *Prolegomena ad Homerum* (1795), to the effect that, rather than being germane to epic tradition itself, the compositional unity of the *Iliad* and the *Odyssey* was due to the work of an editor, and so on. However, a more detailed discussion of this topic oversteps the scope of the present book. For our purpose, it is sufficient that Homer's references to poetry reflect a state of the epic different from that exemplified by his own poems.

Homer and the Epic Tradition

Whether or not the poems of the Epic Cycle as we know them historically preceded the Homeric epics, one thing is certain: both the *Iliad* and the *Odyssey* lean heavily upon the repertoire of Trojan subjects dealt with in the poems of the Cycle. The growing recognition of this fact has been one of the major achievements of the Neoanalytic trend in Homeric scholarship.[20] This does not mean that, as the pioneers of Neoanalysis sometimes suggested, the source of the Homeric poems should necessarily have been the Cyclic poems themselves: it is, indeed, not beyond the bounds of probability that both the Cyclic epics and Homer ultimately drew upon the common stock of traditional subjects concerning the Trojan war.[21] However this may be, there can be no doubt that the debt the Homeric poems owe to the tradition represented by the poems of the Cycle is considerable. This is immediately obvious in the case of the *Odyssey*.

[19] Cf. Stanley (1993), 248–96.
[20] The works most representative of the methods of Neoanalysis are Kakridis (1949) and Kullmann (1960); for comprehensive discussions in English see Kullmann (1984) and Edwards (1990); up-to-date assessment and bibliography can be found in Kullmann (1991).
[21] Cf. Kakridis (1949), 93; Edwards (1990), 311–25; Kullmann (1991), 427–8.

Characteristically, although the *Odyssey* evokes numerous episodes of the Trojan war, it never explicitly touches upon those dealt with in the *Iliad*. Like the subjects referred to by Homer as worth preserving in song (Chapter 3), all the topics recounted by the *Odyssey* singers and story-tellers are borrowed from the Cyclic tradition. In fact, two Trojan themes stand at the centre of *Odyssey* attention—the Fall of Troy, the subject of the Cyclic *Aethiopis*, *Ilias parva*, and *Iliu persis*, and the Returns, the subject of the Cyclic *Nosti*. The *Aethiopis* is evoked in the story about Achilles' funeral told by Agamemnon to Achilles in the Underworld in book 24; *Ilias parva* (the *Little Iliad*) in Odysseus' meeting with Ajax in the Underworld described by Odysseus in book 11 and in the story of Odysseus' entering Troy as a spy told by Helen in book 4; *Iliu persis* in the story of the Wooden Horse told by Menelaus to Telemachus in book 4 and by Odysseus to the ghost of Achilles in Book 11; this same story is also the subject of Demodocus' third song in book 8 of the poem.[22] The Returns are evoked in Nestor's reminiscences and his story of Agamemnon's death in book 3, in Menelaus' reminiscences in book 4, in Agamemnon's account of his own death in book 11 and, of course, in Odysseus' reminiscences embracing books 9-12 of the poem; this is also the subject of a song performed by Phemius in book 1.[23] As a result, the *Odyssey*, besides being a poem of the return of the last of the heroes, also acts as a large-scale compendium of the part of the Epic Cycle that deals with the final stages of the Trojan war and the fate of the survivors.

The way in which the *Iliad* deals with the Cyclic material is different. Note that many an episode from books 2-8 of the *Iliad*, which form a digression from the narrative succession of the story of the wrath of Achilles, is connected with the beginning of the Trojan war. Odysseus' reminiscence of the mustering of the troops at Aulis and the Catalogue of Ships in book 2; the Teichoscopia, the duel of Paris and Menelaus, and the Helen–Paris encounter in book 3; Agamemnon's inspection of the troops in book 4; the Trojan scenes in book 6; the negotiations about the return of Helen

[22] Achilles' funeral, *Od.* 24. 35-92, cf. Allen, v. 106. 9-16; Odysseus and Ajax, 11. 541-64, cf. Allen, v. 106. 20-3; Odysseus the spy, 4. 235-64, cf. Allen, v. 107. 4-7; the Wooden Horse, 4. 265-89, 11. 504-37, 8. 499-520, cf. Allen, v. 107. 16-21, 107. 27-108. 2.

[23] Nestor, *Od.* 3. 103-200, 253-312; Menelaus, 4. 351-585; Agamemnon, 11. 404-34; Phemius' song, 1. 325-7; cf. Allen, v. 108-9.

and the building of the Achaean wall in book 7—each of these episodes provides a retrospective of one of the initial stages of the war which must have been well known to the Homeric audience from traditional sources other than the *Iliad*. Although none of them is of direct relevance to the main theme of the *Iliad*, this does not necessarily mean, as the Analysts have more than once claimed, that these episodes do not constitute an integral part of the poem. Their function is to provide the *Iliad*, whose plot concerns only one episode in the tenth year of the war, with a general historical perspective and thus to turn it into what it is, a poem about the Trojan war as a whole.

The beginning of the war can be evoked in a direct reminiscence, as in Odysseus' recalling of the Aulis episode in *Iliad* 2. 284–332 or Antenor's reminiscence of the embassy of Odysseus and Menelaus to Troy in *Iliad* 3. 204–24, both told in the Cyclic *Cypria*.[24] This technique is largely paralleled in the opening books of the *Odyssey*, where the reminiscences of Nestor and of Menelaus, covering the period between the fall of Troy and the beginning of the *Odyssey* plot, fulfil the same function of supplying information about the initial stages of the Returns. But more often than not the *Iliad* adopts a subtler strategy, in that the episodes properly belonging to the beginning of the war are incorporated into the chronological and narrative setting of its last year and become an integral part of it. Thus, the seduction of Helen by Paris and Aphrodite in book 3, rather than being simply a reminiscence, provides, as it was aptly put by Mark Edwards, 'a reenactment of the original seduction', the proper context of which is the Cyclic *Cypria*.[25] In a similar way, the mustering of the troops described in book 2 or the negotiations about Helen and the building of the Achaean wall described in book 7, all incidents properly belonging to the beginning of the war but introduced so as to suit the context of its last year, can hardly be anything else than such 're-enactments' of the war's initial stages, again closely parallel to the *Cypria* account.[26]

In fact, what we have here is a narrative technique characteristic

---

[24] See Allen, v. 104. 1–3, 105. 3–5.

[25] Edwards (1987a), 196. Cf. Kullmann (1991), 434: 'Aphrodites Aufforderung an Helena, sich in die Kammer zu Paris zu begeben (Γ 383 ff.), ist sozusagen die symbolische Wiederholung der Zusammenführung mit ihm bei der Abfahrt von Sparta, so wie sie die *Kyprien*, sicher nach alter vorhomerischen Sagentradition, erzählten.' For the *Cypria* episode see Allen, v. 103. 2–10.

[26] Cf. Allen, v. 105. 3–5, 17–18.

of the *Iliad* as a whole, because in the second half of the poem the same strategy of 're-enactment' or, to borrow the expression used by Wolfgang Kullmann, 'imitation of a narrative known to us from one of the Cyclic epics', is employed.[27] There, this strategy is used to evoke the last stages of the war, which, again, are not described directly in the *Iliad*. Thus, although the lamentations of Thetis and the Nereids over Achilles in *Iliad* 18. 22–72 are prompted by the death of Patroclus, they evoke Thetis' bewailing of Achilles, described in the Cyclic *Aethiopis*: 'The Achaeans then bury Antilochus and lay out the body of Achilles, while Thetis, arriving with the Muses and her sisters, bewails her son. . . .'[28] Likewise, although the fall of Troy properly belongs with the events described in the Cyclic *Iliu persis*, the death of Hector is represented in *Iliad* 22 as if the city of Troy were already in flames:

So Hector's head was all sullied in the dust. And now his mother tore her hair, and flung the shining mantle away from her head, and raised a great wail when she saw her son. And his dear father groaned pitiably, and around them and all through the city the people were overcome with wailing and groans of lamentation. It was just like it would be if all of beetling Ilios were fired and smouldering from top to bottom.[29]

Above all, however, the 're-enactment' strategy would be true of the encounter between Patroclus and Sarpedon in book 16, the study of which served as a starting-point for Neoanalysis. As was noticed long ago, this episode directly evokes the Achilles–Memnon encounter as described in the Cyclic *Aethiopis*; accordingly, the issue of the relationship between the two epics has been the subject of lively discussion.[30] However this relationship be interpreted, we can be sure of one thing: although it begins *in medias res* and describes only one episode in the tenth year of the Trojan war, the *Iliad* simultaneously functions as an 'imitation' of the war as a whole—an imitation in which the episodes associated with the initial stages of the war are concentrated around the beginning of the poem and those associated with its final stages are concentrated around its end.

What the *Iliad* does for the Trojan war proper, the *Odyssey* does

---

[27] Kullmann (1984), 310.

[28] Allen, v. 106. 11–13; the episode is also evoked in *Od.* 24. 36–97.

[29] *Il.* 22. 405–11, cf. Allen, v. 108. 6–7.

[30] See further Kullmann (1981), 6–11, and (1991), 440–2 (with bibliography); cf. Edwards (1991), 15–19.

for the Returns. We have already pointed out that the reminiscences of Nestor and Menelaus in books 3 and 4 of the poem, in that they cover the period between the fall of Troy and the beginning of the *Odyssey*, essentially fulfil the same function as the episodes evoking the initial stages of the war in books 2–7 of the *Iliad*. The fates of the other survivors continue to loom large in the two Underworld scenes in books 11 and 24 of the *Odyssey*; above all, however, it is the fateful return of Agamemnon that acts in the *Odyssey* background as a mirror image of Odysseus' own successful return home. Thus, Orestes' avenging of his father's death is already set as an example for young Telemachus in book 1, whereas Clytaemnestra's perfidy is opposed to the constancy of Penelope up to the concluding book of the poem. All these supply the *Odyssey* narrative with a suggestive parallel running throughout the entire poem and acting as a counterpoise to its main plot.[31]

Note that by isolating the traditional episodes from their proper context and incorporating them into the story of Odysseus' return, which is after all only one traditional episode among many, Homer empties the episodes so employed of their original function in the saga, thus achieving an effect similar to that achieved in the *Iliad* by means of the strategy of 'imitation'. Yet, as distinct from the *Iliad*, the *Odyssey* poet accomplishes this by skilful organization of the traditional material at his disposal rather than by inventing new variations on already existing subjects. Why do the two Homeric poems differ in this respect? Examination of at least one subject which is generally believed to have been invented by the *Odyssey* poet may help to decide the issue.

The subject in question is supplied by the song of the quarrel between Odysseus and Achilles performed by Demodocus at the beginning of book 8 of the poem:

And when they had eaten and drunk their fill the Muse moved the bard to sing the deeds of heroes. He sang the lay whose fame then reached the broad heaven itself, the quarrel between Odysseus and Achilles, son of Peleus, how once at a sumptuous feast of the gods these two began to wrangle with violent words, and Agamemnon, king of men, rejoiced in secret that the noblest of the Achaeans had fallen out; because this was the sign that Phoebus Apollo had spoken of at his oracle in holy Pytho when the king crossed the stone threshold to ask his counsel; for then the

[31] Telemachus and Orestes, *Od.* 1. 293–302, 3. 301–16; Penelope and Clytaemnestra, 11. 405–34, 441–53, 24. 192–202.

first billow of calamity was rolling towards both Trojans and Danaans because of the counsel of great Zeus.[32]

The theme of Demodocus' song, a quarrel between Odysseus and Achilles, is neither attested to by any reliable tradition nor easily explicable from the internal standpoint of the epics. It is thus not surprising that, alongside attempts to discover the tradition to which it should be attributed, it has often been argued that the subject of Demodocus' first song was simply invented by Homer. Especially influential has been the hypothesis of W. Marg, according to which the quarrel between Odysseus and Achilles was created in order to generate an allusion to the quarrel between Achilles and Agamemnon in book 1 of the *Iliad*.[33] However, Marg's hypothesis, plausible though it is, fails to supply the motive for the invention. In addition to the Wooden Horse, the episode most frequently referred to in the *Odyssey* and sung of by Demodocus at the end of book 8 itself, the poem also touches upon other subjects featuring Odysseus, such as his entering Troy in disguise, his participation in the battle over Achilles' corpse, and his rivalry with Ajax. These are all well-known Trojan subjects, attested in the Epic Cycle. Thus one can argue for Homer's invention of the quarrel between Odysseus and Achilles only if one can provide a satisfactory answer to the following question: what made Homer invent a new subject instead of using one of the well-known Trojan episodes featuring Odysseus referred to elsewhere in the poem?[34]

Note that the subjects mentioned in the poem have one feature in common—they are all concerned with the final stages of the Trojan war. This is also true of the song of the Wooden Horse sung by Demodocus at Odysseus' invitation towards the end of book 8. Characteristically, the point at which the song stops is the arrival of Odysseus and Menelaus at the house of Deïphobus, where Helen

---

[32] *Od.* 8. 73-82.

[33] Marg (1956), 24-5, cf. Von der Mühll (1940), 718. 45-8. That the first song of Demodocus makes an allusion to the *Iliad* was accepted by Rüter (1969: 247-54) and, in a modified form, Nagy (1979: 15-65 and *passim*); both, however, reject the hypothesis that it was invented by Homer. Strauss Clay (1983: 105-6, 241-3), though accepting the hypothesis as a whole, does not agree with Marg's view that the invention was designed to create an allusion to the *Iliad*; Braswell (1982: 130 n. 5) argues that Homer invented the subject of the song in order to prepare the forthcoming quarrel between Odysseus and Euryalus the Phaeacian. Marg's hypothesis was totally rejected by Maehler (1963: 27 n. 1).

[34] Cf. Finkelberg (1987*b*), 128-32.

was found.[35] The song of the Wooden Horse as sung by Demodocus, implying as it does Helen's return to the Greeks, is thus a song about the end of the Trojan war. Significantly, Homer's description of the song of the Quarrel of Odysseus and Achilles ends with the following words: 'for then the first billow of calamity was rolling towards both Trojans and Danaans because of the counsel of great Zeus' (81–2). The relation between the two songs is therefore the relation between the beginning and the end of the Trojan war. That is, while the song by means of which Odysseus is recognized at the end of *Odyssey* 8 deals with the end of the Trojan war, the anticipation of this recognition at the beginning of *Odyssey* 8 is a song dealing with the war's beginning. *Odyssey* 8 thus presents on a miniature scale the same narrative pattern as that on which the monumental edifice of the *Iliad* is based.

While accounting for Homer's preferring this subject to better-known episodes of the Trojan war, the need for a subject featuring Odysseus at the beginning of the war does not necessarily entail invention on the part of the poet. The question is, of course, whether he had sufficient material at his disposal to fulfil the demands of his compositional technique. However, even the most cursory examination of the epic subjects featuring Odysseus at the beginning of the Trojan war reveals that this was not the case. The *Cypria* mentions only two episodes involving Odysseus—his pretending to be mad, in order to avoid joining the Trojan expedition, and the killing of Palamedes.[36] Clearly, neither of these subjects is appropriate to Odysseus 'the sacker of cities', whom the poet obviously intended to portray in Demodocus' songs. Hence, we can infer that it was the requirements of Homer's compositional technique and the lack of traditional material fit to meet these requirements that necessitated his invention of the subject of Demodocus' first song. Considering the striking resemblance between the first song of Demodocus and the quarrel of Agamemnon and Achilles in book 1 of the *Iliad*, there is nothing intrinsically improbable in the idea that the poet invented the subject of Demodocus' song as a deliberate imitation of the *Iliad*.

The case of Demodocus' first song seems to indicate that the poet turns to invention only when the traditional material at his dis-

---

[35] *Od.* 8. 517–20, cf. *Iliu persis*, Allen, v. 108. 1–2.
[36] Allen, v. 103. 25–7; 105. 15–16, fr. 21.

posal is inadequate for his purposes. Note that, as far as the rest
of the *Odyssey* is concerned, there was certainly no lack of
traditional subjects dealing with the Returns which could serve as
the background to Odysseus' story; hence, recourse to invention
would not be essential there. Not so, however, in the case of the
Iliad. It is indeed hard to imagine which Trojan subjects concerning the beginning of the war might fit into the context of its tenth
year wherein the *Iliad* itself is placed. Yet, introduction of such
subjects was demanded by the compositional requirements of the
poet, who, as we have seen, aimed at transforming an episode in
the tenth year of the war into a comprehensive picture of the war
as a whole. This is why, side by side with the reminiscences, the
poet of the *Iliad* also applies the technique of imitation of the
traditional subjects whose proper place is in the poems of the Cycle.
'Imitation' therefore can be defined as a narrative strategy designed
to answer specific requirements of Homeric composition and
characterized by the invention of new episodes modelled on the
traditional ones when no traditional episodes are available. As far
as I can see, this definition would be capable of accounting for the
practice of both the *Iliad* and the *Odyssey*. With this in view, let us
turn to what can count as Homer's own references to the practice
in question.

During Telemachus' visit to the palace of Menelaus in *Odyssey* 4,
Helen proposes to entertain the company by recounting 'plausible
things' (*eoikota*) about Odysseus.[37] Her subsequent story about
meeting Odysseus when the latter penetrated Troy disguised as
a beggar evokes an episode related in the Cyclic *Little Iliad*.[38]
Characteristically, Helen's words present a unique variation of the
formula 'to recount the truth/to recount point after point' discussed in Chapter 4 (pp. 126–9). Note that Helen's 'I shall recount
plausible things' is metrically equivalent to the formula 'I shall
recount the truth', and therefore redundant from the point of view
of formulaic economy.[39] That is to say, what we find in *Odyssey* 4
is the replacement of a traditional formula by a unique expression,
a practice not unparalleled in the epics. Generally speaking, there

[37] *Od.* 4. 235–9. Cf. Emlyn-Jones (1986), 1; Goldhill (1991), 62.
[38] *Od.* 4. 240–64; cf. Allen, v. 107. 4–7: 'Odysseus disfigures himself and goes
into Ilium as a spy, and there being recognized by Helen, plots with her for the
taking of the city; after killing certain of the Trojans, he returns to the ships.'
[39] ἐοικότα γὰρ καταλέξω as against ἀληθείην καταλέξω, both beginning with a
vowel, see Ch. 4 above.

are two ways in which such cases can be interpreted. When the unique expression does not differ in meaning from the traditional formula it has replaced, its emergence must have been due to the poet's failure to summon up the formula appropriate to the context; if, on the other hand, there is a significant difference in meaning between the traditional formula and the unique expression by which it has been replaced, the emergence of the latter must have been due to the poet's wish to express an idea not provided for by his tradition.[40]

As far as the verb *katalegein* ('to recount') evokes the point-by-point narrative succession demanded of a truthful account, its combination with the word *eoikota* ('plausible things') creates a sharp semantic incongruity: what the poet actually says is that what is being dealt with is a plausible story (*eoikota*) cast in the form of a truthful narrative (*katalegein*). In that respect, it comes close to the phrase 'he uttered many lies which resembled truth', applied by Homer to a lying story told by Odysseus to Penelope.[41] In fact, this is only one in a series of lying stories told by Odysseus in the second part of the poem. The following characterization by P. Walcot of a similar story told to Eumaeus in *Odyssey* 14 applies well to all of them: 'Examination shows that Odysseus' second lie is very much a mixture of fact and fiction, if the word "fact" is appropriate in a context where Odysseus appears to draw upon his experiences in making his way back to Ithaca in order to develop his lie'.[42] That is to say, although what Helen tells is an episode from the Trojan saga, the latter is understood as not differing in essence from the 'mixture of fact and fiction' contained in Odysseus' inventions.

At the same time, as R. B. Rutherford points out in his recent commentary on books 19 and 20 of the *Odyssey*, the Egyptian adventures of which Odysseus tells Eumaeus are in fact closer to the true story of Menelaus than to that of Odysseus himself. Rutherford also correctly emphasizes that Odysseus' lying stories

---

[40] See further Finkelberg (1988b), 206–11, and (1989), 192–7.

[41] *Od.* 19. 203 ἴσκε ψεύδεα πολλὰ λέγων ἐτύμοισιν ὁμοῖα.

[42] Walcot (1977), 12–13. See *Od.* 13. 256–86, 14. 191–359, 462–502, 17. 419–44, 19. 164–202. On Odysseus' lying stories as a mixture of fact and fiction see also Goldhill (1991), 37–47; Bowie (1993), 19–20; Pratt (1993), 55–94; on elements shared by most of them see Rutherford (1992), 71–3; on their difference from the true stories told by Odysseus see Emlyn-Jones (1986), 1–10, and Ch. 4 above.

with their notorious anachronisms can even be envisaged in a much broader perspective of the Greek colonizing period of the eighth and seventh centuries. 'The adventures described in book 14 could easily have happened to a Greek soldier of fortune, a mercenary enlisted by the kings of Egypt.'[43] Thus, these stories create a pattern which would apply not only to legendary characters such as Odysseus and Menelaus, but virtually to any traveller making his way along the shores of the Mediterranean in Homer's own time. This seems to indicate that, rather than simply implying the mixing of truth with lies, the expression 'lies resembling truth' stands for a form of narration which attained plausibility by representing typical rather than individual characters and situations.

Thus, the *Odyssey*'s replacing of the traditional expression 'to recount the truth' by the untraditional 'to recount plausible things' and the application of this expression to an episode of the Trojan saga, unique though it is in the Homeric epics, may be seen as a programmatic statement signalling a break with the traditional attitude to epic narrative and indicating that the new poetical practice applied in the Homeric tradition is beginning to rise to the poet's consciousness. By marking a Trojan episode as 'plausible' rather than 'truthful', and by introducing the expression 'lies resembling truth', the *Odyssey* gives legitimation not only to many an episode of the *Iliad* which was classed above as a 're-enactment' or 'imitation' of the original saga, and not only to the song resembling the beginning of the *Iliad* sung by Demodocus in the *Odyssey* itself, but also to Odysseus' replacement in his lying stories of the individual and specific by the typical and generic. Like the images on the Shield of Achilles, all these episodes are only 'similar' to their models without at the same time being reducible to them. Thus, the Homeric tradition, although overtly proclaiming that every utterance of the poet is true by virtue of its origin in divine inspiration, came to the threshold of acknowledging that what it supplied were plausible rather than truthful accounts. As we shall see, the reason for this development lies ultimately in the interpretation given in the Homeric tradition to the inherited idea of the poet's inspiration by the Muses.

[43] Rutherford (1992), 71.

More Strategic Possibilities

In a tradition which makes no provision for the poet's divine inspiration, the guarantee of the song's truthfulness would be the tradition itself. Thus, we have seen that to sing 'what one has heard and exactly as it happened' is the idea passing as a leitmotif through the Yugoslav poets' accounts of their art. Accordingly, in a tradition basing its claim to truthfulness on what the poet heard from his predecessors, the poet's free treatment of the material handed down to him by his tradition can well cast doubt on the veracity of his account: if he sings about things of which he did not hear from his predecessors, the natural conclusion will be that he has invented those things by himself. In Greek tradition, however, 'what happened' amounted not only to 'what the poets heard from their predecessors' but also to 'what the Muse tells to the poets'. Naturally, what the Muse tells to the poets can well be seen as identical to the tradition itself; in that case, the poets' treatment of the traditional material at their disposal would not differ essentially from poetic traditions which possess no concept of divine inspiration. This was obviously the case with Hesiod and the Cycle. At the same time, it is not difficult to see that the idea of the poet's inspiration by the Muse can offer an excellent justification for the poet's creative intervention. Thanks to this idea, each of the poet's innovations would naturally gain the status of divine truth by virtue of its origin in divine inspiration. This was the course taken by the Homeric tradition.

As we have seen, all Greek epic poetry recycled a limited repertoire of canonized subjects dealing with the Heroic age. Since these subjects were not only universally known but also accepted as historical truth, the poets were not at liberty to mould them in a free and independent way: the Trojan war will end with the Trojan rather than the Achaean defeat, Hector will be killed by Achilles and not vice versa, Odysseus will eventually return home, and so on. This is not to say that the poet was not authorized, if he wished, to introduce new subjects that would fit the main outlines of the saga, and to elaborate on the basic 'facts' of the latter without at the same time interfering with their essentials. This is where the role played by inspiration is crucial. As Greek tradition bases its claim to truthfulness on the poet's divine inspiration, the poet's adding to the traditional models at his disposal can well be envisaged, at least initially, not as distortion of the truth but, rather, as the natural effect of the poet's contact with the Muses, who provide him with additional information about events that happened in the past. It goes without saying that a poet who uses the inherited saga in such a manner will eventually transform the tradition into raw material for his poetry. That is to say, the last meeting of Hector and Andromache, formally a mere digression that was almost certainly created by the poet of our *Iliad*, becomes more interesting than the very action from which it was originally a digression. 'The singer who transformed a chronicle transformed it into what was essentially fiction, and fiction cannot be justified, or excused, by an appeal to what happened. Fiction must hold its audience by its intrinsic interest and the way it is presented.'[44]

One further step in the same direction, and we shall find the reality itself transformed into raw material for poetry. This step was taken twice by Homer. In *Iliad* 6, in the course of her meeting with Hector, Helen addresses him, *inter alia*, with the following words:

But come now, come in, brother, and sit here on this chair—since it is your mind more than any that the war's work besets, all for the sake of the bitch that I am and the blind folly of Alexander. On us two Zeus has set a doom of misery, so that in time to come we can be a song for men of future generations.

This avowal is echoed in *Odyssey* 8, in Alcinous' words to Odysseus in Phaeacia, when the latter weeps over hearing Demodocus' songs about himself:

And tell me too why you weep and lament thus bitterly when you hear told what things befell the Argive Danaans and Ilium. These things were the doing of the gods; they spun for mortals this thread of doom that there might be a song for generations hereafter.[45]

It is clear that the idea that the doom of those involved in the Trojan war was ultimately imposed by the gods only to supply a subject for song for future generations, implying as it does that the song has become more privileged than the events in which it originated, allows the work of poetry a degree of ontological independence not envisaged in the 'poetics of truth'.

[44] Hainsworth (1991), 26. Cf. Heubeck (1978).
[45] *Il.* 6. 354–8; *Od.* 8. 577–80.

This was as far as the Homeric tradition allowed itself to go. That going even further would not have been impossible can be seen from the example of the Sanskrit *Ramayana*. Although the poem's creator, Valmiki, is represented there as contemporary with his hero, the poem he composed embraces not only what had happened to Rama up to the point at which the poem starts but also the future unfolding of his story; moreover, this poem is interwoven in more than one way with the real events it is supposed to represent. In particular, Valmiki teaches his poem, which came to him through visionary insight, to Rama's two sons, and they eventually perform it before Rama himself. The *Ramayana* as the audience hears it is therefore identical to the poem's recitation before its protagonist. But this recitation also exerts its influence upon the hero's actual behaviour within the body of the poem: towards the end of the *Ramayana* and as a direct consequence to what has happened in it, Rama sends messengers to bring before him his wife Sita, who had been exiled to the forest because of false accusations against her purity. Sita proves her innocence and is swallowed by the Earth, her mother. The outburst of despair on Rama's part brings Brahma upon the scene, who delivers the following message:

Rama, Rama, do not grieve. Remember your former existence; remember your origin in Viṣṇu. Sita has reached the world of the serpents, but you will undoubtedly be reunited in heaven. You have heard this excellent poem, which will tell you everything—from your birth onwards, your joys and sorrows, and all that is still to be. Listen to the rest of it, all that regards the future. (trans. D. Shulman)

With dawn, the recitation resumes from the very point at which it stopped the day before, that is, from Sita's entering the Earth, and unfolds before Rama the subsequent events of his life up to the moment of his death. The result is a permeating interaction between the poem and the reality, on which David Shulman comments as follows:

In effect, the story itself, or the work of art that embodies it, has finally taken over and substituted its reality for the 'external' or 'objective' one within which the audience lives their usual lives. The story, that has held us, like its hero, captive for thousands of verses, in a lyrical universe of perfect form, ends by presenting an implicit ontology more powerful than our own.[46]

[46] Shulman (1991), 15.

Characteristically, in one of the late versions of the *Ramayana*, at the point when Rama tries to persuade Sita not to accompany him into the forest, Sita responds with the following words: 'Do you know a *Ramayana* in which Sita does not go after Rama into the forest?'[47]

As both Helen's and Alcinous' words show, there is certainly a point at which the Homeric poetic ontology and the ontology of the *Ramayana* would concur. At the same time, as distinct from their Sanskrit counterpart, the Greek epics as a rule do not overstep the conventions of representation expected from a plausible narrative.[48] It is true, of course, that Odysseus too listens to his own story performed by Demodocus in Phaeacia, and it is also true that the song exerts an influence on actual events, in that Odysseus' sorrowful reaction to it prompts his recognition by the Phaeacians, but this is about all. In Homer, the characters are never taken out of their stories, never discuss the narrative conventions of the latter, or command the knowledge of their entire plots: this would be the prerogative of the gods, of the poet himself and, last but not least, of the poet's audience.[49]

Thus, although in Greek tradition the idea of the poet's inspiration by the Muse was an inherited one, the form it acquired in Homer was due to the choice made by the Homeric tradition to the exclusion of the other epic traditions current in Archaic Greece. As distinct from Hesiod and the poets of the Epic Cycle, who preserved epic poetry in its traditional form, at some stage of its development the Homeric tradition departed from the mainstream of the epic tradition and began to offer its audience 'plausible' rather than 'truthful' narratives of past events. And although the Homeric poems never reached the heights of self-consciousness and artistic conventionality characteristic of the Sanskrit epic, there can be no doubt that Homer's transformation of the traditional saga into raw

[47] By personal communication from David Shulman.

[48] On Homer's illusionism see e.g. Hainsworth (1991), 29–30.

[49] The fact of overriding importance in everything concerning our correct understanding of the Greek audience's reaction to traditional subjects is that their point of view was not as a rule identical to the point of view of the characters. Rather, the point of view of the audience, acquainted with the plot of the traditional story and aware that its essentials could not be changed, was that of the poet himself. This distance between the audience and the characters created in the epic, and later in tragedy, the well-known phenomenon of tragic irony, to which Greek poetry owes some of its best effects. On Homer's strategies of foreshadowing and foreknowledge see Rutherford (1982), 152–8.

material for his poems endowed the latter with the status of metaepics.[50]

This is why it is important to recapitulate the features in which the Homeric tradition differed from the other epic traditions of Archaic Greece, and first and foremost from the tradition represented by the poems of the Epic Cycle. The characteristic features of the Homeric poems as discussed above are: the structural unity achieved by rearrangement of the traditional saga in accordance with the requirements of organic composition; the narrative diversity issuing from the extensive use of digressions subordinated to the main action; and the introduction of newly invented episodes made possible by extensive use of the strategy of 'imitation'. One additional characteristic of the Homeric narrative, which formally falls into the category of digressions, deserves special attention.

It is hard to judge from Proclus' summary and the handful of extant fragments to what degree, if any, the Cyclic poems were digressive. Yet, thanks to a piece of evidence supplied by Aristotle in the *Poetics*, we can be certain of at least one thing: the poems of the Epic Cycle contained very little speech. In continuing his discussion of epic poetry in *Poetics* 24, Aristotle writes:

Homer, admirable in all respects, has the special merit of being the only poet who rightly appreciates the part he should take himself. The poet should speak as little as possible in his own person, for it is not this that makes him an imitator (*mimētēs*). Other poets appear themselves upon the scene throughout, and imitate but little and rarely. Homer, after a few prefatory words, at once brings in a man, or woman, or other personage; none of them wanting in characteristic qualities, but each with a character of his own.

As Stephen Halliwell has pointed out, Aristotle's remark that poets other than Homer are very rarely engaged in mimesis can only refer to the composers of other epics, which indicates that the narratives of the latter contained practically no direct speech.[51] The

---

[50] Cf. Bowie (1993: 18), warning against uncritical application to the Homeric poems of the evidence offered by the South Slavic epic tradition: 'We should also take account of the fact that the poems we have must stand at the end of a tradition of which they themselves and their creator(s) cannot have been entirely typical. In many details of their handling of their story and characters, both the *Iliad* and the *Odyssey* are very self-conscious poems; and some awareness of the processes that created them should not be denied to their poet merely on analogy with other cultures.' Cf. Goldhill (1991), 49.

[51] *Poet.* 1460[a]5–11; Halliwell (1986), 126. A similar observation concerning the

extant fragments of the poems of the Epic Cycle corroborate this inference. Take for example the following passage from the *Little Iliad*:

Then the bright son of bold Achilles led the wife of Hector to the hollow ships; but her son he snatched from the bosom of his rich-haired nurse and seized him by the foot and cast him from a tower. So when he had fallen bloody death and hard fate seized on Astyanax. And Neoptolemus chose out Andromache, Hector's well-girded wife, and the chiefs of all the Achaeans gave her to him to hold requiting him with a welcome prize.

J. B. Hainsworth's comment on these lines supplies an excellent example of the reaction of a reader who is accustomed to the pathos and lavishness of the Homeric diction: 'Could not Neoptolemus speak, one wonders. Had Andromache no feelings? Had the poet no feelings?'.[52] Nothing, indeed, could provide a sharper contrast to Homer, in whose poems speeches constitute about two thirds of the entire text and serve as the main means of characterization. Accordingly, the performance of these poems must have involved a high degree of impersonation. This point was especially stressed by J. Herington:

In delivering all such speeches the rhapsode . . . must have become to some extent an impersonator, distinguishing at least between the tones, pitches, and tempos appropriate to the various speakers. And to this day, as a matter of practical experience, anyone who sets himself seriously to declaim a Homeric episode—for instance, the debate in the Greek camp near the opening of the *Iliad*—will be led almost without noticing it into acting out the very different voices and emotions of Agamemnon, Achilles, and Nestor; Homeric verse is built that way.[53]

Later, it will be precisely this characteristic of the Homeric epics that will come to the fore in the theory of mimesis developed by Plato and Aristotle.

As in the case of the later conflict between Plato and the Sophists discussed in Chapter 1, what is 'plausible' for Homer would be 'false' in the eyes of Hesiod and his school. Indeed, the narrative principles on which our *Iliad* and *Odyssey* are based would fit in perfectly well with the concept of false narrative found in Hesiod,

respective proportions of direct speech in Homer and Hesiod was made in Kannicht (1980), 20.

[52] *Ilias parva*, fr. 19. 1–8 Allen, trans. H. G. Evelyn-White; Hainsworth (1970), 97. Cf. also Griffin (1977), 51–2.

[53] Herington (1985), 52.

whose Muses know how to tell not only the truth but also plausible lies: 'We know to tell many lies which resemble truth, but we know to utter true things when we will.'[54] Considering that, as we saw above, the poetry of Hesiod himself was certainly within the limits of the traditional 'poetics of truth', it is difficult not to agree with the *communis opinio* which sees in Hesiod's description of the Muses who know how to tell 'many lies resembling truth' a deliberate criticism of the Homeric school.[55] And although M. L. West is certainly right to claim that 'no Greek ever regarded the Homeric epics as substantially fiction', this general truth is not enough to disprove the view that the alternatives articulated by Hesiod's Muses would correctly account for Hesiod's attitude towards the difference between his own poetry and the kind of poetry produced in the Homeric tradition.[56] Indeed, we have seen that, when tested against the more rigid standards of truth accepted in the school of Hesiod, the Homeric epics can only be recognized as presenting that very combination of 'truth' (that is, the authentic tradition) and 'falsehood' (that is, the poet's plausible inventions along the lines of this tradition) of which the formula 'lies resembling truth' would be an appropriate definition.

In any case, to claim, as some scholars do, that the adoption of both alternatives would properly describe Hesiod's actual practice is in my opinion to misinterpret the message of the Hesiodic lines: since the Muses tell the truth only when they are willing to do this, they would deliver lies only to those to whom they grudge to tell the truth; it follows that it is only on their favourites, such as Hesiod himself, that they would bestow truth about the past.[57] It

---

[54] *Th.* 27-8 ἴδμεν ψεύδεα πολλὰ λέγειν ἐτύμοισιν ὁμοῖα | ἴδμεν δ', εὖτ' ἐθέλωμεν, ἀληθέα γηρύσασθαι.

[55] See e.g. Sikes (1931), 5-6; Latte (1946), 159; Verdenius (1972), 234; Puelma (1989), 74-9, *et al.*

[56] West (1966), 162. It is worth noting in this connection that even if the alternative to his own poetry that Hesiod was thinking of was indeed the kind of poetry produced in the Homeric tradition, this still does not mean that it was necessarily the *Iliad* and the *Odyssey* as we know them that he had in mind.

[57] For a similar interpretation of the Muses' speech as 'Akt des Ausschlusses derer, die eine Offenbarung nicht verdienen' see Rösler (1980), 296-7. After having entertained the possibility that both the 'truth' and the 'lie' of the Muses' speech are meant to relate to Hesiod's own poetry, Pratt (1993: 112) asks a rhetorical question which in my opinion makes it self-evident why the approach she adopts is untenable: 'At the beginning of what would seem to be a very serious religious poem about the nature of the universe, how can Hesiod suggest that his account also contains certain elements of fiction?' For earlier examples of this kind of approach see Stroh (1976), 85-112; Belfiore (1985), 47-57; Heath (1985), 258.

would, of course, be quite another matter if Hesiod's Muses' claim
implied that a recognition of poetic fictionality was traditionally
consistent with the idea of inspiration by the Muses.[58] But such an
interpretation of Hesiod's lines is precluded by the Muses' essential
function as eyewitnesses who supply the poet and through him the
community as a whole with firsthand information about past
events. We saw above that this function of heroic poetry was taken
with the utmost seriousness in Archaic Greece and other traditional societies; we also saw that it was consistent with the Archaic
Greek idea of knowledge as the accumulation of information
(Ch. 3, pp. 71-3, 97-8). If we take into account that the traditional language of epic poetry actually possessed no means of
expressing the idea that poetry may contain lies (Ch. 4, pp.
129-30), the conclusion that follows is that such lies could only
be regarded as a gross deviation from the norm. Of course, it is in
the Muses' power to make a poet fail, but this could hardly be
regarded as their regular practice—otherwise, this would have
made meaningless the very institution of poetry and, accordingly,
the Muses themselves.[59] All this seems to indicate that Hesiod's
introduction of the lying Muses was sharply at variance with what
was traditionally seen as the goddesses' function.

Characteristically, the first part of the Muses' claim, 'we know to
tell many lies which resemble truth', is cast in the same words as
Homer's description of Odysseus' lies to Penelope (cf. n. 41 above).
That is to say, by the time of Hesiod the idea of 'plausible lies'—
the very idea which, though accounting for the practice widely
applied in the *Iliad*, was never explicitly expressed in that poem and
was still innovatory enough for the poet of the *Odyssey* to make
him break up a traditional formula in order that this idea might be
expressed—had acquired the status of a standard expression. After
Hesiod, the expression was taken over, with the characteristic
introduction of *eoikota* instead of the Homeric and Hesiodic *homoia*,
by Xenophanes; Parmenides too uses the word *eoikota* for the

---

[58] See Kannicht (1980), 13-16, 19-21; Bowie (1993), 21-2.

[59] Moreover, there is no reason to suppose that in Greek tradition the punishment imposed by the Muses would have amounted to their inspiring the poet with
lying tales. The only traditional story of such a punishment, that of Thamyris the
Thracian, consisted in the bard's total loss of both the poetic gift and the technical
competence he had formerly possessed: 'they took from him the inspired song and
made him forget the playing of the lyre' (*Il.* 2. 599-600 αὐτὰρ ἀοιδὴν | θεσπεσίην
ἀφέλοντο καὶ ἐκλέλαθον κιθαριστύν). Even Apollo's punishment of Cassandra concerns
not the truthfulness of her prophecies but others' belief in their truthfulness.

description of his own cosmogonical narrative in the part of his poem that deals with the Opinion, whereas Plato takes for granted the form of story-telling (*muthologiai*) in which, 'owing to our ignorance of the truth about antiquity, we liken the false to the true as far as we may and so make it edifying'.[60]

Hesiod's juxtaposition of the Muses' ability to tell the truth with their ability to tell plausible lies amounted to a recognition of the fact that in the epic poetry of his time two alternatives existed: to relate 'truthful', i.e. traditional, stories arranged in the 'point-by-point' narrative succession, or to produce 'plausible' variations on traditional subjects arranged in spatial and periodic rather than temporal and paratactic order.[61] It goes without saying that these are the same alternatives that centuries later were to be distinguished by Aristotle in his juxtaposition of the poems of the Epic Cycle with the poems of Homer. In the sixth century BC, the Homeric poems were codified in Pisistratean Athens for recitation at the highly prestigious Panathenaic festival. This was probably the reason why it was this form of epic poetry rather than the one represented in Hesiod and the Epic Cycle that became canonized in the Classical age and thus gave an impulse to additional developments in both the theory and practice of poetry.

At the same time, it is not difficult to see that this was canonization of a text whose status was more than problematic. It is not only that the Homeric epics overtly professed a view of poetry which they themselves had already ceased to represent. Even more difficult is the fact that, in spite of what Homer himself says about poetry, the kind of epic poetry created in the Homeric tradition could no longer be consistently accounted for in terms of divine inspiration. The Hesiodic idiom of the lying Muses gives the clearest expression of this difficulty. Characteristically, Hesiod does

---

[60] Xenoph. DK 21 B 35 ταῦτα δεδοξάσθω μὲν ἐοικότα τοῖς ἐτύμοισι, cf. Cornford (1937), 30 and n. 2; Parm. DK 28 B 8 60 τόν σοι ἐγὼ διάκοσμον ἐοικότα πάντα φατίζω; Pl. *Rep.* 382d διὰ τὸ μὴ εἰδέναι ὅπῃ τἀληθὲς ἔχει περὶ τῶν παλαιῶν, ἀφομοιοῦντες τῷ ἀληθεῖ τὸ ψεῦδος ὅτι μάλιστα, οὕτω χρήσιμον ποιοῦμεν. Cf. Plut. *Mor.* 16 B–C: 'But, just as in pictures, colour is more stimulating than line-drawing because it is life-like, and creates an illusion (ἀπατηλόν), so in poetry falsehood combined with plausibility (μεμιγμένον πιθανότητι ψεῦδος) is more striking, and gives more satisfaction, than the work which is elaborate in metre and diction, but devoid of myth and fiction (ἀμύθου καὶ ἀπλάστου περὶ μέτρον κατασκευῆς).' Cf. also ibid. 25 B–C.

[61] Cf. Bowie (1993), 21: 'Hesiod is referring to two types of poetry, each in their own terms legitimate. These are heroic narrative epic like Homer's, which offers *etumoisin homoia*, and philosophical poetry like Hesiod's own.'

not admit that the poets themselves can tell lies. The reason is clear: put as simply as possible, this would have amounted to the acknowledgement that there can be poetry which does not originate in divine inspiration. This is why, for Hesiod, whether the poets' accounts are truthful or false, it is nevertheless the Muse who is to be held responsible for these accounts. Thus, paradoxically, Hesiod's conservatism, which caused him to try to preserve at any cost the belief in the poet's divine inspiration, resulted in the extremely unorthodox concept that the Muses were capable of lying.

Obviously, this situation could not last. As Plato put it, 'there is nothing of the lying poet in God'.[62] It is characteristic in this connection that Parmenides, whose goddess is similar to Hesiod's Muses in that she can produce both a truthful and a plausible account, unequivocally ascribes the latter to mortal opinion rather than to herself.[63] In a similar vein, Stesichorus and Pindar, both known for their free handling of traditional subjects, prefer to speak in terms of a collaboration between the Muses and the poet rather than simply ascribing to the goddesses, as a traditional poet would have done, everything they composed (see Ch. 6, p. 171). Emergence of the popular maxim 'the poets lie a lot', generally ascribed to Solon, was no more than the natural outcome of the process which began with the lying Muses of Hesiod.[64] As soon indeed as it was recognized that poetry can tell lies, it was inevitable that eventually it was the poets themselves rather than the Muses who would be held responsible for the lies in their poems. This development, however, lies beyond the scope of both Homer and Hesiod.

[62] *Rep.* 382d9 ποιητὴς μὲν ἄρα ψευδὴς ἐν θεῷ οὐκ ἔνι. Although on the whole I find the interpretation of *Th.* 26–7 proposed in Belfiore (1985: 47–57) untenable (see n. 57 above), I think it plausible that, as she suggests, both in this phrase and in the entire discussion concluding *Republic* 2 it was Hesiod whom Plato specifically had in mind.

[63] DK 28 B 8 60 τόν σοι ἐγὼ διάκοσμον ἐοικότα πάντα φατίζω, as against ibid. 51–2, by which the entire account is introduced: δόξας δ' ἀπὸ τοῦδε βροτείας | μάνθανε κόσμον ἐμῶν ἐπέων ἀπατηλὸν ἀκούων. Cf. Cornford (1937), 30 and n. 1.

[64] Solon 29 West πολλὰ ψεύδονται ἀοιδοί. Cf. West (1966), 162.

6
Towards Fiction

From Hesiod to Pindar

Generally speaking, it is doubtful whether the traditional idiom of
the Muses as attested in Homer and Hesiod can be fully applicable
to the sort of poetry which flourished in the seventh and sixth
centuries BC and which is conventionally labelled as 'lyric'. We saw
that the Muses of the epic tradition were essentially eyewitnesses of
past events, who transferred their knowledge of these events to the
poet and thus guaranteed the truthfulness of his account. Now in
so far as most Greek 'lyric' poetry, both sung and recited, was,
perhaps with the exception of Stesichorus', presumably first person
poetry dealing with the here and now rather than the historical
past, we may well wonder for what particular purpose the 'lyric'
poets would have needed the Muses' help at all. Examination of the
Muses' role in each separate genre of 'lyric' poetry gives us the
answer.

That poetry delivering individual messages needs no recourse
to the Muses' authority is immediately clear in the case of the
monody and the iambus. No invocations of the Muse are found
either in the extant lyrics of Alcaeus and Anacreon or in the iambic
poems of Archilochus, Semonides, and Hipponax. It is true that
several addresses to the Muses and Charites do appear among the
papyrus finds of Sappho's poetry; their fragmentary nature makes
it impossible for us to know their contexts, but it is reasonable to
assume that they are not requests for information (see below).[1] If
we take into account that invocations of the Muse seem to be indispensable even for shorter epic poems such as the Homeric hymns,
this would allow us to conclude that what is dealt with in the

---

[1] Sappho 124 PLF, αὐτὰ δὲ σὺ Καλλίοπα; 127 δεῦρο δηὖτε Μοῖσαι χρύσιον
λίποισαι . . .; 128 δεῦτέ νυν ἄβραι Χάριτες καλλίκομοί τε Μοῖσαι, cf. 103. 8 ἄγναι
Χάριτες Πιέριδε[ς τε] Μοῖ[σαι.

monody and the iambus is a kind of poetry whose status is construed differently from that of the epic.[2]

The case of elegy seems more pertinent. It is true, of course, that Solon, although evoking the Muses at the beginning of one of his moralistic elegies, transforms the traditional invocation into a prayer to the goddesses to give him happiness and good fame,[3] and that no invocations of the Muse are found in the extant elegies of Callinus, Tyrtaeus, or Theognis. Yet, invocations of the Muses concerning the content of the poem do occur in elegy. In conformity with the epic practice, this only concerns the occasions on which the poet finds himself engaged in evoking past events, whether traditional or historical. Thus, Mimnermus turns to the Muses in order to tell of the battle between the defenders of Smyrna and the Lydian host of Gyges, an event of recent history but already beyond living memory, whereas Simonides, in a poem cast in elegiac distichs, asks the Muse's help in relating the story of Heracles.[4]

The practice of the choral lyric is even more relevant. Thus, Alcman introduces the primeval Muses, the daughters of Uranos and Gaia, to deliver a piece of theogony; Stesichorus twice invokes the Muse in order to establish an unorthodox version of Helen's story on her authority, while Ibycus, in an obvious imitation of the Homeric Catalogue of Ships, asks the Muses to tell him of the number of the Achaean ships mustered at Aulis.[5] Choral poetry, however, goes even further than this. More often than connecting their invocations with the content of their songs, the choral poets would rather ask the Muse to 'start' their songs for them. Thus, Alcman asks the 'clear-voiced' Muse to start singing a 'new tune' or 'lovely words'; another choral poet, who could be Stesichorus,

---

[2] See *H. Herm.* 1; *H. Aphr.* 1; *Hymn. Hom.* 9. 1; 14. 2; 17. 1; 19. 1; 20. 1; 31. 1; 32. 1; 33. 1. On narrative elements in monody and iambus see Bowie (1993), 30–5.

[3] Sol. 13. 1–6 West.

[4] Mimn. 13 West; Simon. 17. 1, 2 West. Cf. Bowie (1993), 6–7. It is likely that the new papyrus fragment of an elegiac poem probably by Simonides ('the New Simonides') contained an invocation of the Muse which was placed at the point of transition from the mythological to the historical narrative, dealing with the Persian Wars, see P. J. Parsons in *Oxyrynchus Papyri*, lix (1992), 32. Parsons bases his reconstruction on the model of transition found in the concluding lines of Homeric Hymns. If this parallel is correct (as it seems to be), then Simonides' invocation should, as is invariably the case with the hymns, have addressed the goddess as a stimulus for a new beginning (see below) rather than as a source of information.

[5] Alcm. 5. 25–30; Stesich. 193. 8–11; Ibyc. 282. 23–31 *PMG*.

asks the 'clear-voiced' Muse to start 'lovely hymns of song', and Pindar addresses the same request to his Muse.[6] The similarity of locution, especially between Alcman and 'Stesichorus', suggests that this was probably the standard form of invocation adopted in the choral tradition.

As we saw in Chapter 2, the *Odyssey* evidence shows that the practice of asking the Muse to begin the poet's song was far from being unknown to Homer. But in Homer this was only a subsidiary form of invocation, supplementing the main one, which invariably concerned the content of the epic narrative. What is subsidiary in epic comes to the fore in choral poetry. After quoting an invocation made by Alcman, the orator Aristides paraphrases the poet's words as to the reason for his addressing the Muse: 'He also adds this, that the poet needs the Muse herself at the beginning, in order that he should be made active (*energos*) by her.'[7] It can be suggested in view of this that addresses to the Muses and Charites found among fragments of Sappho's poems (n. 1 above) were meant to serve the same purpose.

Receiving a stimulus from the Muse is thus an additional form of divine inspiration which choral poetry shares with epic. Since we have seen that an invocation concerning the content of the song can also be employed in this genre, it seems reasonable to conclude that, although the emphasis as regards the constituents of the Muses' idiom is placed differently in epic and choral poetry, both proceed from the traditional idea of divine inspiration whose essentials are taken for granted in both genres. Choral poetry thus supplies a full parallel to the idiom of the Muses as we know it from Homer and Hesiod. If we take into account that elegy too has proved quite capable of making use of the Muses as eyewitnesses of past events, this will give us a solid basis for comparison between these two genres, on the one hand, and the genre of epic poetry, on the other.

Our analysis of Homer provides us with criteria for discerning what may count as significant changes in the Greek attitude to poetry, even when these changes were not realized in full by the

---

[6] Alcm. 14 PMG, Μῶσ' ἄγε Μῶσα λίγηα πολυμμελὲς | αἰὲν ἀοιδὲ μέλος | νεοχμὸν ἄρχε παρσένοις ἀείδην, 27 Μῶσ' ἄγε . . . ἄρχ' ἐρατῶν Ϝεπέων, cf. 30; [Stesich.] 278 ἄγε Μοῦσα λίγει' ἄρξον ἀοιδᾶς †ἐρατῶν ὕμνους† | Σαμίων περὶ παίδων ἐρατᾷ φθεγγομένα λύρᾳ; Pind. *Nem.* 3. 10–11 ἄρχε δ', οὐρανοῦ πολυνεφέλα κρέοντι θύγατερ, | δόκιμον ὕμνον.

[7] Alcm. 30 PMG.

poets themselves. Such criteria are found in the semantic oppositions that we have established above for Homer, between 'responsibility' and 'non-responsibility', 'knowledge' and 'ignorance',
'teaching' and 'giving'. The ways in which these oppositions
were employed after Homer may well serve as an indication of
deviations, conscious or unconscious, from the traditional idiom.
Consider now the following. As early as the seventh century BC,
Archilochus says in one of his elegies that he is 'expert' (*epistamenos*) in the gift of the Muses, a statement which, as W. Marg
aptly remarked, deprives Homer's invocation of the Muses of its
traditional content, whereas Archilochus' younger contemporary
Alcman proclaims that he 'invented' the words and tune of his
song.[8] Among the sixth-century poets, Solon gives a characterization of the poet as one who has 'learned' the 'gift of the Muses'
and is 'expert' (*epistamenos*) in the 'metre of the delightful skill
(*sophiē*)'; the Muses of Ibycus are 'perfectly skilled' (*sesophismenai*),
while Theognis is himself 'skilled' (*sophizomenos*) and refers to the
poet as one who possesses 'some excellent knowledge of skill
(*sophiē*).'[9]

Now, if the traditional idiom as found in both Homer and Hesiod
presupposed that the poet does not believe he is individually
responsible for his poetry *qua* poetry, that is, for the 'song' (*aoidē*)
given to him by the Muses, and if, in both Homer and Hesiod, this
song was systematically opposed to skill, teaching, and knowledge,
then the acknowledgement of the poet as responsible for his
activity as found in the choral and elegiac poets and the treatment
of this activity in terms of skill, teaching, and knowledge, can only
mean that the traditional attitude to poetry began to change. True,
to the extent that the traditional idiom was not challenged in a
conscious way, there was no compelling reason for it to be
abandoned: thus, we have seen that the Homeric poems still preserved in full the traditional poetics which they had abandoned in
practice. This is why the Muses continued to be formally invoked
long after Homer.[10] But the erosion of the Muses' idiom is reflected
in combinations, impossible from the standpoint of epic, of terms of
responsibility and appeal to the Muses' authority which are applied

---

[8] Archil. 1. 2 West; Marg (1938), 63. Alcm. 39. 1–2 *PMG*.

[9] Sol. 13. 51–2 West; Ibyc. 282. 23 *PMG*; Thgn. 769–70 West. On *sophiē* as
'skill' see above, Ch. 4.

[10] That the Muses were already 'dead' soon after Homer, in spite of what we
have become accustomed to believe, is argued in Häussler (1973), 117–45.

to the same activity. The ambivalent approach to poetry of the fifth century BC can be discerned here in *statu nascendi*.

Among the choral poets it was, above all, in Pindar that the conflict between the two attitudes towards poetry found both its clearest expression and even some sort of theoretical foundation. On the one hand, Pindar saw himself as a professional (*sophos*), competent in poetic skill (*sophia*) and fully responsible for his work;[11] on the other, he tried to fill the traditional idiom of the Muses with new content by calling himself a 'prophet' of the Muses.[12] In view of this, it is hard to agree with those scholars who conclude, on the basis of this evidence, that Pindar's attitude indicates that his view of poetry was well balanced.[13] It would have been well balanced if professional skill and inspiration by the Muses had, as in Homer, concerned different sides of his activity. But, as is best shown by his 'paradoxical' (to use Verdenius's word) prayer to the Muses, 'grant me an abundant flow of song welling from my own thought', they are not.[14] According to C. M. Bowra, 'Pindar stood midway between two extremes, both of which were familiar in Greece': the belief in the poet's divine inspiration and the view that 'poetry is just a τέχνη to be mastered, like other crafts, by instruction and study'.[15] With Pindar, however, we are already in the fifth century BC.

A piece of evidence supplied by an epic poet unambiguously indicates that the post-Homeric tendency to treat poetry in terms of knowledge can be regarded as relevant to the post-Homeric epic as well. A fragment of the *Persika* by the fifth-century epic poet Choerilus of Samos testifies to the effect that, as distinct from the normal epic practice, there was no formal invocation of the Muse in the first line of the poem; that the poet referred to his narrative as *logos*, ('speech'), rather than as *aoidē*; and that he called himself, in full accordance with the practice of the lyric poets, 'servant of the Muses, expert in song'.[16] Attempts to account

[11] Cf. e.g. *Ol.* 1. 9, 11. 10; *Pyth.* 6. 49, *Pae.* 7b. 15. See Gundert (1935), 38 f., 46 ff., 50 ff., 91 ff.; Bowra (1964), 4-8.

[12] See e.g. *Ol.* 3. 4 νεοσίγαλον εὑρόντι τρόπον as against *Pae.* 6. 6 ἀοίδιμον Πιερίδων προφάταν; cf. also fr. 150 Snell-Maehler, and Bacchy. 9. 3.

[13] Tigerstedt (1970), 175; Murray (1981), 97 ff.

[14] *Nem.* 3. 9 τᾶς ἀφθονίαν ὅπαζε μήτιος ἁμᾶς ἄπο, trans. E. R. Dodds. Verdenius (1983), 42. Cf. also *Ol.* 7. 7-8, where the same song is characterized simultaneously as the 'gift of the Muses' (Μουσᾶν δόσιν) and the 'sweet fruit' of the poet's own mind (γλυκὺν καρπὸν φρενός).　　　　　　　　　　　　　　[15] Bowra (1964), 13.

[16] Fr. la Kinkel ἴδρις ἀοιδῆς Μουσάων θεράπων.

for the peculiarity of Choerilus' expression by arguing that the events he relates were historical rather than mythological seem unwarranted to me.[17] What is termed mythological today was seen by the Greeks as history, and the Trojan war was no less historical in their eyes than the Persian wars described by Choerilus. We have seen that Mimnermus, whose distance from the war of Smyrna against Gyges was approximately the same as that between Choerilus and the Persian wars, nevertheless invoked the Muses in order to sing of this recent historical event. Of course, Mimnermus was altogether traditional in this respect: where a human witness cannot be supplied, the Muses are just as well qualified to sing of events of the recent as well as of the remote past. If, then, it was not the subject-matter of Choerilus' epic that prompted his untraditional attitude, we have reason to conclude that the same processes that were responsible for the innovatory treatment of poetry by the 'lyric' poets influenced epic poetry as well.

It is not out of the question that one of the factors that precipitated these developments so soon after Homer was the introduction of the practice of fixing poetry in writing. As long, indeed, as a poet created his poems by improvising them at the time of performance, his use of traditional language could not be fully deliberate. But entrusting these poems, however orally composed, to the new medium of writing would have necessarily involved conscious effort on the part of the poet. Though the language used in most post-Homeric poetry, and especially in elegy, was, at least at the beginning, traditional,[18] this new poetic self-consciousness could well have stimulated the poet's conception of his work in new terms. At the same time, it may be doubted whether the introduction of writing as such can count as sufficient reason for the emergence of the 'poetics of fiction'. Divine inspiration and the 'poetics of truth' deriving from it can hardly be regarded as intrinsically opposed to the idea of writing, which is after all only a medium, and, as such, capable of conveying both truthful and false messages. It is more likely that it was the tensions generated within the 'poetics of truth' itself by the time of Hesiod that precipitated the poets into thinking of their activity in terms of responsibility and knowledge. That the introduction of writing was chiefly responsible for the

---

[17] Koster (1970), 17–20.
[18] Cf. Page (1964), 117–63.

abandonment of the old concept of inspired poetry as a vehicle for conveying truth was argued in W. Rösler's influential paper 'Die Entdeckung der Fictionalität in der Antike'. According to Rösler's elegant reconstruction, the claim to veracity raised by the new prose genres of history and philosophy, paralleled as it was by criticism of the truthfulness of the oral tradition, undermined the traditional status of the old poetic genres and pushed them out of their former domain into the new sphere of fiction. Yet, attractive as it certainly is, Rösler's hypothesis does not stand the test of the evidence at our disposal. To begin with, as we saw in Chapter 5, realization of the fictitious character of much traditional poetry began within the poetry itself, long before the new prose genres of history and philosophy were firmly established.[19] In addition, Rösler's theory fails to explain why, long after the emergence of Greek prose, philosophical, historical, astonomical, geographical, and other non-fictional compositions cast in verse still constituted an integral part of the Greek and Roman literary scene. As this evidence suggests, the relationship between poetry and prose was in fact much more complicated: while prose indeed almost exclusively specialized in non-fictional genres, poetry continued to preserve its former status as a legitimate medium for both fiction and non-fiction (see further the Afterword below).

Let us now examine more closely the spheres treated by the 'lyric' poets in terms of knowledge. Alcman testifies about himself: 'These words and tune Alcman invented, understanding the tongued speech of partridges.'[20] While the poet's seeing himself as an 'inventor' is entirely new,[21] the division of his activity into the music and the verbal content of song is already well known to us from Homer: in epic poetry the terms of knowledge are consistently applied to the technical side of the poet's activity, including the musical accompaniment to the epic recital (Ch. 2, pp. 50–2). It goes without saying that the choral genre in which Alcman worked was much more closely engaged with music than the simple lyre accompaniment used in epic. 'The tune' (*melos*) of

---

[19] See Rösler (1980), esp. 284–5, 302–8. On criticism of Rösler's position see also Bowie (1993), 11–12, 35–6.

[20] Alcm. 39 *PMG*, Ϝέπη τάδε καὶ μέλος Ἀλκμὰν | εὗρε γεγλωσσαμέναν κακκαβίδων ὄπα συνθέμενος, trans. C. Segal. Cf. Simon. 542. 26 *PMG*.

[21] Cf. Kraus (1955), 78: 'In diesem εὗρε wird zum ersten Mal ausdrücklich der Dichter von dem Vortragenden geschieden. Bis dahin was das Dichtertum anonym unter der Bezeichnung ἀοιδός gegangen.' Cf. also Maehler (1963), 73.

Alcman obviously relates to this side of his activity. The composers of elegy, a declamatory genre accompanied by the flute, obviously could not share this kind of musical competence. Nevertheless, a similar feeling can be discerned in the verses of Solon who says about the poet that he is 'expert' (*epistamenos*) in the 'metre of the delightful skill'.[22] Since this is cast in elegiac distichs, it seems reasonable to infer that the 'metre' meant by Solon is the specific combination of the hexameter and the pentameter employed in this genre. If this inference is correct, this would obviously be a deviation from the traditional practice, because, judging from the complete absence from their poems of any references to this side of their activity, neither Homer nor Hesiod nor any other early hexametric poet seems even to have been conscious of the metre in which they worked. Additional evidence shows that this new consciousness spread not only to the metre.

As we have seen, Alcman claims to be the inventor not only of the tune but also of the 'words' (*epē*) of his song. Pindar, too, speaks of himself as an 'inventor of words', and of his poems and others' as having been 'joined together' out of words by those 'skilled carpenters', the poets.[23] We saw in Chapter 4 that Greek epic poetry had no consciousness of the single word as a unit of song, and that this characteristic is shared by other traditional poetry. In that they claim to be 'inventors' of words, the lyric poets seem to have acquired such consciousness. A similar conclusion follows from the fact that the traditional expression 'the order of song' (*kosmos aoidēs*), also discussed in Chapter 4 (pp. 124–6), begins to be replaced at this period by the expression 'the order of words' (*kosmos epeōn*). Its first attested usage is in Solon, who at the beginning of his famous elegy 'Salamis' defines his poem as an 'order of words': 'I have come in person, a herald from lovely Salamis, delivering a song, an order of words, instead of a speech.'[24] In a similar vein, Parmenides defines that part of his poem which deals with the Opinion as 'the deceiving order of my words', whereas for Pindar his song is 'a many-coloured order of expressions'; finally, Democritus says of Homer that he 'built an order of various words'.[25] Undoubtedly, the very fact that the poets

---

[22] Sol. 13. 52 West, ἱμερτῆς σοφίης μέτρον.

[23] *Ol.* 9. 80 εὑρεσιεπής; cf. *Ol.* 1. 111 εὑρὼν ὁδὸν λόγων. *Pyth.* 3. 113–14 ἐξ ἐπέων κελαδεννῶν τέκτονες οἷα σοφοὶ ἅρμοσαν.

[24] Sol. 1. 2 West, κόσμον ἐπέων ᾠδὴν ἀντ' ἀγορῆς θέμενος, trans B. M. W. Knox.

[25] Parm. DK 28 B 8. 52 κόσμον ἐμῶν ἐπέων ἀπατηλόν; Pind. fr. 194. 2–3 Snell-

begin to see their poems as consisting of words is a clear indication of new developments in their attitude to poetry.

The replacement of the order of events, implied in the traditional expression 'order of song', by the 'order of words' seems to indicate that, as distinct from traditional practice, the song begins to be treated in tectonic categories. As far as our evidence goes, the first Greek poet explicitly to apply the terminology of crafts to his own poetry was Pindar. More than once, he calls the poets 'carpenters' (*tektones*) who construct their songs out of words, and the poem is treated as a meticulously elaborated precious artefact; Pindar was also the first to begin to speak metaphorically of 'the web of song'.[26] Long before Plato subsumed both poetry and fine arts under the common denominator of mimesis, Pindar's contemporary Simonides coined the famous dictum, 'painting is silent poetry, poetry is speaking painting'.[27] How would the traditional poet have accepted the description of poetry in such terms? We have seen that not only does Homer never treat poetry in tectonic categories, but, since in the 'poetics of truth' any deviation from the 'point-by-point' narrative succession would be equivalent to a lie, he applies such categories to false accounts only.[28] That the new conception of the poem as the 'order of words' precludes its identification as a truthful account is also clear from Parmenides who styled his Doxa as 'the deceiving order of my words', while later in the same passage he applies to it the Homeric term for 'plausible' (*eoikota*).[29] That is to say, for the traditional poet, a description of the poet's creative process in the vein of Pindar

---

Maehler, ποικίλον κόσμον . . . λόγων, cf. *Ol.* 11. 13. Democr. DK 68 B 21 ἐπέων κόσμον παντοίων ἐτεκτήνατο. On the later usages of the expression see Kerschensteiner (1962), 10–11.

[26] *Nem.* 3. 4–5 μελιγαρύων τέκτονες | κώμων; *Pyth.* 3. 113–14 ἐξ ἐπέων κελαδεννῶν τέκτονες οἷα σοφοὶ | ἄρμοσαν; fr. 194. 1–3 Snell-Maehler, κεκρότηται χρυσέα κρηπὶς ἱεραῖσιν ἀοιδαῖς· | εἶα τειχίζωμεν ἤδη ποικίλον | κόσμον αὐδάεντα λόγων; *Ol.* 1. 104–5 μή τιν' ἀμφότερα . . . κλυταῖσι δαιδαλώσεμεν ὕμνων πτυχαῖς. Cf. Kerschensteiner (1962), 8–9. On the 'web of song' in choral poetry see now Scheid and Svenbro (1996), 117–19 (with quotations and bibliography).

[27] Plut. *Mor.* 346 F, cf. *Mor.* 18 A. Cf. Detienne (1973), 106–7.

[28] See Ch. 4 above. The fact that terms of this kind begin to be applied to poetry after Homer does not mean that they are relevant to Homer's poetics (as is taken for granted, for example, by Verdenius (1983), 17)—rather, their popularity with post-Homeric writers should be considered as an indication of a change in the Greek attitude towards artistic form, a change which led to the legitimation of fiction in poetry.

[29] Parm. DK 28 B 8. 52, 60. Cf. also Heraclit. DK 22B 28. Cf. Ch. 5, pp. 158–9.

would imply that the poet is engaged in fabricating a false account. This brings us back to the issue of truth and lies dealt with at length in connection with Homer and Hesiod.

When Helen in the *Iliad* and Alcinous in the *Odyssey* say that the tragic doom and suffering of the participants in the Trojan war have been imposed on them by the gods in order that there may be song about these events in future generations, this amounts to recognition that the poem has come to be felt as ontologically independent of the events that stimulated it (Chapter 5). But Homer does not claim that the reality of poetry and the reality of the heroic past do not concur: the events in both cases are the same events, and this is what allows the song, independent though it has become, to retain its status as a truthful account of the past. Not so, for example, in the case of Pindar, according to whom the ontological independence of poetry implies the power of replacing truth with lying, which leads to falsification of the past. Thus, in *Nemean* 7 Pindar claims that the power of Homer's poetry was responsible for a great historical injustice: Homer distorted the truth about the quarrel between Odysseus and Ajax and canonized a version which was biased in favour of Odysseus.[30] Consider also his statement in the first *Olympian*: 'Truly, there are many wonders! Sometimes even the rumour of mortals, stories ornamented with many-coloured lies, deceive and gain the upper hand over the true account. Grace (*Charis*), who makes everything agreeable to men, bestows honour and often makes improbable probable.'[31] The passage is meant to disqualify the primitive (and undoubtedly authentic) version of Pelops' story in order to replace it by a version of Pindar's own making, more agreeable to the religious taste of the poet and his contemporaries: Pelops was taken to Olympus not to be eaten and then returned to life by the gods but because he was kidnapped by Poseidon who fell in love with the handsome youth. Characteristically, in the absence of any address to the Muses, the only factor that can validate Pindar's moralistic recension of the inherited myth is the very Grace of poetry who had once validated the wrong versions of his predecessors. Thus, in the last analysis Pindar's own account can only act as one more in the series of poetic replacements of reality which he so sharply disapproves of in others.[32]

---

[30] *Nem.* 7. 20 ff., cf. 8. 25 ff. Cf. Puelma (1989), 87–8; Pratt (1993), 127–8.
[31] *Ol.* 1. 28–32 (my translation).
[32] For a similar interpretation, see Pratt (1993), 123–6.

'This tale is not true,' Stesichorus proclaims when introducing an entirely new version of Helen's story in his *Palinode*, 'nor did you go in the well-benched ships nor reach the citadels of Troy.'[33] Stesichorus was known for his free handling of traditional subjects, and the same freedom is also characteristic of the work of Pindar and Bacchylides. It seems, indeed, that the choral poets found a solution of their own to the problem of the 'lying Muses' which inevitably arose whenever such a free handling was at issue. Thus, the Muse of Stesichorus sings not 'through' or even 'to' the poet, as do the Muses of Homer and Hesiod, but 'together with' him, while in Pindar's invocations the poet places himself on an equal footing with his Muse, engaging in dialogue with her rather than simply seeing himself as a passive instrument in her hands.[34] This would certainly free the Muses from responsibility for the poet's inventions, thus solving the problem of the 'lying Muses'. The trouble, however, is that this kind of solution would also eventually deprive the Muses of their *raison d'être*. We have indeed seen that in the early Greek tradition it was the Muse who was held responsible for the creative element in the poet's activity. Consequently, the poet's growing awareness of the way in which he expressed himself would have emptied the Muses' idiom of its traditional content. In the new poetic self-consciousness acquired as a result of the poet's free treatment of traditional subjects there was no longer any need for the Muses to account for what, the poets felt, they created themselves. This must have stimulated the poets' conception of their activity in terms of individual responsibility as described above, and would eventually lead to the reformulating of the Muses' idiom in entirely new terms.[35]

It can be seen from the foregoing that epic poetry, on the one hand, and choral and elegiac poetry, on the other, had much in

[33] Stesich. 192 *PMG*, οὐκ ἔστ' ἔτυμος λόγος οὗτος, | οὐδ' ἔβας ἐν νηυσὶν εὐσέλμοις | οὐδ' ἵκεο πέργαμα Τροίας, trans. C. Segal. That Stesichorus was fully aware of the fictitious character of the version he proposed has been convincingly argued by Bowie (1993), 23–8, and Pratt (1993), 132–6.

[34] Stesich. 210 *PMG*, πεδ' ἐμοῦ (μετ' codd.), cf. Lanata (1963), 56; Pind. *Ol.* 3. 3–4, 10. 3–6, 13. 96–7; *Pyth.* 1. 58–9, 4. 3, 11. 41–2; *Nem.* 3. 1–10, 6. 27–9; *Pae.* 6. 54–8.

[35] As was shown by Bing (1988), this inward change was outwardly expressed in the poet's self-image only in the Hellenistic age: 'Poets rethought their methods, modified their goals and, in so doing, created a new aesthetic which affected not only subsequent Greek authors, but the Latin poets of the Augustan Age as well' (p. 11). As we shall see presently, in theoretical poetics the new status of poetry was established even earlier.

common. All three shared a common basis in inspiration by the
Muses and participated in the developments which eventually led
to the erosion of the Muses' idiom. Nevertheless, their ways were
bound to separate. Indeed, by the very nature of the genre in
which they worked, the problem of 'lies resembling truth' could
not be at the centre of the lyric poets' attention, at least not in the
form it assumed as a result of the extensive use of impersonation
in the Homeric epics. It was this problem, however, which became
central to the theories of poetry developed in the fifth and fourth
centuries. Hence, it comes as no surprise that the genres by which
these theories were directly stimulated were epic and dramatic
rather than lyric poetry.

Athens, Fifth Century BC

To appreciate the extent to which the status of the work of poetry
had changed as a result of developments in the seventh and sixth
centuries, consider the outcome of this process as described by
Aristophanes in the second half of the fifth century BC:

Agathon the fair of speech is about to lay the keel of a new drama, yea
with mighty crossbeams shall it be constructed. For behold, he turneth the
verses upon the lathe and sticketh them together; maxim and metaphor
doth he hammer out, yea in melted wax doth he mould his creation: he
rolleth it till it be round; he casteth it. . . .[36]

Aristophanes' description of a contemporary poet at work, parody
though it is, faithfully represents the tendency which had become
pervasive in the fifth century BC to render the poet's creative process
in terms of handicrafts.[37] Undoubtedly, the treatment of poetry in
terms of handicrafts involved much more than simply borrowing
craft metaphors to describe the poet's work. As we have seen,
Plato, for example, regularly places his 'poetry as an art' alongside
the crafts, and Aristotle too, by defining poetry as *technē*, makes it
impossible to draw a clear line between this activity and handicrafts. The situation is described by R. G. Collingwood as follows.
Defining craft as 'the power to produce a preconceived result by

[36] *Thesm.* 49-57, trans. R. Harriott.
[37] Cf. Harriott (1969), 97: 'By the last years of the fifth century almost the whole
range of Greek crafts is called into service for the description of the literature.' For
the list of examples see ibid. 104. This tendency can be traced back to Pindar, see
Svenbro (1976), 186 ff.

means of consciously controlled and directed actions', he blames
the Greek philosophers, primarily Plato and Aristotle, for extending
the 'philosophy of crafts' they had invented to the art of poetry:
'they took it for granted that poetry, the only art which they discussed in detail, was a kind of craft, and spoke of this craft as
ποιητικὴ τέχνη, poet-craft.'[38] The question, however, is whether the
Greeks had any alternative to construing poetry in terms of crafts.

From the standpoint of the traditional classification of human
activities, the fact that poetry begins to be treated in terms of individual responsibility, knowledge, and teaching indicates that its
class membership begins to shift from the class of activities for
which man is *not* held individually responsible to the opposed class
of activities for which he *is* held responsible. In other words,
poetry begins to be conceived in the same way as sports, handicrafts, skills, and practical wisdom were conceived in Homer (see
Chapter 2). But poetry, unlike many of man's activities, is also a
productive activity, that is, an activity resulting in something that
can be approached in its own right, independently of the activity
from which it originated. If I am correct in asserting that the
transition from inspiration to art involved more than a mere
exchange of one idea for another, this change in class membership
would have been inseparable from a change in the status of the
product of the poetic activity, the poem. That is to say, when the
poet ceases to be regarded as not responsible for his activity, this
will inevitably result in the assimilation of poetry to the productive
activities for which man is held responsible. As we saw in Chapter
4, the only such activity available to the Greeks was the artisan's
technē. It was inevitable, then, that when the poets began to consider themselves responsible for their activity, they also began to
think of it in terms of craftsmanship. Consequently, the product of
this activity, the poem, began to be conceived on the model of the
artefact. As we saw in Chapter 1, everything points to this shift in
the status of poetry as taking place in the fifth century BC.[39]

---

[38] Collingwood (1938), 15, 17, 18. For criticism of Collingwood's position from
the standpoint of aesthetics see Janaway (1995), 36–57.

[39] That post-Homeric poetics differs from the poetics of Homer in that it begins
to be formulated in terms of craftsmanship has also been argued by Svenbro (1976).
However, Svenbro (p. 5) sees Aristotle's *Poetics* as 'le point où se perd finalement le
souvenir de la configuration sociale qui a engendré la conception du poète comme
poiētēs, comme "producteur" (au sense artisanal).' That is, to apply the terminology
used in this book, according to Svenbro the development of Greek poetics takes the
following form: 'poetics of truth' (Homer, Hesiod) > 'poetics of fiction' (from Hesiod

This was a period of cultural upheaval. In every facet of the spiritual life of the age a struggle between 'old' and 'new' was taking place. Ideas and beliefs that had been the basis of Greek tradition for centuries were being called into question, and doubt was being cast on what had recently been incontestable, self-evident. The traditional boundaries between 'human' and 'super-human' were overstepped as the scope of human endeavour, of spheres perceived to be under human control, widened consider-ably.[40] Traditionally, man was considered passive, and social history was regarded either as a process of degeneration or as an endlessly recurring cycle. Now, human inventiveness was seen as responsible for the progression from savage disorder and material want to civilized society enjoying the rule of laws (*nomoi*) and the prosperity made possible by useful arts (*technai*).[41] Traditionally, human life was believed to be permanently open to divine inter-vention, which diminished man's personal responsibility for his actions, while fate and the 'jealousy of the gods' undermined the difference between the just and the unjust man. Now, man is recognized as the true cause of his actions, right or wrong, and justice (*dikaiosunē*) becomes the safest guarantee of a happy life.[42] Traditionally, the personal qualities of man were thought to be pre-determined either by 'divine gift' or by birth, but now, the idea that they are influenced by training and man's own efforts begins to take hold, and whether or not virtue can be taught becomes one of the most hotly debated issues of the age.[43]

Although it is true that it is the nature of rhetoric rather than

to Aristotle) > poetics of Aristotle. The exact nature of Aristotle's poetics and its relationship to the preceding attitudes to poetry are left unexplained. It seems that Svenbro's preoccupation with social and class agendas (sharply criticized by Murray (1981), 99) prevented him from realizing that the poetics of Aristotle was in fact the culmination of the understanding of poetry in terms of craftsmanship, which he documented at length for Simonides and Pindar.

[40] Generally, this process is conveyed by the *nomos : phusis* dichotomy. For com-prehensive treatment of this subject see Heiniman (1945). See also Nestle (1941); Guthrie (1969), 55-134; Kerferd (1981), 11-30.

[41] See Democr. DK 68 B 5; Protag. in Pl. *Prot.* 320c-322e; Archelaus, DK 60 A 4; Prodic. DK 84 B 5; Hippoc. *De prisca med.* 3; Aesch. *PV.* 442-68, 478-506; Soph. *Ant.* 332-71; Eur. *Supp.* 201-13; Critias, DK 88 B 25; Gorg. DK 82 B 11a, 30. Cf. Dodds (1973), 2-4.

[42] Aeschylus was the first to raise this Socratic theme against the 'old' view that divine punishment threatens just and unjust men equally (*Ag.* 750-62).

[43] See Democr. DK 68 B 59, B 157, B 179, B 242; Protag. DK 80 B 3, B 10; Critias, DK 88 B 9; *Dialexeis* 90. 6 DK; Eur. *Supp.* 911-17. Cf. Guthrie (1969), 250-60; Kerferd (1988), 131-8.

that of poetry that engaged fifth-century thinkers, the radical changes that were taking place were not without influence on contemporary approaches to poetry. Thus, the very definition of poetry as 'art' (*technē*) brings it into the context of the opposition between 'nature' and 'art' which the theories of human progress presupposed. The exact place of poetry in the doctrines of human progress is among the non-useful arts, which appeared, according to some, in the later stage of evolution.[44] The discussion of the nature of the virtues seems to be of even greater moment. As in the question of whether virtue can be taught, what is at issue in the case of poetry is the line between what is and what is not under the individual's control:

First of all, one needs natural endowment (*phunai*), and this belongs to chance; the rest, however, is in man's own control, namely, he has to become both a seeker after noble things and an industrious man, to start learning as early as possible and pursue it a long time.[45]

We have seen that Homer too drew a clear-cut line between what is and what is not under the individual's control. Yet, we have good reason to believe that in the period under consideration the traditional classification of human activities as attested in Homer was undergoing radical redistribution. The case of courage can be taken as an example. We saw above that Homeric man's valour (*tharsos, alkē*) was not conceived as exercised deliberately. It was instantly 'put' or 'thrown' into someone's heart, 'sent' or 'breathed' into him, and a man could be 'filled' with it exactly as he could be filled with anger or physical strength. Yet, after the fifth century BC 'courage' (*andreia*) is unambiguously treated as exercised deliberately, which indicates that it has moved from the class of activities for which man is not considered responsible to the class of activities for which he is considered responsible. Characteristically, in his discussion of courage in the *Nicomachean Ethics*, Aristotle refuses to class under courage the very manifestations of Homeric man's valour that we discussed in Chapter 2, arguing that they fall short of courage proper because their only

[44] Cf. Democr. DK 68 B 144; Isoc. *Paneg.* 40; Pl. *Rep.* 373ab; *Epin.* 974d; Arist. *Metaph.* 982^{b}22. On this subject see Koller (1954), 145–8; Luria (1970), 552–3. It may be added that some of Euripides' claims in the *Frogs* (see esp. ll. 939–79) have much in common with the pattern of the cultural hero, or *heuretēs* ('inventor'), of theories of human progress. On the 'inventor' see Kleingünter (1933).

[45] *Anonymus Iamblichi* 89 1, 2 DK (my translation).

source is passion.[46] In view of this, it is reasonable to suppose that the change in the Greek attitude to poetry, prepared by new developments in poetic practice itself, was made possible by the cultural transformation that Greece underwent in the fifth century BC. This enables us to set the Greek attitude to poetry within a concrete historical perspective.

During the first half of the fifth century, a radical shift occurred in the Greek terms designating poetry, the poet, and the poem. Up to this point, the generally accepted terms had been 'to sing' (*aeidein*), 'the singer' (*aoidos*), and 'the song' (*aoidē*), but now these terms began to be replaced by 'to make' (*poiein*), 'the maker' (*poiētēs*), and 'the thing made' (*poiēma*).[47] It is reasonable to suppose that this terminological shift echoed significant changes in the poet's status, which influenced Greek views on the nature of poetry in a way thus described by Gregory Nagy:

Whereas the *aoidos* had remained in the sacral realm of prophecy, as evidenced by the institutional dependence of the *aoidos* on the divine inspiration of the muse, the *poiētēs* entered the desacralized realm of poetry as we are used to it, where the very notion of inspiration is but a literary convention. The *poiētēs* was a professional; he was a master of *technē*, the work of an artisan.[48]

The change in the professional terminology was paralleled by the emergence of new directions in the literary practice of the Greeks. The first half of the fifth century BC was a time of rapid development in the new genre of prose writing. Prose writing was directly stimulated by the art of rhetoric, the beginnings of which lie in this very period. Since the acknowledged goal of rhetoric was persuasion (*peithō*), it put forward a principle of plausibility (*eikos*) disconnected from either truth or falsehood, the origins of which can be traced as far back as Homer.

But it is above all the emergence of another literary genre, that of dramatic poetry, which occurred at around the same time, that

---

[46] *Eth. Nic.* 1116[b]24–1117[a]5.

[47] ποίησις Hdt. 2. 82, 2. 23; ποιητής Hdt. 2. 53; ποίημα Cratinus 186 Kock; see also ποιεῖν, 'to compose poems', in Hdt. 1. 23, 4. 14, 6. 21.

[48] Nagy (1989), 23–4. Cf. Detienne's remark on Simonides: 'la volonté de pratiquer la poésie comme un métier, cette réflexion sur la poésie, sa fonction, son objet propre consomme la rupture avec la tradition du poète inspiré, qui dit l'*Alétheia* aussi naturellement qu'il respire', in Detienne (1973), 109. Cf. also de Romilly (1973), 160: 'La poésie, devenue τέχνη, est tout naturellement devenue ouvrière d'ἀπάτη.'

seems to have influenced Greek views on the nature of poetic activity. It was in reference to dramatic poetry that Gorgias gave definitive expression to the change in the Greek attitude to poetry. 'Tragedy', Gorgias said, 'is a deceit (*apatē*) in which the deceiver is more just than one who did not deceive, and the deceived is more wise than one who was not deceived.'[49] True, the poets had been said to 'lie' since the time of Hesiod. But the 'lies' of the poets were always seen as a misrepresentation of some reality, as a distortion of the truth. With Gorgias, for the first time fiction is legitimized as an autonomous sphere which cannot be evaluated by using ordinary standards of 'truth' and 'falsehood'.[50] In a similar vein, the anonymous author of the Sophistic treatise *Dissoi logoi* holds that 'the poets compose their poems not for the sake of truth but for the sake of pleasure', and he places poetry among the arts which draw no distinction between just and unjust; that it was first and foremost tragic poetry that he had in mind follows from his saying in the same context, that 'in tragic poetry and in painting the one who deceives most while making likenesses of truth is the very best'.[51]

Is it possible to correlate these references to poetry with the actual experience of the contemporary audience? The following incident is illuminating in this respect. In 493 BC, approximately a year after the fall of Miletus to the Persians, a tragedy by Phrynichus on this subject was produced on the Athenian stage. What happened next is described by Herodotus as follows:

The Athenians, on the other hand, showed themselves beyond measure afflicted at the fall of Miletus, expressing this, in many ways, and especially by their treatment of Phrynichus. For when the latter composed and brought out upon the stage his drama, *The Capture of Miletus*, the whole theatre burst into tears, and the people sentenced him to pay a fine of a thousand drachmas, for recalling to them their own misfortunes (*oikeia kaka*). They likewise made a law, that no one should ever again exhibit that piece.[52]

The parallelism between this historical episode and Alcinous' interrupting Demodocus' performances in *Odyssey* 8 is striking.

[49] DK 82 B 23 (my translation).
[50] Cf. Taplin (1985), 167–8, and above, Ch. 1, pp. 25–6.
[51] *Dialexeis* 90. 3. 17 DK, cf. 2. 28; 90. 3. 10. Cf. Detienne (1973), 107; Puelma (1989), 91–2.
[52] Hdt. 6. 21, trans. G. Rawlinson, with minor changes.

The reason for Odysseus' weeping on hearing songs about the Trojan war was the same as the reason for the Athenians' reaction to Phrynichus' tragedy: on both occasions, the performance reminded the audience of 'their own misfortunes' and was ruled out of order for this very reason. We cannot be sure, of course, that it was this particular incident that eventually brought the Athenian dramatists to exclude historical subjects from their repertoire. The fact is, however, that with the exception of the *Phoenissae* by Phrynichus (476) and Aeschylus' *Persae* (472), no other tragedies on a historical subject seem to have been produced in fifth-century Athens. All the subjects performed on the Attic stage up to the end of the fifth century were traditional.

But this is not to say that the Athenian audience wished to avoid *every* form of emotional involvement with what was happening on the tragic stage. In this connection, two Platonic passages, one from the *Ion* and the other from *Republic* 10, are especially illuminating. The passage from *Ion* describes how both Ion himself and his audiences react to the rhapsode's recitation of Homer. Socrates poses the following question to Ion:

Suppose you are reciting epic poetry well, and thrill the spectators most deeply. You are chanting, say, the story of Odysseus as he leaped up to the dais, unmasked himself to the suitors, and poured the arrows out before his feet, or of Achilles rushing upon Hector, or one of the pitiful passages, about Andromache, or Hecuba, or Priam. When you chant these, are you in your senses (*emphrōn*)? Or are you carried out of yourself, and does not your soul in an ecstasy (*enthousiazousa*) conceive herself to be engaged in the actions you relate, whether they are in Ithaca, or Troy, or wherever the story puts them?

Ion acknowledges that, indeed, he weeps whenever he recites a pitiful story and his hair stands on end with fear whenever a story of terror is told; he also admits that the same effect is produced in his audiences as well:

As I look down at them from the stage above, I see them, every time, weeping, casting terrible glances, stricken with amazement at the deeds recounted. In fact, I have to give them very close attention, for if I set them weeping, I myself shall laugh when I get my money, but if they laugh, it is I who have to weep at losing it.[53]

[53] *Ion* 535be, trans. L. Cooper.

Causing emotional turmoil in his listeners is therefore the very thing the rhapsode is paid for. *Republic* 10 is even more specific on this point:

I think you know that the very best of us, when we hear Homer or some other of the makers of tragedy imitating one of the heroes who is in grief, and is delivering a long tirade in his lamentations or chanting and beating his breast, are delighted, and abandon ourselves and accompany the action with sympathy and eagerly praise as an excellent poet the one who most strongly affects us in this way.[54]

On the surface, Plato's description of the Athenian audience's reaction disagrees with the Phrynichus incident recorded by Herodotus. There, the poet was punished because his play produced emotional distress in the audience; here, the poets are praised and earn their very living only if they succeed in eliciting such emotional reaction. But, of course, the contradiction is only imaginary. In the case of *The Capture of Miletus*, the action on the stage concerned the Athenians' *oikeia kaka*, 'their own troubles', so that it could not create the emotional distance between the audience and the performance which alone would allow them to enjoy the play. Not so in the case of the traditional subjects. Comparison between the Athenians' reaction to the tragedy of Phrynichus, on the one hand, and to the performance of traditional subjects, on the other, indicates with great precision what kind of effect they regarded as most favourable for poetry. To feel pleasure at a poetic performance, the spectators should be able, in Plato's words, to 'abandon themselves and accompany the action with sympathy' without at the same time losing the safe distance between the action and themselves. 'There comes over the audience of poetry', Gorgias wrote in his *Encomium of Helen*, 'a fearful horror and tearful pity and doleful yearning. By means of the discourse their spirit feels a personal emotion on account of the good and bad fortune of others.'[55] Oliver Taplin comments on this: 'he [Gorgias] has put his finger on one of the most vital and remarkable features of this experience: that the emotions are generous—altruistic almost—that we feel disturbed personally for

---

[54] *Rep.* 605d, trans. P. Shorey, with minor changes. Cf. Herington (1985), 10–14.

[55] Gorg. DK 82 B 11. 9 ἐπ' ἀλλοτρίων τε πραγμάτων καὶ σωμάτων εὐτυχίαις καὶ δυσπραγίαις ἴδιόν τι πάθημα διὰ τῶν λόγων ἔπαθεν ἡ ψυχή, trans. O. Taplin.

other people, for people who have no direct connection with us and indeed belong to another world from ours.'[56]

That is to say, no pleasure is produced by poetry either when it represents events which arouse too direct an emotional involvement or when the events represented arouse no emotional involvement at all. Such were the limits set to the effect of poetry by the taste of the fifth-century Greek audience. It is evident that such an attitude could only be developed in an audience accustomed to a considerable degree of artistic illusion on the part of the poetic performance, and also experienced enough to make this illusion the source of pleasure. Characteristically, Gorgias' definition of tragic *apatē* is evoked by Plutarch in order to support an argument that only a cultivated audience is susceptible to an effect of this kind:

For the element of deception (*to apatēlon*) in it [*sc.* poetry] does not gain any hold on utterly witless and foolish persons. This is the ground of Simonides' answer to the man who said to him, 'Why are the Thessalians the only people whom you do not deceive?' His answer was, 'Oh, they are too ignorant to be deceived by me'; and Gorgias called tragedy a deception etc.[57]

To be sure, not every state in fifth-century Greece was fit to provide such an audience. Thus, on the evidence of Plato's dialogues, Thessaly is 'the part of Greece where the man who best knows how to impart horsemanship would be most highly esteemed, and would make most money'; the Cretans 'are not much given to cultivating verse of alien origin [sc. of Homer]', while the Spartans, although holding Homer in high esteem, took the greatest pleasure 'in the genealogies of heroes and of men, and in stories of the foundations of cities in olden times', that is, in the kind of performance a follower of Hesiod would be able to supply; and in any case their national poet was the 'most divine' Tyrtaeus and not Homer who described a life that was 'decidedly Ionian rather than Laconian'.[58]

Codification of the *Iliad* and the *Odyssey* under Pisistratus granted to the Athenian state a monopoly over the standard text of Homer and to its citizens a close familiarity with the Homeric poems, not to mention the fact that tragedy as we know it was exclusively a local development. The Panhellenic festivals, in the

[56] Taplin (1985), 168 (Taplin's italics).
[57] Plut. *Mor.* 15 C–D.
[58] Thessalians, *Hipp. Mai.* 284a; Cretans, *Laws* 680c; Spartans, *Laws* 680c, 629ab; *Hipp. Mai.* 285d, cf. 285b, 281b.

course of which both Homer and tragedy were performed, were among the central events of the public life of the city and of the whole of Greece. 'There had probably never been before, in the Greek world, such a concentration of diverse musical and poetic talent within a single city as now existed in Athens.'[59] We saw in Chapter 5 that at some stage the Homeric tradition turned to an extensive use of impersonation unparalleled in other epic traditions, and both Plato and Aristotle testify to the effect that this was why artistic illusion became a norm in the rhapsodic performances of the Homeric poems. The tragedians took over the standards of representation established in the performances of Homer and continued to work along the same lines. They were guided in their work by the taste of their audience, which, to follow the line of Plutarch's argument, was wise enough to demand from what was presented on the stage a degree of artistic illusion allowing for neither too close an involvement in the theatrical performance nor a total emotional estrangement from it. The introduction of a category that once and for all disentangled poetry from the 'truth : lie' dichotomy came next. This category, which emerged as a direct reaction to what was happening on the Attic stage, was Plato's category of mimesis.

A Competitor of Reality

As we have seen, poetry was challenged by philosophers and historians from the times of Xenophanes and Hecataeus onwards. The reason is clear—like epic poetry, both early history and early philosophy claimed to be media for conveying truth. As long, however, as the discussion was premised on the 'true : false' dichotomy, poetry could meet the challenge: though declared false prophets and false witnesses, the poets nevertheless remained prophets and witnesses. The nature and the final outcome of this 'ancient quarrel'[60] between partisans of truth was most clearly expressed by Plato.

In Plato's eyes, philosophy was 'the greatest of activities taking their rise in the Muses'[61] and, hence, both twin sister and rival of

---

[59] Herington (1985), 96.
[60] Pl. *Rep.* 607b.
[61] *Phd.* 61a μεγίστη μουσικῆς.

inspired poetry, in that both aspired to beget the highest truth through contact with the divine. In a sense, the central conflict of Plato's poetics as presented in Chapter 1, the conflict between inspired poetry as depicted in the *Ion* and poetry as an art as introduced in the *Republic*, can be understood as an outcome of his successive attempts to separate poetry from philosophy by assigning to poetry its own sphere of competence. Note that in both the *Ion* and the *Republic* Plato tries to answer the same question: 'What is the sphere in which the poet is competent?' The answer of the *Ion* is in full agreement with tradition: there is no such sphere at all. The theory of poetic enthusiasm, in which the poet's ignorance constituted the only barrier between the poet and the highest wisdom, was a natural corollary of this answer.[62] In the *Republic*, however, Plato's answer is that the sphere of the poet's competence is mimesis, which he defines as a pseudo-craft employing words, harmonies, rhythms, and metres for the production of images of things. Both poetry and fine arts could now be subsumed under this new sphere. Since such an activity could pose no challenge to philosophy, the latter attained the desired status of sole medium for conveying divine truth. It is with this conclusion in view that Plato's formulation of the new status of poetry as a mimetic art should be approached.

In everything concerning the relation between mimesis and reality, book 10 of the *Republic* is essential. Here, Plato sets out to prove that works of mimetic art are at a third remove from reality and therefore devoid of any value. The work of fine art should be placed first after the idea of the artefact and second after the work of the craftsman who produces the artefact; by the same token, the work of poetry should be placed first after the idea of justice and second after the activity of the king.[63] But did Plato really mean

[62] The issue of the inspired poet's ignorance leads one to enquire into Plato's understanding of the situation of the inspired philosopher in this specific respect. His answer can be suggested on the basis of *Tim.* 71e–72a: 'And herein is a proof that God has given the art of divination not to the wisdom, but to the foolishness (*aphrosunē*) of man. No man, when in his wits, attains prophetic truth and inspiration, but when he receives the inspired word, either his intelligence (*phronēsis*) is enthralled in sleep or he is demented by some distemper or possession (*enthousiasmos*). And he who would understand what he remembers to have been said, whether in a dream or when he was awake, by the prophetic and inspired nature, or would analyse by reason (*logismos*) the meaning of the apparitions which he has seen, and what indications they afford to this man or that, of past, present, or future good and evil, must first recover his wits', trans. B. Jowett.

[63] *Rep.* 597be.

that, as is often supposed, the picture of a couch is an exact copy of the real couch made by the craftsman? In fact, his argument concerning the relation between the work of mimetic art and reality is not as straightforward as many are ready to believe.

Plato's argument in *Republic* 10 falls into two parts. He begins with a description of the mimetic artist who aims at creating a likeness of reality; yet, judging by what he says in *Republic* 10, Plato does not think it possible that mimesis is capable of producing exact replicas of its models. This is true not only of the painter who imitates the couch made by the craftsman but also of the kind of mimesis in which the craftsman himself, imitating the one and only idea of the couch, is involved. According to Plato, the work of both is only 'a dim adumbration in comparison with truth'.[64] It is to this context that the famous comparison of mimetic art with the mirror belongs:

> this same handicraftsman is not only able to make all implements, but he produces all plants and animals, including himself, and thereto earth and heaven and the gods and all things in heaven and in Hades under the earth . . . . it is something that the craftsman can make everywhere and quickly. You could do it most quickly if you should choose to take a mirror and carry it about everywhere. You will speedily produce the sun and all the things in the sky, and speedily the earth and yourself and the other animals and implements and plants and all the objects of which we just now spoke.[65]

The immediate conclusion of this illustration is that it is the appearance rather than the reality that can be produced in this way.[66] But it is often overlooked that the premiss from which Plato proceeds in this and similar contexts is that *any* mimetic reproduction involves distortion of the reproducer's model, thus turning every form of reproduction into no more than 'dim adumbration'. This is especially true of the kind of reproduction supplied by the object's reflection in a mirror because, according to the view expressed by Plato more than once, in virtue of the fact that it exchanges left for right and vice versa the reflection in the mirror is actually a standard example of distortion of reality.[67] Thus, art's being at third remove from reality amounts to the distortion of reality necessarily involved in any reproduction of it.

---

[64] *Rep.* 597b καὶ τοῦτο ἄμυδρόν τι τυγχάνει ὂν πρὸς ἀλήθειαν.
[65] Ibid. 596ce.
[66] Ibid. 596e φαινόμενα, οὐ μέντοι ὄντα γέ που τῇ ἀληθείᾳ.
[67] See *Theaet.* 193c; *Tim.* 46a, 71b; cf. *Soph.* 239d.

The second part of Plato's argument concerns only mimetic art and deals with the artist who has no intention of reproducing the exact likeness of his model. His argument runs as follows. Whereas a real couch is always the same, although it appears different 'according as you view it from the side or the front or in any other way', what the picture of a couch reproduces is only this very appearance without the sameness of the actual couch. Accordingly, such a picture is nothing more than a phantom:

Then the mimetic art is far removed from truth, and this, it seems, is the reason why it can produce everything, because it touches or lays hold of only a small part of the object and that a phantom (*eidōlon*), as, for example, a painter, we say, will paint us a cobbler, a carpenter, and other craftsmen, though he himself has no expertness in any of these arts, but nevertheless if he were a good painter, by exhibiting at a distance his picture of a carpenter he would deceive children and foolish men, and make them believe it to be a real carpenter.[68]

Obviously, neither the mirror-like imitation nor, moreover, the imitation which deliberately misrepresents its model can be regarded as an exact reproduction of the object it imitates. No such thing as the exact copy or replica of a real thing is therefore possible.

Both arguments are recapitulated and taken further in the *Sophist*. In this dialogue, which continues the discussion of the ontological status of the representational arts begun in *Republic* 10, Plato goes to great trouble in his efforts to distinguish between divine, or natural, and artistic creation, with the sole purpose of eliminating the mimetic artist's claim, known to us already from the *Republic*, that he is able 'to create everything' by his art.[69] Yet, he cannot avoid the conclusion that, in so far as objects of art cannot be envisaged as replicas of already existing things, their existence produces an ontological problem. Returning to the two arguments of art's relation to reality introduced in *Republic* 10, Plato divides mimetic art into the making of likenesses (*eikastikē*) and the making of semblances (*phantastikē*). Although the likeness (*eikōn*) presumably distorts reality by virtue of being two removes from it, as far as the artist is engaged in 'creating a copy that conforms to the proportions of the original in all three dimensions

---

[68] *Rep.* 598bc, cf. also 598a. Cf. n. 80 below.

[69] *Soph.* 231b–236c, 239c–240b, 264b–268c. Cf. the discussion in Cornford (1935), 187–99, 320–31.

and giving moreover the proper colour to every part',[70] the object of art created in this way ostensibly possesses no ontological status of its own and thus poses no real ontological problem. Not so, however, in the case of those sculptors or painters whose works are of colossal size:

If they were to reproduce the true proportions of a well-made figure, as you know, the upper parts would look too small, and the lower too large, because we see the one at a distance, the other close at hand . . . . So artists, leaving the truth to take care of itself, do in fact put into the images they make, not the real proportions, but those that will appear beautiful.[71]

The semblance, or 'phantom' (*phantasma*), thus produced does not simply blur the reality as the likeness does, but also distorts it in a much more substantial manner. Further on in the same dialogue, Plato admits, again in full accordance with *Republic* 10, that even the images created by mirror-like imitation, that is, those that do not deliberately distort the proportions of their model, cannot be regarded as this model's truthful representations. The conclusion, again, is that there is no way in which the creation of the exact likeness of a given natural object can be possible.[72] There is thus no reality of which the imitation can be considered to be a copy. This fact turns the existence of the work of mimetic art into a real ontological *aporia*:

The truth is, my friend, that we are faced with an extremely difficult question. The 'appearing' or 'seeming' without really 'being', and the saying of something which yet is not true—all these expressions have always been and still are deeply involved in perplexity (*aporia*). It is extremely hard, Theaetetus, to find correct terms in which one may say or think that falsehoods (*pseudē*) have a real existence, without being caught in a contradiction by the mere utterance of such words.[73]

But as far as those 'falsehoods' cannot be regarded as 'another truth', to put it into Plato's own words,[74] they should inevitably be credited with some sort of real existence. This, in fact, is the conclusion Plato eventually arrives at in the *Sophist*. His reasoning is quite simple. In so far as images of art cannot be regarded as copies of really existing things (and we have seen that Plato envisages

---

[70] *Soph.* 235d, trans. F. M. Cornford.
[71] Ibid. 235e–236a.   [72] Ibid. 239d–240a.   [73] Ibid. 236e–237a.
[74] Ibid. 240a τὸ πρὸς τἀληθινὸν ἀφωμοιόμενον ἕτερον τοιοῦτον . . . ἕτερον τοιοῦτον ἀληθινόν.

no condition on which this can be possible), these images cannot be regarded as reflections of reality any more than lies can be regarded as a reflection of truth. Or, to put it again in Plato's own words,

anyone who talks of false statements or false judgements as being images (*eidōla*) or likenesses (*eikones*) or copies (*mimēmata*) or semblances (*phantasmata*), or of any of the arts concerned with such things, can hardly escape becoming a laughing-stock by being forced to contradict himself.[75]

Accordingly, images of art should be credited with some sort of independent existence of their own.[76]

At the same time, there can be little room for doubt that it was not only metaphysical issues that were in Plato's mind when he was coming to his conclusions concerning the status of poetry. This can already be seen from the apparent lack of coherence with which he treats the issue of mimesis in the *Republic* for, as we saw in Chapter 1, it is only through the use of the mixed criterion combining the relation of poetry to reality with its effect on the human soul that he eventually manages to banish almost any form of poetry from his ideal state. The effect of poetry on the human soul was thus no less important to him than its problematic status in respect of reality. This seems to indicate that Plato's concept of mimesis cannot be properly understood if it is reduced to the ontological status of the work of art alone.

At this stage of our discussion we can no longer state simply that according to Plato the effect of poetry was pleasure: we should define what exactly this pleasure meant in Plato's eyes. The first and more obvious answer is found, again, in *Republic* 10: Homer and tragedy act upon the inferior, i.e. the irrational, part of the soul, in that they present characters who openly express the emotions which we are expected to suppress in real life, and thus destroy the superior, i.e. the rational, part of it.[77] Using the same kind of terminology as Herodotus in his description of the Athenian decree against Phrynichus and as Gorgias in his description of the effect of poetry in the *Encomium of Helen*, Plato writes:

(You will be able to understand why poetry produces the effect it does) if you would take into account that the part of the soul which in the former

---

[75] *Soph.* 241de.
[76] Ibid. 240bc, cf. 264cd.
[77] *Rep.* 603c–606d. Cf. Janaway (1995), 151.

case, in our own misfortunes (*en tais oikeiais sumphorais*), was forcibly
restrained, and which has always hungered for tears and a good cry and
satisfaction, because it is its nature to desire these things, is the very
element in us that the poets satisfy and delight, while the best element in
our nature, since it has never been properly educated by reason or even
by habit, now relaxes its guard over the plaintive part, inasmuch as it is
being engaged in contemplating the sufferings of others (*allotria pathē*) and
it is no shame to itself to praise and pity another who, claiming to be a
good man, abandons himself to excess in his grief—on the contrary, it
thinks that this vicarious pleasure is so much clear gain, and would not
consent to forfeit it by disdaining the poem altogether. That is, I think,
because few are capable of reflecting that our own emotions inevitably get
advantage from those of the others. For after feeding fat the emotion of
pity there, it is not easy to restrain it in our own sufferings.[78]

It can be seen from this passage that, although the eagerness of the
soul to indulge in emotions is obviously seen by Plato as perfectly
natural, the process by which the emotions of the characters in
Homer and tragedy take hold of the spectators' souls is represented
by him as a sort of contamination: 'our own emotions inevitably
get advantage from those of the others.' It can also be seen that in
Plato's eyes the effect caused by poetry is not simply to arouse the
emotions of fear and pity but to cause an audience actually to
identify itself with the characters who experience such emotions:
this is where the pleasure caused by poetry finally comes from. 'We
are delighted, and abandon ourselves and accompany the action
with sympathy'—this description in *Republic* 10 gives the clearest
idea of the degree of emotional involvement experienced by the
Athenian audience when Homer and tragedy were being performed.[79] This is where the illusion (*apatē*) created by mimetic art
on the ontological level meets pleasure (*hedonē*) as its essential effect
on the teleological level. Just as a good painter, by exhibiting at a
distance his picture of a carpenter, 'would deceive children and
foolish men, and make them believe it to be a real carpenter',[80] so

---

[78] *Rep.* 606ab. Cf. *Phileb.* 48a.

[79] *Rep.* 605d χαίρομέν τε καὶ ἐνδόντες ἡμᾶς αὐτοὺς ἑπόμεθα συμπάσχοντες. Cf. Plut.
Mor. 16 D–E: 'whereas he who always remembers and keeps clearly in mind the
sorcery of the poetic art in dealing with falsehood (τῆς ποιητικῆς τὴν περὶ τὸ ψεῦδος
γοητείαν) . . . will check himself when he is feeling wroth at Apollo in behalf of the
foremost of the Achaeans . . . he will cease to shed tears over the dead Achilles and
over Agamemnon' etc.

[80] Pl. *Rep.* 598c παῖδάς γε καὶ ἄφρονας ἀνθρώπους . . . ἐξαπατῷ ἂν τῷ δοκεῖν ὡς
ἀληθῶς τέκτονα εἶναι.

also a good poet, by exposing his audiences to an illusionary reality created by his art, would make them lose their identities and be transported into a reality which has no direct correspondence to their real lives. It is only in virtue of its ability to cause the audience to sympathize with fictitious events as if they were real that poetry is presented as a full-scale competitor to real life. If my previous argument is correct, this was exactly where Plato saw the greatest danger of all.

Book 7 of the *Laws* contains the following imaginary answer by the legislator to the writers of tragedy that he has banished from his city:

Respected visitors, we are ourselves poets, or makers (*poiētai*), of a tragedy, and that the finest and best we know how to make. In fact, our own polity has been constructed as a mimesis of a noble and perfect life; that is what we hold to be in truth the most real of tragedies. Thus you are poets, or makers, and we also are poets and makers of the same things, rival artists (*antitechnoi*) and rival actors (*antagōnistai*) in the finest of all dramas, one which indeed can be produced only by a code of true law— or at least that is our faith.[81]

In accordance with the traditional idea of the 'living artefact' (see Chapter 4), Plato sets art and life against one another as full-scale rivals presenting identical ontological claims. Thus, paradoxically, having disposed of inspired poetry by firmly establishing the status of poetry as a mimetic art, Plato has provided poetry with even greater power than it had before—the ability to create a product possessing an independent ontological status and therefore able to compete with the reality of which it is supposed to be an imitation.

This would seem to explain why the only form of mimesis that Plato was prepared to accept was mimesis of things that have no counterpart in reality. In a memorable passage from the *Timaeus*, to which Christopher Gill has paid due attention, Plato complains that poets fail to create edifying myths on a par with his own myth of Atlantis:

everyone can see that they [the poets] are a tribe of imitators, and will imitate best and most easily the life in which they have been brought up, while that which is beyond the range of a man's education he finds hard to carry out in action, and still harder adequately to represent in language.[82]

[81] *Laws* 817b, trans. A. E. Taylor.
[82] *Tim.* 19d. See Gill (1979), 64–78.

The poets thus fall short of the standards of mimesis set by Plato, and the same would presumably be true of their public as well. In a passage of the *Republic* already quoted above, Plato speaks of a variety of story-telling (*muthologiai*) in which, 'owing to our ignorance of the truth about antiquity, we liken the false to the true as far as we may and so make it edifying', thus formulating the principle on which his own practice of myth-making was based.[83] Although the terminology evoking the ancient idiom of 'lies resembling truth' (see Chapter 5), as used in this and similar Platonic descriptions, indicates that the ontological status of the accounts created in such a manner would be indistinguishable from the ontological status of works of mimetic art, they would not compete with reality by virtue of their being purely fictitious and therefore presenting no real danger.

There can be no doubt that Plato's theory of mimetic poetry acted as the groundwork for Aristotle's *Poetics*. But, equally, there can be no doubt that the *Poetics* in its turn acted as what Richard Janko defined as a 'reformulation and reversal of Plato's position'.[84] Like Plato, Aristotle recognized that the work of poetry had come to possess an ontological status of its own, but while in Plato this amounted to the emergence of a threatening rival to reality, for Aristotle the representation of 'what might have happened' was more philosophical and therefore potentially more cognitively valuable than the actual events. Again like Plato, Aristotle saw that, by virtue of its ability to cause the audience to identify themselves with the characters, mimetic poetry exerts a profound emotional influence on the human soul; but while Plato interpreted this influence as a contamination of the soul by the emotions of fear and pity causing the spectators to lose their identities, Aristotle saw that if the action represented in poetry is of the right, 'philosophical', kind, these very emotions can purge the soul and thus allow an ordinary man, by sharing for a while the edifying experience of the characters, to arrive at the kind of pleasure which comes as close as possible to the purest pleasure experienced by the philosopher.[85]

---

[83] *Rep.* 382d, cf. *Tim.* 29cd and Ch. 5 n. 60. On this subject see esp. Belfiore (1985), 48–54; Gill (1993), 51-66. Note that both Parmenides' Doxa and the cosmogonical myth of the *Timaeus* would fall into the category of mimesis thus understood.

[84] Janko (1987), p. xiv.

[85] As was pointed out by Janko (1987, p. vii; cf. pp. xvi-xx), both the discovery

One can hardly improve on Stephen Halliwell's definition of the significance of Aristotle's *Poetics*:

Aristotle marks a new and important phase in the approach to Greek poetry, for he wishes neither to return to the traditional estimation of poets as wise and knowledgeable guides to life nor to assent to an outright rejection of poetry of the kind Plato had moved towards. Well used as we now are to various forms of aestheticism, which grant to poetry and the other arts a strong degree of autonomy, it is difficult for us to appreciate the nature of the evaluative problem facing Aristotle in his theory of poetry, or the originality with which he tackled it. The problem was effectively to define the status of poetry in such a way as to free it from the moral and other objections which its critics had brought against it, yet without slipping back into a conventional account of the privileged nature of poetic knowledge.[86]

At the same time, it should not be forgotten that, original though it was, the *Poetics* was not a one-man achievement. The *Poetics* would not have acquired its present form without the inherited Greek views of creation by craftsmanship and of the 'living artefact'; without the idea and the practice of 'lies resembling truth' developed in the Homeric tradition; without the intellectual revolution of the fifth century BC and the new assessment of the status of poetry aroused in the course of it; and, last but not least, without the idiosyncrasies of the Athenian crowd, the principal consumer of the epic and tragic performances. Above all, however, the *Poetics* would not have acquired its present form without the titanic struggle led by Plato against both inspired and mimetic poetry, a struggle in the course of which the concept of literary fiction was born.

After Aristotle, scientific and artistic discourses were separated, and it was generally acknowledged that each had its own specific requirements. The character of these requirements is illuminated by Ammonius' account of the way in which Aristotle's disciple Theophrastus distinguished between what is demanded of poetry and rhetoric, on the one hand, and of philosophy, on the other. According to Theophrastus, the primary task of the poet and

of new texts pertaining to the issue of *katharsis* and the reassessment of some previously known evidence support the new scholarly consensus, rapidly gaining in strength over recent years, in favour of interpreting of the tragic *katharsis* as having a quasi-homoeopathic effect on the human soul. See also Halliwell (1986), 184–201. On pleasure in Aristotle see Ch. 1, pp. 13–17.

[86] Halliwell (1987), 177. Cf. Janko (1987), p. ix.

orator is to choose 'more solemn words, rather than common and vulgar', and to combine them with each other 'in a harmonious way', whereas the main concern of the philosopher is 'to refute the lie and to demonstrate the truth'.[87] Theophrastus' formulation faithfully reflects the new consensus as regards the status of poetry, a consensus which consolidated soon after Aristotle and remained valid throughout the Hellenistic and the Roman periods. This was a consensus which treated poetry as a branch of rhetoric. The shift of the focus of interest from the inner structure of the poem to its style, from 'the order of song' to the 'order of words', which occurred as a result of this attitude, naturally acted against the holistic principles on which Aristotle's *Poetics* was based.[88] This (and not simply because the treatise as such, together with the other esoteric works of Aristotle, was not widely known in antiquity) seems to be the main reason why the ideas expressed in the *Poetics* exerted a considerably lesser influence on Hellenistic and Roman than on modern European culture.[89]

---

[87] *Ammonii in Arist. De Interpretatione comm.* 65, 31-66, 9 Busse.

[88] Cf. Halliwell (1986), 289: 'Such a view [sc. the rhetorical view of poetry] . . . has a tendency to drive a wedge between style and content, and to emphasise the former at the expense of the latter. One consequence of this is a concern with discrete linguistic effects rather than coherent structures . . .'. That the unit of the text that the Hellenistic or Roman reader had before his eyes was a single passage rather than the work of poetry as a whole has been convincingly argued in the dissertation by Amiel Vardi, 'Aulus Gellius as Reader of Poetry' (Jerusalem, 1993), 95-100 (in Hebrew).

[89] On the reception of the *Poetics* see Fuhrmann (1973), 121-6; Halliwell (1986), 287-91; Janko (1987), 175.

Afterword

Bernard Williams was probably right when he remarked, rather melancholically, in his *Shame and Necessity*, that 'it is too late to assume that the Greek past must be interesting just because it is "ours" '.[1] Nevertheless, whether we like it or not, our own civilization still has a much greater cultural affinity for Greek tradition than, say, for the myths of the American Indians, and the impact of this affinity on the very form taken by many a modern discourse, however original the latter may seem at any given moment, cannot be simply ignored. The modern mode of thought has been influenced by ancient Greek thought to such a degree that not a few cultural choices being made even now are still conditioned by the categorial framework inherited from the Greeks, and not a few modern dilemmas are clearly foreshadowed in the very civilization in which this categorial framework was created. The concept of literary fiction is one such case.

From about 1500, the *Poetics* of Aristotle became a seminal document that dominated Western thought on poetry and art in general in the subsequent three centuries. The discovery of the *Poetics* and its incorporation into the critical theory of the Renaissance was paralleled by the weakening of the Platonic tendency in approaching art which was influential with the early humanists: 'As the sixteenth century advances, a younger text, Aristotle's *Poetics*, comes to vie with Plato's dialogues for domination in matters theoretical—at least insofar as the theory of poetry is concerned.'[2] The influence exerted by the *Poetics* in the forma-

---

[1] Williams (1993), 3.

[2] Weinberg (1961), 348; cf. Curtius (1953), 241; Fuhrmann (1973), 197–211. Similarly, Halliwell (1986: 304), while pointing out in his discussion of French neo-classicism that Aristotle's *Poetics* cannot validly be described as the only source of this influential trend, emphasizes at the same time that 'most neo-classicists were broadly aligned with Aristotle as regards the ancient debate over the relation between "art" and "nature" in poetic composition', and that 'as a system of principles implying a conception of the poet's productive powers' . . . *les règles* of neo-classicism were 'opposed to neo-Platonic notion of inspiration'.

tive years of modern European history made the Greek 'poetics of fiction' an integral part of the Western tradition. And, however acute the theoretical acrimonies of a given historical period might be,[3] the idea of fiction as an autonomous phenomenon acting as a reality *sui generis* has proved flexible enough not only to stimulate some of the best works of European literature written in the traditional genres of epic and drama but also to embrace forms of literary practice unforeseen by Aristotle, first and foremost the new genre of the novel.

In the first hundred years following the recovery of the *Poetics*, the application of Aristotelian categories to the new narrative genre of the romance, which arose in the Middle Ages, had already stimulated debates which led to a considerable enlargement of the scope of critical reference in comparison to what Aristotle offered.[4] Rethinking the romance in Aristotelian terms came next. There can be no better illustration of this than the simultaneous rejection and revival of the genre as presented by Cervantes in *Don Quixote*. In the programmatic two-part speech of the canon, which concludes chapter 47 of volume 1, the romances are first severely criticized for falling short of the classical standards of verisimilitude, imitation of nature, organic form, and artistic style, and the conclusion is that they are 'destitute of anything that resembles art', and therefore 'deserve to be banished from the Christian state as not being of public utility'.[5] As a second thought, however, the canon admits that in spite of all their deficiencies the romances are possessed of an incomparable narrative potential, 'for they offered a broad and spacious field over which the author's pen might run without impediment, describing shipwrecks, tempests, battles, and encounters . . . the author could relate now a lamentable and tragic event and now some joyful and unexpected occurrence' etc.[6]

---

[3] The famous Quarrel of the Ancients and the Moderns which was carried on in France and England at the end of the 17th and beginning of the 18th cent. immediately comes to mind in this connection. However, it is often overlooked that the actual debate was concerned with the claim of vernacular literatures to become an integral part of the canon rather than with questioning the classical poetics on which the canon itself was based: accordingly, the claims of the 'moderns' presented no real threat to the 'poetics of fiction'. On the Quarrel of the Ancients and the Moderns see e.g. Highet (1949), 261–88.

[4] See Weinberg (1961), 635–714, 954–1073.

[5] Cervantes (1949), 426. Cf. Fielding (below, n. 11): 'Such are those voluminous works, commonly called Romances . . ., which contain, as I apprehend, very little instruction or entertainment.'

[6] Cervantes (1949), 427.

Accordingly, he offers a revision of the genre which will make of it the crowning achievement of all literary writing:

All of which being done in an easy-flowing style, with a skilled inventiveness that draws insofar as possible upon the truth of things, the result would surely be a web woven of beautiful and variegated threads, one which when completed would exhibit such a perfect beauty of form as to attain the most worth-while goal of all writing, which as I have said is at once to instruct and to entertain. These books, indeed, by their very nature, provided the author with an unlimited field in which to try his hand at the epic, lyric, tragic, and comic genres and depict in turn all the moods that are represented by these most sweet and pleasing branches of poetry and oratory; for the epic may be written in prose as well as in verse.[7]

It was this impregnation of the romance with the Aristotelian principle of verisimilitude that made the genre of the novel possible. In this respect I cannot but agree with Richard Janko that 'his [Aristotle's] analysis . . . would still be relevant even to a culture based exclusively on media like cinema or television.'[8] This does not mean, however, that Aristotle's analysis would be applicable to every genre recognized as literary in our own days. To see this, let us return to the final outcome of the processes described in this book.

On the one hand, poetry which conveyed 'truth' became a form of philosophical expression and thus indistinguishable from philosophical discourse cast in prose. In the *Phaedrus*, for example, 'philosopher' is in fact an inclusive term, comprising both the philosopher proper and the poet who composes 'with a knowledge of the truth', as opposed to the poet 'who has nothing to show of more value than the literary works on whose phrases he spends hours, twisting them this way and that, pasting them together and pulling them apart', which is yet another expression of the opposition between the *mousikos* and the *poiētikos*. For Aristotle, too, a poet-philosopher like Empedocles is a philosopher rather than a poet. Or, as Plutarch put it: 'The verses of Empedocles and of Parmenides, the *Antidotes against Poisons* of Nicander, and the maxims of Theognis, are merely compositions (*logoi*) which have borrowed from poetic art its metre and lofty style as a vehicle in order to avoid plodding along in prose.'[9] On the other hand, such

---

[7] Cervantes 427-8.   [8] Janko (1987), p. ix.
[9] Plut. *Mor.* 16 c. Cf. Pl. *Phdr.* 278be; Arist. Poet. 1447ᵇ16-22.

prose genres as the mime of Sophron and the Socratic dialogue, the only two forms of prose fiction which existed in Aristotle's time, are treated by him as belonging to 'poetry', and as much can be gathered from Plato's treatment of his own myths.[10]

That is to say, 'poetry' had come to cover all fiction, whether or not it was cast in verse. Thus, delimiting the realm of poetry in accordance with the principle of mimesis amounted to acknowledging that, to be recognized as such, 'poetry' should be able to create a self-sufficient world of its own, every participant of which abandons his own world for a while and is transported, after the manner of Don Quixote, into the illusionary world of fiction. This is how the 'Aristotelian galaxy' of fiction, which dominated Western tradition until the emergence of the Romantic movement at the end of the eighteenth and beginning of the nineteenth century, began.

To outline with greater precision the limits of poetry as envisaged in the 'poetics of fiction' it would be sufficient to point out that consistent application of the criterion of mimesis would mean admitting into the realm of poetry the novels of, say, Tolstoy, but excluding from it the poems of, say, Hölderlin. This is why Fielding was quite consistent when, following Cervantes, he argued in his 'Author's Preface' to *Joseph Andrews* that it is immaterial whether epic or drama be cast in verse or in prose, and defined his own novel, 'written in imitation of the manner of Cervantes, author of Don Quixote', as 'a comic epic poem in prose'.[11]

We have seen that the Greek word *poiēsis*, which began to designate poetry from the first half of the fifth century BC, was in fact more akin to our idea of fine literature than to that of poetry proper. In Greece, prose was a relatively young medium, which emerged only with the introduction of writing, and therefore much later than the traditional poetic genres, and which from its very beginning specialized in history, philosophy, medicine, rhetoric, and other forms of non-fiction. Well beyond the end of the Classical period, the distinction between 'fiction' and 'non-fiction' still coincided for all practical purposes with that between mimetic

[10] See the fragments from the lost Aristotelian treatise *On Poets* collected in Janko (1987), 56; cf. Halliwell (1986), 127; Janko (1987), 69–70. On Plato's myth-making see Gill (1979), 64–77.

[11] Fielding (1939), p. xxxii. See also *Tom Jones*, the introductory chapters to books 4 and 5, respectively: 'this heroic, historical, prosaic poem' and 'prosai-comi-epic writing'.

poetry and prose, and this is obviously why 'poetry' could act in Aristotle as an inclusive term capable of encompassing the few existing samples of prose fiction as well. The potential of prose as a medium for literary fiction was not actualized in full until the emergence of the Hellenistic novel fairly late in antiquity. It is not out of the question, therefore, that it was because of this very lateness that the Hellenistic novel was never given a status of its own in ancient literary theory.[12] By defining the new genre of the novel as a 'prosaic epic', the early modern theorists have thus filled the classificatory gap left by the ancient literary critics.

It is, of course, not a mere chance that the literary genre that eventually undermined the monopoly of the 'poetics of fiction' over Western thought, and thus opened the way to new developments in the theory of poetry, was the very genre that was excluded from Aristotle's *Poetics* in virtue of its referring to reality in too direct a way and therefore being deficient from the point of view of mimesis. I mean, of course, lyric, or 'inspired', poetry. As has been amply demonstrated by M. H. Abrams in *The Mirror and the Lamp*, with the rise of the Romantic movement at the end of the eighteenth and beginning of the nineteenth century the lyric became the privileged poetic form and a paradigm of poetry as such.[13] This ascendancy of the lyric was inseparable from the revival of the idea of inspiration as the true and only source of the poet's creativity rather than simply a conventional device. And, as soon as poets began to see the source of their creative ability in inspiration, they renewed the ancient claim that poetry is akin to prophecy in that it is a privileged vehicle for delivering truth. Thus the Romantic revival of the concept of poetic inspiration amounted, in a sense, to the revival of the pre-Aristotelian 'poetics of truth'.[14]

Yet, as was stressed in Chapter 1, the difference between the ancient and the modern concepts of inspiration can be stated thus: while in the former the individual is seen as the instrument of a

[12] On this subject see especially Morgan (1993), 175–229.

[13] Abrams (1953), 70–155.

[14] Cf. Fuhrmann (1973), 189: 'Die Epoche des poetologischen Aristotelismus, die von den Gelehrten und Dichtern des Cinquecento eingeleit wurde, erreichte im 17. Jahrhundert, in Frankreich unter Ludwig XIV., ihren Höhepunkt; sie endete in der zweiten Hälfte des 18. Jahrhunderts, als der Geniekult des Sturm und Drang mit der platonischen Enthusiasmuslehre Ernst machte und man den Grundsatz verkündete, dass sich ein jedes Genie selbst die Gesetze seiner Werke vorschreibe.' Cf. Halliwell (1986), 315–16.

divine force, in the latter the individual is rather the instrument of latent forces within his own self (pp. 18-19 above). It is immaterial whether these forces are seen in an excess of hot black bile, as in the ancient rationalists and their followers from the Renaissance until modern times,[15] or in man's unconscious self or some innate powers, as in more recent doctrines. In any case, the truth the poet delivers would be of a particular rather than a universal character. Consider, indeed, Abrams's characterization of the dominant attitude of Romanticism:

The first test any poem must pass is no longer, 'Is it true to nature?' or 'Is it appropriate to the requirements either of the best judges or the generality of mankind?' but a criterion looking in a different direction; namely, 'Is it sincere? Is it genuine? Does it match the intention, the feeling, and the actual state of mind of the poet while composing?'[16]

The modern return to the 'poetics of truth' was thus accompanied by the molecularization of universal truth into myriads of private truths, a process which eventually involved the prose genres as well.[17]

The rebirth of the 'poetics of truth' was not, however, the end of the 'Aristotelian galaxy' of fiction. As far as the practice of art was concerned, the contrary would rather be true. Just as the crisis of inspired poetry in the fifth century BC precipitated the idea of poetry as a state of possession, so also the crisis of the Aristotelian approach to literature precipitated the rapid growth of realistic and then naturalistic fiction which allowed for an even more intense identification of the reader with the characters than, say, the Enlightenment novel. This signalled the beginning of a breach between high and low forms of art which was actualized in full with the birth of modernism at the end of the nineteenth and beginning of the twentieth century. The emergence of non-figurative art, undeniably the most conspicuous feature of the modernist movement, acted as a direct negation of the principles on which the 'poetics of fiction' was based. For theorists of art, 'mimetic' became an almost abusive word, designating everything

[15] See Russell (1981), 70; R. Klibansky, E. Panofsky, and F. Saxl, *Saturn and Melancholy: Studies in the History of Natural Philosophy, Religion, and Art* (New York, 1964), 217-74.

[16] Abrams (1953), 23; see also 312-20.

[17] That much of modern prose is 'less closely related to the traditional forms of fiction than to lyric poetry' was argued by Booth (1983), 63, cf. 393.

that is characteristic of an uncultivated taste. It is, however, highly symptomatic that the rise of modernism was paralleled by the world-wide spread of mimesis-based mass culture, of which the new medium of cinema has become the principal vehicle. The coming of 'hyperreality', whose blurring of the distinction between illusion and real life has already surpassed the worst of Plato's fears, seems to be the next stage.[18] The phenomenon of two cultures, the 'high' and the 'low', that has arisen as a result of these developments, was not, however, without precedent.

It is only too rarely taken into account that for both Plato and his circle contemporary drama was first and foremost a vulgar spectacle, specially tailored to appeal to the taste of the Athenian mob.[19] In an episode of the *Symposium*, the tragic poet Agathon, who only a day before had stood with 'ease and dignity' before a vast audience as a participant in the tragic competition, is represented as being shy to speak before a small group of friends, because 'a man of any judgement cares more for a handful of brains than an army of blockheads'.[20] The ironic encouragement he gets from Socrates is even more symptomatic:

Oh, I should never make such a mistake, Socrates assured him, as to credit you, my dear Agathon, with ideas that smacked of the illiterate (*agroikoi*). I've no doubt that if you found yourself in what you really considered intellectual company, you'd be more impressed by their opinion than by the mob's. But we, alas, can't claim to be your intelligent minority, for we were there too, you know, helping to swell that very crowd.[21]

The 'intellectuals' (*sophoi*) and the 'crowd' (*hoi polloi*) are the two keywords not only in this specific discussion but also in Plato's general attitude to Attic drama. If even a mere visit to the theatre of Dionysus caused the intellectuals to be contaminated by the inferiority of the crowd's favourite spectacle, what shall we say of the uneducated crowd itself, easily lured by artistic illusion into confusing reality and dramatic performance? This is why the influence of mimetic poetry on the rational powers of an ordinary man was

[18] I use the term 'hyperreality' in the sense employed by Umberto Eco in his essay 'Travels in Hyperreality' (Eco (1986), 3–58).

[19] *Gorg.* 502cd; *Rep.* 602b; *Laws* 658d, 817c.

[20] *Symp.* 194b5 νοῦν ἔχοντι ὀλίγοι ἔμφρονες πολλῶν ἀφρόνων φοβερώτεροι, trans. M. Joyce. Aristotle, *Eth. Eud.* 1232^b6–7, ascribes similar words to the Attic orator Antiphon, a man of strong oligarchic convictions and a friend of Agathon.

[21] *Symp.* 194c.

seen by Plato as no less destructive than that of the demagogues, and mimetic poetry on the whole as socially dangerous.[22] Here again, he did not differ from Aristophanes, another member of the circle of fifth-century Athenian intellectuals immortalized in the *Symposium*. The *Frogs*' portrayal of Euripides' fans in Hades, however exaggerated for the purposes of comic performance, is without doubt characteristic of Aristophanes' general attitude:

> But when Euripides came down, he kept
> Flourishing off before the highwaymen,
> Thieves, burglars, parricides—these form our mob
> In Hades—till with listening to his twists
> And turns, and pleas and counterpleas, they went
> Mad on the man, and hailed him first and wisest.[23]

This was the same Euripides, it should be remembered, who was admired by the Greek population of Sicily to such a degree that many Athenians taken prisoner during the Sicilian expedition had their lives spared or were released from slavery only because they were able to quote from memory excerpts from his dramas.[24]

Yet, this does not mean that Plato saw no way in which art could satisfy the taste of the intellectual élite; however, it could not be done by means of the mimetic art dear to the heart of the general public. In the *Laws*, he says that the 'finest Muse' is the one that 'delights the best men, the properly educated', and in the *Philebus*, that the beauty of abstract geometrical forms and colours 'is not what most people would understand as such, not the beauty of a living creature or a picture'.[25] Thus, the intellectuals and the crowd are each equipped with separate aesthetic niches of their own. To quote Julia Annas, 'Plato talks here [in *Republic* 10] as though all poetry, including Homer, were utterly stupid. It is as if he were regarding them all as something like the products of a mass culture like TV shows, something so essentially banal that it is hard to see what could be distinctively worth having about a good specimen.'[26]

To be sure, Aristotle could hardly count as one of the ordinary consumers of mimetic art: after all, he too belonged with those who could attain the highest pleasure of all, the pleasure of theoretical contemplation given only to the philosopher. Moreover,

---

[22] *Gorg.* 502 bd. Cf. Annas 1982, 1–28.   [23] *Frogs* 771–6.
[24] Plut. *Nicias* 29.   [25] *Laws* 658e; *Phileb.* 51c.   [26] Annas (1982), 18.

as Halliwell has convincingly argued, it can be gathered from the *Poetics* that Aristotle's actual feelings about the tastes of the Athenian audience were often not very different from those expressed by Plato.[27] While discussing in the *Politics* the dangers of professional performance of music, Aristotle wrote:

The players themselves may also become vulgar in the process. The standard by which they fix their aim is a bad standard: the commonness of the audience tends to debase the quality of the music; and the artists themselves, with their eyes on the audience, are affected by it—affected not only in mind, but also even in body, as they move and swing to suit the taste of their hearers.[28]

On the whole, however, Aristotle applied to art what Ernest Barker aptly called 'the democratic argument in aesthetics', namely, that 'the many (*hoi polloi*) are better judges [than a single man] of music and poetry: some appreciate one part, some another, and all together appreciate all'.[29]

Although he had in mind the same forms of poetic practice and proceeded from the same theoretical premisses as regards mimetic art as Plato did, Aristotle was prepared to see that, if properly treated, the very mimetic art that Plato saw as the greatest social danger could become a great benefit for society. Consider, for example, his discussion of tragic plots in *Poetics* 13:

A perfect tragedy should . . . imitate actions which excite pity and fear, this being the distinctive mark of tragic imitation. It follows plainly, in the first place, that the change of fortune presented must not be the spectacle of a virtuous man brought from prosperity to adversity: for this moves neither pity nor fear; it is merely repulsive (*miaron*). Nor, again, that of a bad man passing from adversity to prosperity: for nothing can be more alien to the spirit of Tragedy; it possesses no single tragic quality; it neither satisfies the sense of humanity (*philanthrōpon*) nor calls for pity and fear. Nor, again, should the downfall of the utter villain be exhibited. A plot of this kind would, doubtless, satisfy the sense of humanity (*philanthrōpon*), but it would inspire neither pity nor fear; for pity is aroused by unmerited misfortune, fear by the misfortune of a man like ourselves. Such an event, therefore, will be neither pitiful nor terrible.

---

[27] Halliwell (1986), 169-70.
[28] *Pol.* 1341[b]14-19; cf. 1342[a]17-27.
[29] Ibid. 1281[b]8-10. Cf. Barker (1946), 128: 'just as, in Athenian practice, the people at large were asked not only to pronounce on politics in the assembly, but also to vote on architectural plans and (through judges drawn by lot from a large panel) to award the dramatic prizes in the theater.'

There remains, then, the character between these two extremes,—that of a man who is not eminently good and just, yet whose misfortune is brought about not by vice or depravity, but by some error or frailty.[30]

Besides the properly tragic criteria, those of mimesis and of pity and fear, Aristotle introduces two additional ones, 'the repulsive' and 'the not humane', which prove effective enough to allow him to channel tragic pleasure in such a way that the emotions experienced by the spectators in the course of their identification with the characters would elevate and improve their souls rather than pollute and corrupt them as in Plato's model.[31]

Plato's total rejection of Attic tragedy as a low form of art is an important caveat which should be taken into account by every theorist of art. It seems, indeed, that the examples of Plato and Aristotle show two alternative ways in which the phenomenon of mass culture can be approached. The Platonic way is to cherish the prejudice of the partisans of 'high culture' against the products of popular and mass art and thus to perpetuate the gap between so-called 'high' and 'low' culture—the gap that has already pushed the mimetic art of our own days into the very realm of amusement that Aristotle unambiguously disqualified for not being an end (*telos*) in itself and therefore not leading to the pleasure proper to man.[32] As distinct from this, the pleasure proper to poetry is not instrumental to something else and is accordingly an end in itself. The Aristotelian way is thus to bring popular art back into the mainstream of high culture and re-establish it in its traditional unifying function of a form of art which both answers the moral and aesthetic standards of society and is universally enjoyed for its own sake.

---

[30] *Poet.* 1452ᵇ30-1453ᵃ10.

[31] See *Pol.* 1340ᵃ36-9: 'The young should be discouraged from looking at the works of Pauso, and encouraged to study the works of Polygnotus or any other painter or sculptor who depicts moral character (εἴ τις . . . ἐστὶν ἠθικός).' Cf. ibid. 1336ᵇ11-22.

[32] In Aristotle's eyes, amusement (*paidia*) is 'a sort of relaxation, and we need relaxation because we cannot work continuously. Relaxation, then, is not an end (*telos*); for it is taken for the sake of activity.' *Eth. Nic.* 1176ᵇ34-1177ᵃ1. Cf. *Pol.* 1337ᵇ28-1338ᵃ9, 1339ᵇ15-40, and Ch. 1 above, pp. 14-17. Cf. also Barker (1946), 323-4.

References

ABRAMS, M. H. (1953), *The Mirror and the Lamp: Romantic Theory and the Critical Tradition* (Oxford).

ADKINS, A. W. H. (1972), 'Truth, *KOΣMOΣ* and *APETH* in the Homeric Poems', *CQ* 22: 5–18.

ALLAN, D. J. (1970), *The Philosophy of Aristotle*, 2nd edn. (Oxford).

ANNAS, J. (1982), 'Plato on the Triviality of Literature', in Moravcsik and Temko (1982), 1–28.

ASMIS, E. (1992), 'Plato on Poetic Creativity', in R. Kraut (ed.), *The Cambridge Companion to Plato* (Cambridge), 338–64.

ATKINS, J. W. (1934), *Literary Criticism in Antiquity*, i. (London).

AUSTIN, N. (1966), 'The Function of Digressions in the Iliad', *GRBS* 7: 295–312

BARKER, E. (1946), *The Politics of Aristotle: Translated with an Introduction, Notes, and Appendixes* (Oxford).

BARMEYER, E. (1968), *Die Musen: Ein Beitrag zur Inspirationstheorie* (Munich)

BELFIORE, E. (1983), 'Plato's Greatest Accusation Against Poetry', in F. J. Pelletier and J. King-Farlow (eds.), *New Essays on Plato* (Guelph, Ontario), 39–62

——(1985), ' "Lies Unlike the Truth": Plato on Hesiod, *Theogony* 27', *TAPA* 115: 47–57.

BETHE, E. (1914), *Homer: Dichtung und Sage*, i: *Ilias* (Leipzig and Berlin).

BING, P. (1988), *The Well-Read Muse: Present and Past in Callimachus and the Hellenistic Poets* (Göttingen).

BOAS, F. (1955), *Primitive Art* (New York).

BOOTH, W. C. (1983), *The Rhetoric of Fiction*, 2nd edn. (Chicago).

BOWIE, E. L. (1993), 'Lies, Fiction and Slander in Early Greek Poetry', in Gill and Wiseman (1993), 1–37.

BOWRA, C. M. (1952), *Heroic Poetry* (London).

——(1955), *Inspiration and Poetry* (London).

——(1963), 'Composition', in A. J. B. Wace and F. H. Stubbings (eds.), *A Companion to Homer* (London), 38–74.

——(1964), *Pindar* (Oxford).

BRASWELL, B. K. (1982), 'The Song of Ares and Aphrodite: Theme and Relevance to *Odyssey* 8', *Hermes*, 110: 129–37.

BUSCHOR, E. (1944), *Die Musen des Jenseits* (Munich).

BUTCHER, S. H. (1904), *Harvard Lectures on Greek Subjects* (London).

——(1951), *Aristotle's Theory of Poetry and Fine Art*, 4th edn. (New York).

CALHOUN, G. M. (1938), 'The Poet and the Muses in Homer', *CP* 33: 157–66.

CERVANTES SAAVEDRA, MIGUEL DE (1949), *The Ingenious Gentleman Don Quixote de la Mancha*, trans. Samuel Putnam, i. (New York).

CHADWICK, N. K. (1962), *Poetry and Prophecy* (Cambridge).

—— and ZHIRMUNSKY, V. (1969), *Oral Epics of Central Asia* (Cambridge).

CHANTRAINE, P. (1968), *Dictionnaire étymologique de la langue grecque* (Paris).

CLAY, D. (1988), 'The Archaeology of the Temple of Juno in Carthage', *CP* 83: 195–205

COLLINGWOOD, R. G. (1938), *The Principles of Art* (Oxford).

CORNFORD, F. M. (1935), *Plato's Theory of Knowledge* (London).

——(1937), *Plato's Cosmology* (London).

——(1952), *Principium Sapientiae: The Origins of Greek Philosophical Thought* (Cambridge).

CULLER, J. (1975), *Structuralist Poetics: Structuralism, Linguistics and the Study of Literature* (London).

CURTIUS, E. R. (1953), *European Literature and the Latin Middle Ages*, trans. W. R. Trask (New York).

DELATTE, A. (1934), *Les Conceptions de l'enthousiasme chez les philosophes présocratiques* (Paris).

DENNISTON, J. D. and PAGE, D. (eds.) (1957), *Aeschylus: Agamemnon* (Oxford).

DETIENNE, M. (1973), *Les Maîtres de vérité dans la Grèce archaïque*, 2nd edn. (Paris).

—— and VERNANT, J.-P. (1978), *Cunning Intelligence in Greek Culture and Society*, trans. J. Lloyd (Hassocks).

DIHLE, A. (1982), *The Theory of Will in Classical Antiquity* (Berkeley and Los Angeles).

DODDS, E. R. (1951), *The Greeks and the Irrational* (Berkeley and Los Angeles).

——(1973), *The Ancient Concepts of Progress and Other Essays on Greek Literature and Belief* (Oxford).

ECKERMAN, J. P. (1955), *Gespräche mit Goethe in den letzten Jahren seines Lebens* (Wiesbaden).

ECO, U. (1986), *Faith in Fakes: Travels in Hyperreality*, trans. W. Weaver (London).

EDWARDS, M. W. (1980), 'The Structure of Homeric Catalogues', *TAPA* 110: 81–103.

——(1987a), *Homer: Poet of the Iliad* (Baltimore and London).

—— (1987*b*), '*ΤΟΠΟΣ* and Transformation in Homer', in J. M. Bremer, I. J. F. de Jong, and J. Kalff (eds.), *Homer: Beyond Oral Poetry* (Amsterdam), 47–60.

—— (1990), 'Neoanalysis and Beyond', *CA* 9: 311–25.

—— (1991), *The Iliad: A Commentary*, (Cambridge).

ELSE, G. F. (1957), *Aristotle's Poetics: The Argument* (Cambridge, Mass.).

EMLYN-JONES, C. (1986), 'True and Lying Tales in the Odyssey', *GR* 33: 1–10.

FALTER, O. (1934) *Der Dichter und sein Gott bei den Griechen und Römern* (Würzburg).

FENIK, B. (1968), *Typical Battle Scenes in the Iliad* (Wiesbaden).

—— (1978*a*) (ed.), *Homer, Tradition and Invention* (Leiden).

—— (1978*b*), 'Stylization and Variety', in Fenik (1978*a*), 68–90.

FERRARI, G. R. F. (1989), 'Plato and Poetry', in Kennedy (1989), 92–148.

FIELDING, H. (1939), *The History of the Adventures of Joseph Andrews and of his Friend Mr. Abraham Adams* (New York).

FINKELBERG, M. (1987*a*), 'Homer's View of the Epic Narrative: Some Formulaic Evidence', *CP* 82: (135–8).

—— (1987*b*), 'The First Song of Demodocus', *Mnemosyne*, 40: 128–32.

—— (1988*a*), 'Enchantment and Other Effects of Poetry in the Homeric *Odyssey*', *SCI* 8/9: 1–10.

—— (1988*b*), 'A Note on Some Metrical Irregularities in Homer', *CP* 83: 206–11.

—— (1989), 'Formulaic and Nonformulaic Elements in Homer', *CP* 84: 179–97.

—— (1990), 'A Creative Oral Poet and the Muse', *AJP* 111: 293–303.

—— (1991), 'Royal Succession in Heroic Greece', *CQ* 41: 303–16.

—— (1991–2), 'How Could Achilles' Fame Have Been Lost?', *SCI* 11: 22–37.

—— (1994), 'The Shield of Achilles, or Homer's View of Representation in Art', *SCI* 13: 1–6.

—— (1995), 'Patterns of Human Error in Homer', *JHS* 115: 15–28.

FINLEY, M. I., (1970), 'Metals in the Ancient World', *JRSA* (Sept.): 597–605.

—— (1978), *The World of Odysseus*, 2nd edn. (Harmondsworth).

FINNEGAN, R. (1977), *Oral Poetry: Its Nature, Significance and Social Context* (Cambridge).

FINSLER, G. (1900), *Platon und die aristotelische Poetik* (Leipzig).

FLASHAR, H. (1958), *Der Dialog Ion als Zeugnis platonischer Philosophie* (Berlin).

FORD, A. (1992), *Homer: The Poetry of the Past* (Ithaca, NY, and London).

FOUCAULT, M. (1970) *The Order of Things*, a translation of id., *Les Mots et les choses* (New York; orig. pub. 1966).

FOUCAULT, M. (1976), *The Archaeology of Knowledge*, trans. A. M. Sheridan Smith (New York).

FOURNIER, H. (1946), *Les Verbes 'dire' en grec ancien* (Paris).

FRÄNKEL, H. (1962), *Early Greek Poetry and Philosophy: A History of Greek Epic, Lyric, and Prose to the Middle of the Fifth Century*, trans. M. Hadas and J. Willis (New York and London).

FRIEDLÄNDER, P. (1964), *Plato*, ii, trans. H. Meyerhoff (New York).

——(1969) *Plato*, iii, trans. H. Meyerhoff (New York).

FRONTISI-DUCROUX, F. (1975), *Dédale: Mythologie de l'artisan en Grèce ancienne* (Paris).

FUHRMANN, M. (1973), *Einführung in die antike Dichtungstheorie* (Darmstadt).

GILL, C. (1979), 'Plato's Atlantis Story and the Birth of Fiction', *Philosophy and Literature*, 3: 64–78.

——(1993), 'Plato on Falsehood—not Fiction', in Gill and Wiseman (1993), 38–87.

——and WISEMAN, T. P. (eds.) (1993), *Lies and Fiction in the Ancient World* (Austin, Tex.).

GOETHE, J. W. (1974), *Werke in zwölf Bänden*, xi (Berlin and Weimar).

GOLDHILL, S. (1991), *The Poet's Voice: Essays on Poetics and Greek Literature* (Cambridge).

GOMME, A. W. (1951), *The Greek Attitude to Poetry and History* (Berkeley and Los Angeles).

GRAY, D. H. F. (1954), 'Metal-Working in Homer', *JHS* 74: 1–15.

GRESSETH, G. K. (1970), 'The Homeric Sirens', *TAPA* 101: 203–18.

GRIFFIN, J. (1977), 'The Epic Cycle and the Uniqueness of Homer', *JHS* 97: 39–53.

——(1980), *Homer on Life and Death* (Oxford).

——(1995), *Homer: Iliad Book Nine* (Oxford).

GRUBE, G. M. A. (1935), *Plato's Thought* (London).

GUNDERT, H. (1935), *Pindar und sein Dichterberuf* (Frankfurt am Main).

GUTHRIE, W. K. C. (1969), *A History of Greek Philosophy*, iii (Cambridge).

HACKFORTH, R. (1952), *Plato's Phaedrus* (Cambridge).

HAINSWORTH, J. B. (1970), 'The Criticism of an Oral Homer', *JHS* 90: 90–8.

——(1984), 'The Fallibility of an Oral Heroic Tradition', in L. Foxhall and J. K. Davies, *The Trojan War: Its Historicity and Context* (Bristol), 111–35.

——(1991), *The Idea of Epic* (Berkeley and Los Angeles).

HALLIWELL, S. (1986), *Aristotle's Poetics* (London).

——(1987), *The Poetics of Aristotle: Translation and Commentary* (London).

HARRIOTT, R. (1969), *Poetry and Criticism before Plato* (London).

HARRISON, E. L. (1960), 'Notes on Homeric Psychology', *Phoenix*, 14: 63–80.

HÄUSSLER, R. (1973), 'Der Tod der Musen', *AA* 19: 117-45.

HAVELOCK, E. A. (1963), *Preface to Plato* (Cambridge, Mass.).

HEATH, M. (1985), 'Hesiod's Didactic Poetry', *CQ* 35: 245-63.

——(1989), *Unity in Greek Poetics* (Oxford).

HEINIMAN, F. (1945), *Nomos und Physis* (Basle).

HEITSCH, E. (1966), 'Das Wissen des Xenophanes', *RhM* 109: 193-236.

HERINGTON, J. (1985), *Poetry into Drama: Early Tragedy and the Greek Poetic Tradition* (Berkeley and Los Angeles).

HEUBECK, A. (1978), 'Homeric Studies Today: Results and Prospects', in Fenik (1978a), 1-17.

HIGHET, G. (1949), *The Classical Tradition: Greek and Roman Influences on Western Literature* (Oxford).

HIMMELMANN, N. (1969), 'Über bildende Kunst in der homerischen Gesellschaft', *Abhandlungen der geistes- und sozialwissenschaftlichen Klasse der Akademie der Wissenschaften und der Literatur in Mainz*, 7: 3-49

HOEKSTRA, A. (1965), *Homeric Modifications of Formulaic Prototypes* (Amsterdam).

HULTON, J. (1982), *Aristotle's Poetics: Translation and Introduction* (New York and London).

JAEGER, W. (1947), *Paideia*, i, trans. G. Highet (Oxford).

JAHN, T. (1987), *Zum Wortfeld 'Seele-Geist' in der Sprache Homers* (Munich).

JANAWAY, Chr. (1995), *Images of Excellence: Plato's Critique of the Arts* (Oxford).

JANKO, R. 1987, *Aristotle: Poetics* (Indianapolis and Cambridge).

KAKRIDIS, J. T. (1949), *Homeric Researches* (Lund).

KANNICHT, R. (1980), 'Die alte Streit zwischen Poesie und Philosophie', *Altertums-Unterricht*, 23/6: 6-36.

KENNEDY, G. A. (1989), (ed.), *The Cambridge History of Literary Criticism* (Cambridge)

KERFERD, G. B. (1981), *The Sophistic Movement* (Cambridge).

KERSCHENSTEINER, J. (1962), *ΚΟΣΜΟΣ: Quellenkritische Untersuchungen zu den Vorsokratikern* (Munich).

KIRK, G. S. (1962), *Heraclitus: The Cosmic Fragments* (Cambridge).

——(1976), *Homer and the Oral Tradition* (Cambridge).

——(1978), 'The Formal Duels in Books 3 and 7 of the Iliad', in Fenik (1978a), 18-40.

——(1990), *The Iliad: A Commentary*, ii (Cambridge).

KLEINGÜNTER, A. (1933), *ΠΡΩΤΟΣ ΕΥΡΕΤΗΣ* (Leipzig).

KOLLER, H. (1954), *Die Mimesis in der Antike* (Berne).

——(1963), *Musik und Dichtung im alten Griechenland* (Berne and Munich).

KOSTER, S. (1970), *Antike Epostheorien* (Wiesbaden).

KRANZ, W. (1967), *Studien zur antiken Literatur und ihrer Fortwirken* (Heidelberg).

KRAUS, W. (1955), 'Die Auffassung des Dichterberufs im frühen Griechentum', *WS* 68: 65-87.

KRISCHER, T. (1965), '*ΕΤΥΜΟΣ* und *ΑΛΗΘΗΣ*', *Philologus*, 109: 161-74.

——(1971), *Formale Konventionen der homerischen Epik*, (Munich).

KULLMANN, W. (1956), *Das Wirken der Götter in der Ilias* (Berlin).

——(1960), *Die Quellen der Ilias* (Wiesbaden).

——(1981), 'Zur Methode des Neoanalyse in der Homerforschung', *WS* 15: 5-42.

——(1984), 'Oral Poetry Theory and Neoanalysis in Homeric Research', *GRBS* 25: 307-23

——(1991), 'Ergebnisse der motivgeschichtlichen Forschung zu Homer', in J. Latacz (ed.), *Zweihundert Jahre Homer-Forschung* (Stuttgart and Leipzig), 425-55.

LANATA, G. (1963), *Poetica pre-platonica: Testimonianze e frammenti* (Florence).

LATTE, K. (1946), 'Hesiods Dichterweihe', *AA* 2: 152-63.

LESKY, A. (1961), *Göttliche und menschliche Motivation im homerischen Epos* (Heidelberg).

LIEBERG, G. (1982), *Poeta Creator: Studien zur einer Figur der antiken Dichtung* (Amsterdam).

LLOYD, G. E. R. (1966), *Polarity and Analogy* (Cambridge).

LORD, A. B. (1954) (ed.), *Serbo-Croatian Heroic Songs Collected by Milman Parry*, i (Cambridge, Mass.).

——(1960), *The Singer of Tales* (Cambridge, Mass.).

——(1974) (ed.), *Serbo-Croatian Heroic Songs Collected by Milman Parry*, iii (Cambridge, Mass.).

LOVEJOY, A. O. (1936), *The Great Chain of Being: A Study of the History of an Idea*, (Cambridge, Mass.).

LUCAS, D. W. (1968), *Aristotle, Poetics: Introduction, Commentary and Appendixes* (Oxford).

LURIA, S. (1970), *Democritea* (Leningrad).

MACLEOD, C. (1982), *Homer: Iliad, Book XXIV* (Cambridge).

——(1983), *Collected Essays* (Oxford).

MAEHLER, H. (1963), *Die Auffassung des Dichterberufs im frühen Griechentum* (Göttingen).

MARG, W. (1938), *Der Charakter in der Sprache der frühgriechischen Dichtung* (Würzburg).

——(1956), 'Das erste Lied des Demodokos', in *Navicula Chiloniensis: Studia philologa Felici Jacoby . . . oblata* (Leiden), 16-29.

MAZON, P. (1943), *Introduction à l'Iliade* (Paris).

MINTON, W. W. (1960), 'Homer's Invocations of the Muses: Traditional Patterns', *TAPA* 91: 292-309.

—— (1962), 'Invocation and Catalogue in Hesiod and Homer', *TAPA* 93: 188-212.

MONRO, D. B. (1891), *A Grammar of the Homeric Dialect*, 2nd edn., (Oxford).

MORAVCSIK, J., and TEMKO, P. (1982) (eds.), *Plato on Beauty, Wisdom, and the Arts* (Totowa, NJ).

MORGAN, J. R. (1993), 'Make-believe and Make Believe: The Fictionality of the Greek Novels', in Gill and Wiseman (1993), 175-229.

MORRIS, S. P. (1992), *Daidalos and the Origins of Greek Art* (Princeton).

MURRAY, P. (1981), 'Poetic Inspiration in Early Greece', *JHS* 101: 87-100.

—— (1996), *Plato on Poetry: Ion; Republic 376e-398b9; Republic 595-608b10* (Cambridge).

MYRES, J. H. (1952), 'The Pattern of the *Odyssey*', *JHS* 72: 1-19.

NAGY, G. (1974), *Comparative Studies in Greek and Indic Meter* (Cambridge, Mass.).

—— (1979), *The Best of the Achaeans* (Baltimore).

—— (1989), 'Early Greek Views of Poets and Poetry', in Kennedy (1989), 1-77.

NESTLE, W. (1941), *Vom Mythos zum Logos*, 2nd edn. (Stuttgart).

NILSSON, M. P. (1935), 'Early Orphism and Kindred Religious Movements', *HThR* 28: 181-230.

—— (1949), *A History of Greek Religion* (Oxford).

—— (1951), 'Götter und Psychologie bei Homer', in *Opuscula Selecta*, i (Lund).

NOTOPOULOS, J. A (1949), 'Parataxis in Homer', *TAPA* 80: 1-23.

—— (1951), 'Continuity and Interconnection in Homeric Oral Composition', *TAPA* 82: 81-102.

—— (1964), 'Towards a Poetics of Early Greek Oral Poetry', *HSCP* 68: 46-65.

NUSSBAUM, M. C. (1982), '"This Story Isn't True": Poetry, Goodness, and Understanding in Plato's *Phaedrus*', in Moravcsik and Temko (1982), 79-124.

ORTEGA Y GASSET, J. (1956), *The Dehumanization of Art and Other Writings on Art and Culture* (New York).

OTTO, W. (1971), *Die Musen*, 3rd edn. (Darmstadt).

PADEL, R. (1992), *In and Out of Mind: Greek Images of the Tragic Self* (Princeton).

PAGE, D. L. (1950), *The Homeric Odyssey* (Oxford).

—— (1959), *History and the Homeric Iliad* (Berkeley and Los Angeles).

—— (1964), 'Archilochus and the Oral Tradition', in *Archiloque* (Entretiens Fondation Hardt, 10; Geneva), 117-63.

PANOFSKY, E. (1968), *Idea: A Concept in Art Theory*, trans. J. J. S. Peake (New York).

PARRY, A. (1966), 'Have we Homer's *Iliad*?', *YCS* 20: 177-216.

PARRY, M. (1971), *The Making of Homeric Verse*, ed. A. Parry (Oxford).

PELLICCIA, H. (1995), *Mind, Body, and Speech in Homer and Pindar* (Göttingen).

PHILIPP, H. (1968), *Tektonon Daidala: Der bildende Künstler und sein Werk im vorplatonischen Schrifttum* (Berlin).

POHLENZ, M. (1965), 'Die Anfänge der griechischen Poetik', in *Kleine Schriften*, ii (Hildesheim).

POLLARD, J. R. T. (1952), 'Muses and Sirens', *CR* NS 2: 60-3.

POLLITT, J. J. (1972), *Art and Experience in Classical Greece* (Cambridge).

——(1974), *The Ancient View of Greek Art* (New Haven and London).

PRATT, L. H. (1993), *Lying and Poetry from Homer to Pindar: Falsehood and Deception in Archaic Greek Poetics* (Ann Arbor).

PUCCI, P. (1979), 'The Song of the Sirens', *Arethusa*, 12: 121-32.

PUELMA, M. (1989), 'Der Dichter und die Wahrheit in der griechischen Poetik von Homer bis Aristoteles', *MH* 46: 65-100.

RADERMACHER, L. (1967), *Aristophanes' Frösche: Einleitung, Text und Kommentar*, 3rd edn. (Graz, Vienna, and Cologne).

REINHARDT, K. (1961), *Die Ilias und ihr Dichter* (Göttingen).

RENEHAN, R. (1987), 'The *Heldentod* in Homer: One Heroic Ideal', *CP* 82: 99-116.

ROMILLY, J. DE (1973), 'Gorgias et le pouvoir de la poésie', *JHS* 93: 155-62.

ROSENMEYER, T. G. (1955), 'Gorgias, Aeschylus, and Apate', *AJP* 76: 225-60.

RÖSLER, W. (1980), 'Die Entdeckung der Fictionalität in der Antike', *Poetica*, 12: 283-319.

RUSSELL, D. A. (1981), *Criticism in Antiquity* (Berkeley and Los Angeles).

RUSSO J., and SIMON B. (1968), 'Homeric Psychology and the Oral Epic Tradition', *JHI* 29: 483-98.

RÜTER, K. (1969), *Odysseeinterpretationen* (Göttingen).

RUTHERFORD, R. B. (1982), 'Tragic Form and Feeling in the *Iliad*', *JHS* 102: 145-60.

——(1992), *Homer: Odyssey, Books XIX and XX* (Cambridge)

SCHADEWALDT W. (1951), *Von Homers Welt und Werk: Aufzätze und Auslegungen zur homerischen Frage*, 2nd edn. (Stuttgart).

——(1966), *Iliasstudien*, 3rd edn. (Berlin).

SCHEID, J., and SVENBRO, J. (1996), *The Craft of Zeus: Myths of Weaving and Fabric*, trans. C. Volk (Cambridge, Mass.).

SCHMIDT M. (1955-) 'Autodidaktos', in *LfgrE* s.v.

SCHMITT, R. (1967), *Dichtung und Dichtersprache in indogermanischer Zeit* (Wiesbaden), 1967.

SCHRADE H. (1952), *Götter und Menschen Homers* (Stuttgart).

SCHWEITZER, B. (1963), *Zur Kunst der Antike*, i-ii (Tübingen).

SEALEY, R. (1957), 'From Phemios to Ion', *REG* 70: 312-55.

SHARPLES, R. W. (1983), ' "But why has my spirit spoken with me thus?":
Homeric Decision-making', *GR* 30: 1-7.

SHIPP, G. P. (1972), *Studies in the Language of Homer*, 2nd edn.
(Cambridge).

SHULMAN, D. (1991), 'Towards a Historical Poetics of the Sanskrit Epics',
International Folklore Review, 8: 9-17.

SIKES E. E. (1931), *The Greek View of Poetry* (London).

SNELL B. (1924), *Die Ausdrücke für den Begriff des Wissens in der vorplatonischen Philosophie* (Berlin).

——(1953), *The Discovery of the Mind in Greek Philosophy and Literature*
trans. T. G. Rosenmeyer (New York).

SOLMSEN, F. (1963), 'Nature as Craftsman in Greek Thought', *JHI* 24:
473-96.

SPERDUTI, A. (1950), 'The Divine Nature of Poetry in Antiquity', *TAPA* 81:
209-41.

STÄHLIN, F. (1901), *Die Stellung der Poesie in der platonischen Philosophie*
(Munich).

STANFORD, W. B. (1967), *The Odyssey of Homer*, i (London).

STANLEY, K. (1993), *The Shield of Homer: Narrative Structure in the Iliad*
(Princeton).

STRAUSS CLAY, J. (1983), *The Wrath of Athena* (Princeton).

STROH, W. (1976), 'Hesiods lügende Musen', in H. Görgemanns and A.
Schmidt (eds.), *Studien zum antiken Epos* (Meisenheim am Glan), 85-112.

SVENBRO, J. (1976), *La Parole et le marbre* (Lund).

TAPLIN, O. (1985), *Greek Tragedy in Action* (London).

TATE, J. (1928), 'Imitation in Plato's *Republic*', *CQ* 23: 16-23.

——(1929), 'Plato and Allegorical Interpretation', *CQ* 23: 142-54.

——(1932), 'Plato and Imitation', *CQ* 26: 161-9.

TAYLOR, A. (1960), *Plato: The Man and his Work*, 7th edn. (London).

TIGERSTEDT, E. N. (1969), *Plato's Idea of Poetical Inspiration* (Helsinki).

——(1970), 'Furor Poeticus: Poetic Inspiration in Greek Literature before
Democritus and Plato', *JHI* 31: 163-78.

UNTERSTEINER M. (1954), *The Sophists*, trans. K. Freeman (Oxford).

VERDENIUS, W. J. (1949), *Mimesis: Plato's Doctrine of Artistic Imitation and
its Meaning to Us* (Leiden).

——(1972), 'Notes on the Proem of Hesiod's *Theogony*', *Mnemosyne*, 25:
225-60.

——(1983), 'The Principles of Greek Literary Criticism', *Mnemosyne*, 36:
14-59.

VERNANT, J. P. (1965), *Mythe et pensée chez les Grecs*, 2 vols. (Paris).

VICAIRE, P. (1960), *Platon: Critique littéraire* (Paris).

VON DER MÜHLL, P. (1940), 'Odyssee', *RE* Suppl. 7: 696-768.

WALCOT, P. (1977), 'Odysseus and the Art of Lying', *AS* 8: 1–19.

WALSH, G. B. (1984), *The Varieties of Enchantment: Early Greek Views on the Nature and Function of Poetry* (Chapel Hill, NC, and London).

WEBSTER, T. B. L. (1939), 'Greek Theories of Art and Literature down to 400 B.C.', *CQ* 33: 166–79.

WEHRLI, F. (1957), 'Die antike Kunsttheorie und das Schöpferische', *MH* 14: 39–49.

WEINBERG, B. (1961), *A History of Literary Criticism in the Italian Renaissance*, 2 vols. (Chicago).

WEST, M. L. (1966), *Hesiod: Theogony* (Oxford).

——(1981), 'The Singing of Homer and the Modes of Early Greek Music', *JHS* 101: 113–29.

——(1985), *The Hesiodic Catalogue of Women* (Oxford).

WHITMAN, C. H. (1958), *Homer and the Heroic Tradition* (Cambridge, Mass.).

WILAMOWITZ, U. von (1931–2), *Der Glaube der Hellenen*, 2 vols. (Berlin).

WILLIAMS, B. (1993), *Shame and Necessity* (Berkeley and Los Angeles).

Index of Passages Cited

Aeschylus
    Agamemnon
        750–62: 174 n. 42
        990–3: 56
Alcman
    5. 25–30 PMG: 72, 162
    14 PMG: 162–3
    27 PMG: 162–3
    30 PMG: 163
    39 PMG: 167
    39. 1–2 PMG: 164
Ammonii in Arist. De Interpretatione
    comm. 65, 31–66, 9 Busse:
        190–1
Anonymus Jamblichi
    89 1, 2 DK: 175
Archilochus
    1. 2 West: 164
Aristophanes
    Frogs
        771–6: 199
        814–29: 7–8
        1078–86: 9
    Thesmophoriazousae
        49–57: 172
Aristotle
    Nicomachean Ethics
        1105^{a}27–32: 13
        1113^{b}30–3: 66
        1116^{b}24–1117^{a}5: 175–6
        1140^{a}21–2: 29
        1174^{b}31–4: 14
        1175^{a}19–21: 14
        1175^{b}1–16: 14–15
        1175^{b}24–9: 15
        1176^{a}22–3: 16
        1176^{a}26–8: 16
        1176^{b}5–6: 16
        1176^{b}34–1177^{a}1: 201 n. 32
        1177^{b}19–21: 16
    Physics
        199^{a}15: 120

Poetics
    1447^{b}16–22: 194
    1451^{a}23–30: 138
    1451^{a}37–^{b}11: 12–13, 121
    1451^{b}5–7: 13
    1451^{b}19–25: 23
    1451^{b}29–32: 22–3, 73
    1452^{b}30–1453^{a}10: 200–1
    1453^{b}10–11: 14
    1459^{a}30–^{b}7: 138
    1460^{a}5–11: 155
    1460^{a}18–19: 13
    1460^{b}13–23: 13
    1460^{b}32–3: 13, 122
Politics
    1281^{b}8–10: 200
    1337^{a}2–3: 120
    1338^{a}9–23: 16
    1340^{a}36–9: 201 n. 31
    1341^{b}14–19: 200
The Bible
    Exodus
        31: 1–5 39
Choerilus of Samos
    fr. 1a Kinkel: 165
Democritus
    DK 68 B 21: 168–9
Diodorus Siculus
    4. 72. 4: 84 n. 47
Dissoi logoi (Dialexeis)
    90. 3. 17 DK: 12 n. 43, 177
Epic Cycle
    Aethiopis
        Allen, v. 106. 11–13: 144
    Cypria
        fr. 1 Allen: 74
        Allen, v. 104. 21–105. 7:
            137
    Ilias parva
        fr. 19. 1–8 Allen: 156
        Allen, v. 107. 4–7: 148 n.
            38

Galen
  de Usu Partium 11. 14 p. 158. 2
    Helmreich: 107
Gorgias
  DK 82 B 11. 9. 20–1: 12
  DK 82 B 11. 9. 21–5: 179
  DK 82 B 23: 177
Heraclitus
  DK 22 A 22: 25
  DK 22 B 28: 130
  DK 22 B 40: 25, 62 n. 98
Herodotus
  6. 21: 177
  7. 36. 4: 125 n. 99
Hesiod
  Aspis
    166: 117
    206: 117
    290: 118
    306–11: 117
  Erga
    648–9: 48
    649: 58
    661–2: 48
    662: 58
  Theogony
    22: 58
    27–8: 25, 70, 72 n. 13, 157
    28: 58
    30–3: 58
    30–1: 58
    31–2: 34
    33–4: 58
Homer
  Iliad
    1. 1–5: 132
    1. 1: 122
    1. 234–7: 103
    2. 119–22: 75
    2. 119: 80
    2. 155–6: 80
    2. 324–9: 77–8
    2. 325: 81
    2. 484–7: 48
    2. 484–7: 71
    2. 595–600: 50–1
    2. 599–600: 158 n. 59
    3. 61–2: 105
    3. 65–6: 42
    3. 222: 124
    3. 353–4: 81
    4. 105–8: 103
    4. 482–6: 103

  6. 354–8: 74, 77, 152
  6. 357–8: 82
  6. 444–5: 45
  7. 44–5: 47
  7. 142: 109
  7. 237–41: 46
  9. 109–10: 36 n. 8, 64 n. 102
  9. 119: 36 n. 8
  9. 255–6: 64 n. 102
  9. 410–16: 78
  9. 438–43: 44
  9. 496: 64 n. 102
  9. 524: 57
  9. 635–7: 64 n. 102
  11. 24–8: 112
  11. 408: 44
  11. 604: 135 n. 5
  12. 237–42: 47
  13. 431–2: 85
  15. 411–12: 43
  16. 31–2: 85
  18. 379: 130 n. 119
  18. 417–20: 114
  18. 509–40: 113
  18. 516–18: 114
  18. 539: 115
  18. 541–9: 115–16
  18. 548: 115
  19. 86–9: 35
  19. 218–19: 40–1
  20. 203–5: 41, 57
  22. 304–5: 75, 81
  22. 405–11: 144
  23. 306–25: 109
  23. 307–9: 43
  23. 311–18: 109
  23. 315: 105
  23. 570–611: 109
  Odyssey
    1. 10: 53
    1. 152: 89
    1. 200–2: 41, 47
    1. 325–6: 94 n. 77
    1. 337–8: 51, 57
    1. 337: 94
    1. 346–50: 70
    1. 346–9: 55
    1. 351–2: 94
    3. 250: 109
    3. 432: 105
    4. 235–9: 148
    4. 595–8: 93
    4. 597–8: 94 n. 80, 123 n. 89

6. 232-4: 43
7. 332-3: 84
8. 44-5: 43 n. 34, 55
8. 73-82: 145-6
8. 81-2: 147
8. 74: 51, 93
8. 90-1: 93
8. 99: 89
8. 170: 130
8. 175: 130
8. 329-32: 109
8. 481: 51
8. 487-91: 71
8. 487-98: 124
8. 489: 51
8. 496-8: 126-7
8. 499-503: 53
8. 536-43: 90
8. 577-80: 74, 77, 152
8. 579-80: 84, 85
9. 408: 109
10. 14-15: 92-3
11. 330-1: 94
11. 366: 130
11. 367-72: 93
11. 367: 129
11. 368: 51, 127, 129
11. 370-6: 92
11. 373-6: 94
11. 380-1: 94
11. 609-14: 112
12. 39-52: 96
12. 183-93: 96
12. 189-91: 95
12. 192-3: 91 n. 67
12. 450-3: 93
14. 131: 130
17. 270-1: 89
17. 383-6: 101
17. 382-5: 93
17. 385: 91
17. 515-21: 92
17. 518-21: 91
19. 203: 149
19. 228-9: 116
19. 229-31: 117
19. 589-90: 92
20. 70-2: 42
21. 253-5: 75-6, 83
21. 406-9: 50
21. 430: 89
22. 345-9: 54
23. 159-62: 43

23. 189: 102
23. 190-2: 103
23. 195-6: 104 n. 14
23. 308-9: 92
24. 194-202: 76
24. 433: 83
Homeric Hymns
  H. Herm.
    428-33: 124
    440-2: 43 n. 36
  H. Hom. 7
    58-9: 125
Ibycus
  282. 23-31 *PMG*: 162
  282. 23 *PMG*: 164
Mimnermus
  13 West: 72, 162
Orpheus
  DK B 1: 125
Parmenides
  DK 28 B 8 51-2: 160 n. 63
  DK 28 B 8 52: 168, 169
  DK 28 B 8 60: 159 n. 60, 160 n.
    63, 169
Pindar
  Ol. 1. 28-32: 170
  Ol. 1. 104-5: 169 n. 26
  Ol. 1. 111: 168
  Ol. 7. 7-8: 165 n. 14
  Ol. 9. 80: 168
  Pyth. 3. 113-14: 168, 169
  Nem. 3. 4-5: 169
  Nem. 3. 9: 165
  Nem. 3. 10-11: 163 n. 6
  Nem. 7. 20-7: 170
  Parth. 2. 14-15: 120
  fr. 194. 1-3 Snell-Maehler: 168,
    169 n. 26
Plato
  Apology
    22c: 3 n. 8
  Gorgias
    502bd: 199
  Hippias Maior
    284a: 180
    285d: 180
  Ion
    530d: 125
    535be: 178
  Laws
    629ab: 180
    658e: 199
    680c: 180

719c: 6 n. 19
817b: 188
Phaedo
61a: 181
Phaedrus
235c: 8 n. 25
244c: 2
245a: 2, 125
248de: 1
278be: 194
Philebus
51c: 199
Republic
382d: 159, 189
382d 9: 160
382e: 6
394bc: 4
394d: 5
595a: 4
596ce: 183
597be: 182
597b: 183
598bc: 184
598c: 187
605d: 179, 187
606ab: 186-7
606e-607e: 5
607a: 5
607b: 181
Sophist
235d: 184-5
235e-236a: 120, 185
236e-237a: 185
240a: 185
241de: 186
Symposium
194b5: 198
194c: 198

Timaeus
19d: 120, 188
48a: 107
71e-72a: 182 n. 62
Plutarch
Moralia
15 C-D: 180
16 B-C: 159 n. 60
16 C: 194
16 D-E: 187 n. 79
31 F: 45 n. 43
346 F: 169
397 A: 22
Protagoras
DK 80 A 30: 26
Sappho
103. 8 *PLF*: 161 n. 1
124 *PLF*: 161 n. 1
127 *PLF*: 161 n. 1
128 *PLF*: 161 n. 1
Simonides
17. 1, 2 West: 162
Solon
1. 2 West: 168
13. 1-6 West: 162
13. 51-2 West: 164
13. 52 West: 168
29 West: 25, 160
Stesichorus
192 *PMG*: 171
193. 8-11 *PMG*: 162
210 *PMG*: 171
278 *PMG*: 162-3
Theognis
769-70 West: 164
Xenophanes
DK 21 B 11: 25
DK 21 B 35: 159 n. 60

General Index

Abrams, M. H. 196, 197
Achilles 25-6, 34-5, 40-3, 45, 49 n.
   58, 57, 62, 64-5, 81-2, 135-7,
   142, 144, 151, 156, 178, 187 n.
   79
   character of 132-3
   fame of 78-9, 84-8
   and the plot of the *Iliad* 131-3
   Quarrel of Odysseus and Achilles, *see*
   Demodocus
   Shield of, 112-17, 119-20, 135,
   150, 189
Aeschylus 7-10, 174 n. 42, 178
Aethiopis 142, 144
   see also Epic Cycle
Agamemnon 75, 80, 83-4, 108-9,
   112, 125 n. 98, 132, 137, 142,
   145-7, 156
   apology of 35-6, 65
Agathon 6 n. 19, 9, 11, 23, 172,
   198
Alcinous 51, 55, 74, 77, 83-5, 90,
   92-5, 97, 112, 116-17, 127,
   129-30, 152, 154, 170, 177
Alcman 72, 162-4, 167-8
   see also choral lyric
alēthēs, alētheiē 127-8
   see also truth
Annas, J. 7 n. 22, 199
aoidē 51-3, 56, 58, 86, 125-6, 164,
   168, 176
   see also 'singing'
apatē 12, 177, 180, 187
   see also illusion, artistic
Archilochus 162, 164
Aristophanes 6-11, 18, 26, 172, 199
Aristotle 21-3, 26, 29, 31-2, 66, 73,
   120-2, 172-3, 175, 181, 191-6
   on the Cyclic epics 138, 155-6,
   159
   on inspiration 6 n. 19, 11
   and lyric poetry 11, 194-6

on moral impact of poetry 12,
   14-17, 200-1
and organic form 12, 110, 121-2,
   130, 137-9, 155
and Plato 10-11, 17, 189-90,
   199-201
on pleasure 12-17, 23, 189, 201
Poetics, its influence 191-4
see also unity, of the *Iliad* and the
   Odyssey
art 13, 23-4, 29, 60-1, 113-16,
   120-2, 130, 172-3
and inspiration 1-3, 5-11, 17-18,
   21-6, 28-31, 68, 99,
and nature, *see* nature
and reality 10, 22-4, 118, 182-9
see also crafts, craftsmanship;
   Creator, creation; *technē*
artefact 102-4, 106, 111-12, 136,
   169, 173, 182
   see also 'living artefact'
Athens, the Athenians 9, 32, 159,
   172, 177-80, 186-7, 190,
   198-200
Atkins, J. W. 28, 116
Austin, N. 135

Barker, E. 16 n. 62, 200
Belfiore, E. 72 n. 13, 160 n. 62
Bible, The 39, 98, 107-8
Bing, P. 171 n. 35
Booth, W. C. 24, 197 n. 17
Bowie, E. L. 54 n. 74, 155 n. 50, 159
   n. 61, 162 n. 2, 171 n. 33
Bowra, C. M. 19, 22, 165
Butcher, S. H. 29, 120

carpentry, carpenter 101-5, 108,
   126, 130, 168-9, 184, 187
   see also crafts, craftsmanship
catalogue-like sequence, *see* 'point-by-
   point' narrative

Catalogue of Ships 28, 48, 52, 71, 75, 123, 138, 142, 162
Cervantes, *Don Quixote* 21, 193, 195
Choerilus of Samos 165-6
choral poetry 11 n. 38, 162-5, 167, 169, 171
  see also lyric poetry
Clytaemnestra 76-7, 79, 82-3, 145
Collingwood, R. G. 24, 172-3
courage 37-8, 44, 61, 175-6
  see also martial activities
crafts, craftsmanship 38-45, 102-10, 112-13, 115-16, 182-3, 190
  and poetry 3-4, 31, 49, 59, 61-2, 100-1, 110-11, 121, 165, 169, 172-4
  see also *sophiē*; *technē*
Creator, creation 33, 100, 102-8, 111, 190
  artist as creator 105-6, 110-11, 184, 188
Culler, J. 30, 38 n. 18
cunning 105, 108-10
  see also *technē*
Cypria 73-4, 80, 137-8, 143, 147
  see also Epic Cycle

Daedalus 115-16
Delatte, A. 18 n. 65
dēmioergoi 90-1, 98, 101
Demiurge 106-7
  see also Creator, creation
Democritus 18 n. 65, 56 n. 82, 168
Demodocus 34, 49, 53, 55, 71, 90, 92-5, 124-6, 129, 140, 142, 150, 152, 154, 177
  Quarrel of Odysseus and Achilles 51, 93, 145-7
Detienne, M. 108, 176 n. 48
digressions, in Homer 134-5, 142, 152, 155
Dodds, E. R. 37 n. 16, 47, 63-4, 98-9
dramatic poetry 4-5, 10, 172, 176-7, 193, 195
  see also genres, literary; tragedy

Eco, U. 198 n. 18
Edwards, M. W. 119, 122 n. 86, 135 n. 5, 141 n. 20, 143
eikos, eoikota 12-13, 148-9, 158, 176
  see also plausibility
elegiac poetry 162-4, 166, 168, 171
  see also lyric poetry

Else, G. F. 10, 23, 29 n. 91
emotions, aroused by poetry 10, 179, 186-7, 189, 201
  see also impersonation
emotions, motivation of 36-9, 41, 44, 48-9, 58-60
enchantment, in Homer 91-8
Epic Cycle 137-42, 144, 146, 148, 151, 155-6, 159
epic poetry 4-5, 10, 14 n. 51, 161-3, 165-8, 171, 193-6
  see also genres, literary
Euripides 8-9, 175 n. 44, 199
eyewitness 51, 62, 71-3, 75, 79, 97-9, 158, 161, 163, 166

feast, in Homer 89-92, 95
fiction 1, 23-6, 32-3, 73, 122, 149-50, 157-9, 167, 169 n. 28, 177, 190, 192-3, 195-7
  see also 'poetics of fiction'
Fielding, H. 195
Finley, M. 83 n. 43, 87 n. 53, 90 n. 61, 101 n. 3
Finnegan, R. 72 n. 10, 89, 121 n. 81
firsthand evidence, *see* eyewitness
Ford, A. 51 n. 64, 126 n. 102
formulae, Homeric 50, 55 n. 80, 126-8, 148-9, 158
Foucault, M. 32, 38
Fränkel, H. 72 n. 12, 77
Friedländer, P. 4 n. 10, 18 n. 65
Frontisi-Ducroux, F. 103-4 n. 12, 104 n. 19, 113 nn. 49 and 52
Fuhrmann, M. 196 n. 14

Galen 56, 107
genres, literary 4, 10, 23 n. 78, 167, 193-7
Gill, C. 23 n. 78, 129 n. 114, 188
'giving', in Homer 42-5, 47, 49, 52, 54, 58, 60, 164
glory, see *kleos*
Goethe 23-4
Gomme, A. W. 78
Gorgias 12, 21, 177, 179-80, 186
Griffin, J. 82, 88

Hainsworth, J. B. 59-60 n. 94, 89, 121, 139, 152, 154 n. 48, 156
Halliwell, S. 11 n. 38, 13 n. 44, 23 n. 79, 29 n. 91, 105 n. 23, 111, 155, 190-2, 200

handicrafts, *see* crafts, craftsmanship
Harriott, R. 8 n. 25, 172 n. 37
Havelock, E. A. 50, 60-1, 102 n. 8
Heath, M. 135 n. 5
Hecataeus of Miletus 25-6, 181
Hector 45-7, 75, 79, 81-2, 85-7,
    131-2, 135-7, 144, 151-2, 156,
    178
Helen 34-5, 74, 77, 79, 82, 85, 87,
    134, 137, 142-3, 146-9, 152,
    154, 162, 170-1
Heraclitus 22, 25-6, 62 n. 98, 130
Herington, J. 156, 181
Heroic age 73-4
Hesiod 9, 18, 25-8, 72, 74, 106, 109
    n. 35, 117, 119-20, 161, 163-4,
    168, 173 n. 39, 177, 180
    and inspiration 34, 48, 58, 171
    and the 'lying Muses' 7, 22 n. 75,
        70, 157-60
    and the 'poetics of truth' 137, 139,
        151, 154, 156-7, 159, 166, 170
    Shield of Heracles 117-18
Heubeck, A. 133
history 73, 82-3, 86-8, 99, 161-2,
    166-7, 181
    and poetry 12-13, 23, 73, 121,
        178
Hoekstra, A. 64 n. 103
Homeric Hymns 161-2
    Hymn to Dionysus 125-6
    Hymn to Hermes 43 n. 36, 50-1,
        72 n. 13, 124-5
Homeric Question 140-1
Horace 19 n. 68, 21

iambic poetry 161-2
    see also lyric poetry
Ibycus 162, 164
Ilias parva (the Little Iliad) 87 n. 51,
    138, 142, 148, 156
    see also Epic Cycle
Iliu persis 142, 144
    see also Epic Cycle
illusion, artistic 12, 32, 113 n. 52,
    116, 154 n. 48, 159 n. 60,
    180-1, 187-8, 195, 198
imitation, *see* mimesis
imitation, in Homer 144-5, 147-8,
    150, 155
impersonation, in Homer and tragedy
    4-6, 10, 155-6, 172, 181
improvisation, *see* performance

insight, motivation of 36, 38, 41, 44,
    47-8, 59-60
inspiration 2-4, 10-11, 21-2, 54,
    60-1, 71, 73, 99, 158-60, 163,
    165-6, 172-3, 176
    the ancient and the modern concepts
        of 18-19, 196
    and art, *see* art
    and artistic creativity 68-9, 150-1,
        154
    and mimesis, in Plato 6-7
    and philosophy 181-2
    and possession 18-20
    in war 45
instincts, motivation of, *see* emotions
invocations 27-8, 48, 53, 71, 75,
    125 n. 95, 132, 135, 165
    and catalogue-like sequence 122-3,
        130
    in lyric poetry 161-4, 170-1
    see also Muse(s)

Jaeger, W. 37 n. 11, 77, 138 n. 11
Jahn, T. 63 n. 101
Janaway, Chr. 3 n. 8, 7 n. 22, 173 n.
    38
Janko, R. 10 n. 35, 189-90, 194-5

Kakridis, J. Th. 132 n. 2, 140
kleos 74-6, 78-9, 84 n. 47
knowledge 3, 28, 40-1, 43-52, 56,
    60-5, 67, 97-8, 100, 105, 110,
    164-7, 173
    of the past 41, 57, 59-60, 69,
        71-2, 74, 98-9, 161
    of the Sirens 95-8
    see also eyewitness; self
kosmos, kata kosmon 21, 124-6, 129,
    168
    see also 'point-by-point' narrative
Krischer, T. 122 n. 86, 127
Kullmann, W. 141 n. 20, 143-4

Lévi-Strauss, C. 115
lies 13, 25, 129, 139, 149-50,
    157-60, 169-70, 172, 186,
    189-91
    and fiction 25 n. 83, 177, 181
'living artefact' 115-16, 118-20,
    188, 190
Lord, A. B. 49, 52-3 nn. 69-71, 69,
    123, 141
Lucas, D. W. 11 n. 37, 122 n. 82

lyre, playing of 43 n. 36, 49-2, 57, 59, 167
see also music
lyric poetry 2, 4-5, 7, 10-11, 59, 161-2, 165-8, 172, 194, 196-7
see also genres, literary

Macleod, C. 94 n. 80, 129 n. 115
Maehler, H. 81 n. 36
Mahabharata 71
Marg, W. 146, 164
martial activities, motivation of 34, 44-6
mass culture 32, 198-9, 201
Mazon, P. 132-3
Menelaus 79, 81-2, 93-4, 108-9, 125 n. 98, 133-5, 142-3, 145-6, 148-50
mental organs 36 n. 8, 48, 55
see also thumos
mimesis, mimetic 1, 10-13, 17, 32, 155-6, 169, 179, 181, 187-90, 195, 198-201
and imitation 24, 107-8, 118, 120, 193
and non-mimetic poetry 3-5, 11, 26, 196-9
in the *Republic* 3-7, 182-4; in the *Sophist* 184-6
see also eikos; impersonation; 'living artefact'
Mimnermus 72, 162, 166
Minton, W. W. 122
modernism in art 197-8
moira, kata moiran 124, 126-9
morphē 129-30
motivations, Homeric 36-40, 42, 44, 48
Murray, P. 5 n. 17, 6 n. 19, 20 n. 70, 174 n. 39
Muse(s) 1-2, 18, 32, 34, 49, 53-4, 68, 75, 117, 144-5, 150, 154, 161, 165, 176, 181
erosion of their idiom 164-5, 171-2
'gift' of 52, 57-8
invocations of, *see* invocations
and knowledge 6-7, 51, 70-3, 98-9, 157-60
and poetic creativity 69-70, 151-2
and the Sirens 95
see also Hesiod; eyewitness; inspiration; 'point-by-point' narrative

music 3, 16, 50, 88-9, 91, 167-8, 181, 200
Myres, J. H. 136

Nagy, G. 76, 140, 176
nature 43 n. 36, 56 n. 82, 106-7
and art 24, 33, 103-4, 108-11, 118, 120, 175, 184
Neoanalysis 141, 144
neoclassicism 21, 192 n. 2
Nestor 36 n. 8, 41, 43, 46, 62, 79 n. 32, 94 n. 78, 109, 112, 129, 156
reminiscences of 133, 135, 142-3, 145
Nilsson, M. P. 35, 63, 91 n. 68, 106
Nosti 80, 142
see also Epic Cycle; Returns
Notopoulos, J. A. 121, 137 n. 9
novel 23, 193-7
Hellenistic 23, 111 n. 41, 196

Odysseus 40, 44, 50, 52-4, 64 n. 102, 71, 74-7, 79, 83-4, 86-7, 90-4, 102-4, 108-9, 124, 126, 142-3, 148, 152, 154, 170, 178
the brooch of 111-12, 116-17
and the plot of the *Odyssey* 133-4, 136, 138, 145, 148, 151
Quarrel of Odysseus and Achilles, *see* Demodocus
and the Sirens, *see* Sirens
as a story-teller 51, 91-4, 97, 129-30, 149-50, 158
oimē, oimai 51-2, 55, 57-8, 79, 86, 93, 140
oral poetry, poets 49-50, 52-3, 60, 68-9, 89, 99, 121, 123, 126, 139-41, 166-7
Fijian 71-2
Kara-Kirghiz 72
South Slavic 49, 52 n. 71, 70 n. 4, 139, 151, 155 n. 50
organic form, *see* Aristotle
Ortega y Gasset 24

Padel, R. 65 n. 104, 98 n. 90
Page, D. L. 69 n. 2, 130 n. 118
painting, and poetry 3, 7, 13, 169, 177, 183-5, 187
Pandora 106, 118
Panofsky, E. 24, 118
parataxis 121-2, 130, 137 n. 9, 159

Paris 79, 81–2, 85, 87, 135, 142–3
Parmenides 158–60, 168–9, 189 n. 83
Parry, M. 92, 126 n. 102, 141
Patroclus 34, 42, 45, 47, 85, 132, 135–6, 144
Pelliccia, H. 36 n. 8, 65 n. 104
Penelope 51, 55, 57 n. 87, 70, 76–7, 79, 82–3, 92–4, 97, 145, 149, 158
performance 49–50, 53, 57, 59–60, 70, 88–95, 98–9, 121
see also oral poetry
Phaeacia, the Phaeacians 71, 74, 79, 84, 90, 92–3, 120, 124, 133–4, 146 n. 33, 152, 154
see also Alcinous
Phemius 49, 51, 61, 70, 72, 93–4, 140, 142
plea of 54–7
philosophy, philosopher 1–2, 7–8, 25 n. 83, 167, 181–2, 189–91, 194–5, 199
Phrynichus 177–9, 186
Pindar 120, 160, 163, 165, 168–72, 174 n. 39
Pisistratus 159, 180
Plato 10–13, 15, 17–19, 21, 23, 26, 32, 111, 120, 156, 159–60, 169, 172–3, 180–1, 192, 195–6
Apology 3
Gorgias 4
Ion 3, 27, 125, 178, 182
Laws 6 n. 19, 188, 199
Meno 3
Phaedrus 1–4, 8–9, 125, 194
Philebus 125, 199
Republic 3–5, 178–9, 182–4, 186–7
Sophist 184–6
Symposium 198–9
Timaeus 106–7, 188–9
see also Aristotle; inspiration; mimesis; pleasure; psychology; truth
plausibility 12–13, 17–18, 23, 25, 148–50, 154, 156–60, 169, 176
see also fiction; lies; representation
pleasure 18, 25, 179–80, 199, 201
in Aristotle, *see* Aristotle
in Homer 28, 88–98
in Plato 5, 17, 21, 186–7
in the Sophists 12, 42, 177
Plutarch 22, 45 n. 43, 159 n. 60, 180–1, 194

Pollitt, J. J. 119
poiēsis 176, 195
'poetics of fiction' 25–7, 31, 68, 99–101, 111, 120–2, 166, 173 n. 39, 193, 195–7
'poetics of truth' 24–7, 31–2, 68, 121–2, 134, 152, 166, 169, 173 n. 39,
in Hesiod 136–7, 157
in Homer 99–101, 130–1
in modern literature 196–7
in South Slavic poetry 139
'point-by-point' narrative 122–3, 125, 127, 129–31, 134, 138, 149, 159, 169
see also truth
possession, *see* inspiration
practical wisdom, motivation of 38, 40–1, 44 n. 39, 49, 57, 59–60, 62
Pratt, L. H. 23 n. 78, 25 n. 83, 129 n. 114, 157 n. 57, 171–2, nn. 32, 33
prophecy 1–3, 19, 22 n. 75, 41, 45–9, 165, 176, 181–2, 196
prose 167, 176, 194–7
Protagoras 12, 26
psychology of poetry, in Plato 4–5, 7, 10, 186–9
see also emotions; pleasure

Quarrel of the Ancients and the Moderns 193 n. 3

Ramayana 153–4
Reinhardt, K. 81 n. 37, 136 n. 7
Renaissance 192, 197
representation, of the specific in the light of the generic 118–20, 150
see also art and reality; 'living artefact'; mimesis
responsibility and non-responsibility 30, 35–6, 38–42, 44, 65, 100, 102, 174–6
in poetry 7, 19–22, 27, 30, 48–9, 53, 57–61, 164–6, 171, 173
Returns 77, 83, 142–3, 145, 148
rhetoric 12, 174, 176, 190–1
Romanticism 32, 105, 107, 195–7
romance 193–4
Rösler, W. 157 n. 57, 166–7
Russell, D. A. 19, 22 n. 73, 197 n. 15

Rutherford, R. B. 149–50, 154 n. 49

Sappho 22, 161, 163
Schadewaldt, W. 70 n. 6, 95 n. 82
Schrade, H. 56 n. 82, 113 n. 52
Schweitzer, B. 101 n. 1, 119 n. 75
self, in Homer 32–3, 63–7
    see also responsibility and non-
    responsibility; *thumos*
Shulman, D. 153–4
'singing', in Homer 52, 56, 58–61,
    68, 88–9, 91, 93, 97, 100
Simonides 162, 169, 174 n. 39, 176
    n. 48, 180
Sirens 28, 57 n. 87, 74, 91–2, 95–8
Snell, B. 44 n. 39, 73 n. 15, 97, 102
    n. 8
Solon 25–6, 102 n. 8, 160, 162,
    164, 168
song, see *aoidē*
sophiē, sophia 50, 102, 164–5
Sophists 1, 6 n. 19, 9, 11–12, 17–18,
    26, 156, 177
    see also Agathon; Euripides; Gorgias;
    Protagoras
soul, see psychology of poetry; self
South Slavic poetry, see oral poetry
speeches, in Homer 134, 155–6
sports, motivation of 38–40, 43–6,
    49, 60, 65, 100, 173
Stanford, W. B. 98, 130 n. 117
Stesichorus 1 n. 2, 160–3, 171
story-telling, and poetry 57, 91–3
    see also Odysseus
Svenbro, J. 173–4 n. 39

Taplin, O. 179
'teaching' 41–4, 47 n. 49, 49, 51,
    54–60 100, 164, 173
    see also knowledge
technē 2, 7–8, 29, 50, 60, 101–2,
    105, 108, 118, 172–6
    see also *sophiē*
Telemachus 34, 55, 70, 93–4, 133–4,
    142, 145, 148
Thamyris 50, 158 n. 59
theogonies and cosmogonies, Greek
    72, 125–6, 162
Theophrastus 190–1

thumos 34–7, 39, 43 n. 34, 45, 55–6,
    63–5
Tigerstedt, E. N. 2 n. 6, 7 n. 22,
    19–20
tragedy, Attic 5, 7, 10–12, 14, 23,
    138, 177–81, 186–8, 190, 194,
    198, 200–1
    tragic irony 154 n. 49
Trojan war 71, 73–4, 77–84, 86,
    132, 136, 141–4, 146–7, 151–2,
    166, 170, 178
the historicity of 87–8
truth, in poetry 17–18, 21–2, 32,
    167, 189–91, 194
    in Aristotle 12–13, 73,
    in Hesiod 156–61
    in Homer 69–73, 88, 127–30,
    148–52, 154
    in choral poetry 170–2
    in Plato 4, 7, 11, 181–6
    in the Sophists 12, 177
    see also 'poetics of truth'

unity, of the *Iliad* and the *Odyssey*
    131–41, 155

Vardi, A. 191 n. 88
Verdenius, W. J. 6, 17, 77 n. 27,
    165, 169 n. 28
Vernant, J.-P. 108, 110

Walcot, P. 149
Webster, T. B. L. 75
West, M. L. 34 n. 3, 59 n. 93, 87,
    137 n. 9, 157
Western tradition 27, 32–3, 107,
    192–3, 195–6
Whitman, C. H. 136
Williams, B. 192
Wolf, F. A. 141
word, as a unit of speech 123–4,
    168–9, 191
writing, introduction of 166–7, 195

Xenophanes 25–6, 158–9, 181

Yugoslav poetry, see South Slavic
    poetry